Cuba's Ties to
a Changing World

Cuba's Ties to a Changing World

edited by
Donna Rich Kaplowitz

Lynne Rienner Publishers ■ Boulder & London

Published in the United States of America in 1993 by
Lynne Rienner Publishers, Inc.
1800 30th Street, Boulder, Colorado 80301

and in the United Kingdom by
Lynne Rienner Publishers, Inc.
3 Henrietta Street, Covent Garden, London WC2E 8LU

Library of Congress Cataloging-in-Publication Data
Cuba's ties to a changing world / edited by Donna Rich Kaplowitz.
   p.   cm.
   Includes bibliographical references and index.
   ISBN 1-55587-389-8 (alk. paper)
   1. Cuba—Foreign relations—1959– . 2. Cuba—Foreign economic
relations. I. Kaplowitz, Donna Rich, 1962– .
F1788.C8243   1993
327.7291—dc20   92-42003
                                                CIP

British Cataloguing in Publication Data
A Cataloguing in Publication record for this book
is available from the British Library.

Printed and bound in the United States of America

The paper used in this publication meets the requirements
of the American National Standard for Permanence of
Paper for Printed Library Materials Z39.48-1984.

Contents

v

Illustrations

Preface

Although Cuba lies only 90 miles off the U.S. coast, it is often necessary to go much farther than that to obtain information about the island. The end of the Cold War has dramatically altered the face of Cuban foreign policy, and Cuban officials guard information about the island even more closely than they did five years ago, or even one year ago. This book is an attempt to discern Cuba's new ties to a changing world. It brings together articles written by scholars from around the world who have carefully researched their respective country's or region's relations with Cuba.

The book is the result of contributions of many people. It would not have been possible without the enthusiasm and interest of the authors of each chapter. The efforts of each scholar have made the book a reality.

A special thanks goes to the people at the Ford Foundation, especially Cynthia Sanborn and Rebecca Nichols, who provided financial support for this project. Lynne Rienner, Kate Watts, Gia Hamilton, and Sally Jaskold at Lynne Rienner Publishers have also helped with the project.

Miguel Nuñez of the Cuban Interests Section and Dorene Earhard of the U.S. Treasury Department were accessible and helpful.

The Latin American Studies Program at Johns Hopkins University School of Advanced International Studies was also instrumental in the production of this book. Wayne S. Smith gave me the opportunity to oversee the project from its conception to its completion and provided insight and encouragement throughout. Riordan Roett provided intellectual guidance, Francine Marshall helped in innumerable ways, and Anne McKinney and Diane Monash provided essential logistical support.

I also owe thanks to Philip Brenner, who taught me many years ago how to ask the right questions.

A debt of gratitude is owed also to my mother, Paula Rich, who has believed in me from the beginning, and my father, Arthur Rich, who would have so loved to discuss each and every idea in this book.

And finally I thank my husband, Michael Kaplowitz, who provided substantive support throughout, space when necessary, and friendship all along.

D. R. K.

Acronyms

ANC	African National Congress (South Africa)
CANF	Cuban American National Foundation
CARDI	Caribbean Agricultural Research and Development Institute
CARICOM	Caribbean Community and Common Market
CARITAG	Caribbean Trade Advisory Group
CDB	Caribbean Development Bank
CDCC	Caribbean Development Cooperation Committee
CDU	Caribbean Democratic Union
CIA	Central Intelligence Agency
CLAPTUR	Latin American Confederation of Tourism Press
CMEA	Council for Mutual Economic Assistance
CNI	National Confederation of Industry
COCOM	Coordinating Committee for Export Control
COMECON	Council for Mutual Economic Assistance Countries
CTO	Caribbean Tourism Organization
EC	European Economic Community
ECLAC	Economic Commission for Latin America and the Caribbean
EP	European Parliament
EPLF	Eritrean People's Liberation Forces
ERP	Popular Revolutionary Army
FAO	Food and Agriculture Organization
FAR	Fuerzas Armadas Revolucionarias (Revolutionary Armed Forces) (Cuba and Guatemala)
FES	Friedrich Ebert Foundation
FLN	Algerian Liberation Front
FMLN	Farabundo Martí Front for National Liberation (El Salvador)
FNLA	National Front for the Liberation of Angola

FOX	London Futures and Options Exchange
FRELIMO	Front for the Liberation of Mozambique
FSLN	Sandinista Front for National Liberation (Nicaragua)
GDP	Gross domestic product
GDR	German Democratic Republic
GLACSEC	Group of Latin American and Caribbean Sugar Exporting Countries
GNP	Gross national product
GSP	General System of Preferences
HDI	Human Development Index
JICA	Japan International Cooperation Agency
LAIA	Latin American Integration Association
LDC	Less-developed country
MINREX	Cuban Ministry of Foreign Relations
MPLA	Popular Movement for the Liberation of Angola
NAM	Nonaligned Movement
NGO	Nongovernmental organization
OAS	Organization of American States
OAU	Organization of African Unity
ODA	Official Development Assistance
OECS	Organization of Eastern Caribbean States
OLADE	Latin American Energy Organization
OPEC	Organization of Petroleum Exporting Countries
PCC	Cuban Communist Party
PLO	Palestine Liberation Organization
PRC	People's Republic of China
PRI	Institutional Revolutionary Party (Mexico)
PSP	Partido Socialista Popular (Popular Socialist Party) (Cuba)
PTIA	Protection of Trading Interests Act
RENAMO	Mozambique National Resistance
SALT	Strategic Arms Limitation Talks
SELA	Latin American Economic System
UNITA	National Union for the Total Independence of Angola

1

Cuba's Foreign Policy: Old Goals, New Strategies

DONNA RICH KAPLOWITZ

GOALS REMAIN, STRATEGIES CHANGE

On October 16, 1953, Fidel Castro, then a virtually unknown twenty-seven-year-old university student, delivered his now-famous "History Will Absolve Me" speech. In it, he alerted Cubans to the existence of a new nationalist movement, defined a revolutionary agenda, and set the process of change in motion.

In January 1962, in response to Cuba's expulsion from the Organization of American States, Pres. Fidel Castro issued the "Second Declaration of Havana." This set forth the basis for Cuba's foreign policy. "The duty of every revolutionary is to make revolution," Castro said. Cuban foreign policy would henceforth be epitomized by the slogan "turning the Andes into the Sierra Maestra."[1]

Thirty years later—almost to the day—in January 1992, Fidel Castro articulated a new Cuban foreign policy, reversing three decades of strategy. He declared that Cuba would no longer support revolutionary movements but instead would devote all its resources to solving the island's domestic difficulties.[2]

This book examines Cuba's new foreign policy. In the last few years, Cuba's methods of achieving its foreign-policy goals have undergone fundamental change. Gone are the days of fiery ideological proclamations, which have been replaced by policy statements and actions that resemble capitalism far more than socialism. Cuba is clearly taking slow, positive steps toward becoming a member of the international marketplace.

Although Cuban foreign policy appears to have changed drastically in the last two years, Cuba's goals remain the same. The island's most important concern remains the survival of the Revolution, with economic development closely linked to this goal. Cubans believe that the security of the Revolution is inseparable from the strength of their economy.[3] Hence, security and economic development are the two main, if not entwined, goals of the Cuban Revolution and the current Cuban government.

Economics was of prime importance to the young revolutionary government because of its commitment to provide for the people, as outlined in the "History Will Absolve Me" speech—Castro's first domestic (and foreign-policy) speech. The provision of adequate nutrition, health care, housing, and employment for the people would serve to strengthen domestic security.

Today, in the face of a mounting economic crisis, the Cuban foreign-policy establishment recognizes that the survival of the Revolution continues to depend on that most basic economic foundation. A Cuban diplomat recently said, "If the people go hungry in Cuba—then I don't know if the Revolution will be able to survive."[4] However, though the regime's ultimate goal—survival—has not changed, the methods of achieving it have been altered dramatically.

BRIEF BACKGROUND ON CUBAN FOREIGN POLICY

The United States has always been the most serious threat to the survival of Fidel Castro's government and therefore has significantly influenced Cuban foreign policy. Though there has not been a direct U.S. military attack against the island since 1961 at the Bay of Pigs, Cubans continue to believe that a U.S. invasion is possible. This concern has fundamentally shaped Cuban foreign policy by forcing the island to dedicate scarce resources to military preparedness, by forcing it to look elsewhere for protection, and by propelling it to promote the emergence of friendly governments. Aside from invasion, U.S. aggression has come in many other forms: assassination attempts, chemical warfare, and UN denunciations, to name a few. However, the thirty-year-old U.S. economic embargo of Cuba is perhaps the most effective type of anti-Cuban aggression and has profoundly influenced Cuban foreign policy.

In the face of U.S. animosity and Cuba's revolutionary goals, the island has employed three primary means to achieve political and economic security: strong ties with the Eastern bloc, proletarian internationalism, and South-South cooperation. More recently, Cuba has promoted ties with developed countries as a method to ensure security.

Increasing Ties to the Socialist Bloc

Castro did not come to power an avowed communist (see Chapter 8). However, his nationalist ideas were threatening to U.S. business and political interests. Castro's goal of sparking revolution in Latin America succeeded mostly in fueling the ire of the colossus to its north. In an effort to gain security for its revolution under fire, Cuba turned to the Soviet Union, the only country powerful enough to confront the United States. On April 16, 1961, one day before the U.S.-sponsored Bay of Pigs invasion, Castro declared the socialist nature of the Cuban Revolution. The Soviets, apprehensive at first, slowly moved in after the retreat of the United States. Despite the ideological differences between Cuba and the Soviet Union in the 1960s, by the end of the decade the Cuban-Soviet alliance was cemented. Doing more than providing military support, the Soviet bloc also filled the gap left by the U.S. economic embargo of the island. Cuba shaped its economy around the Council for Mutual Economic Assistance (CMEA, the Eastern bloc's equivalent to the European Economic Community). Cuba's economic alignment with the Socialist bloc was complete by 1972, when Cuba became the first non-European member of the CMEA.

Cuba's relationship with the Soviet bloc was not without costs. Havana's reputation as a leader of the Third World was tarnished by its close association with Moscow, especially when Cuba failed to condemn the Soviet invasion of Afghanistan. Also, its close alignment with Moscow in the Ethiopian conflict alienated much of the Third World (see Chapter 4). Moreover, the breakup of the Eastern bloc in 1989–1991 left Cuba isolated both economically and politically. In that period, Cuba's imports from the Soviet Union plummeted 70 percent—from $5.6 billion to $1.7 billion.[5] Cuba lost 50 percent of its buying power when the Soviet Union collapsed, and, probably more important, it lost the vital sugar-for-oil barter trade arrangement. Havana can no longer rely on Moscow for its security and is therefore searching for new allies. To attract them and to survive in today's changing world, Cuba has been forced, once again, to reorient its economy, this time toward the capitalist economic model.

Proletarian Internationalism

Proletarian internationalism has been defined as a "commitment to help one's ideological brethren in other countries to seize power and consolidate their regimes."[6] The notion evolved through the 1960s and 1970s to become a major strategy in Cuba's attempts to achieve its foreign- and domestic-policy goals. Proletarian internationalism has taken many forms over time, including military aid, civilian assistance programs, and mediation efforts. Regardless of the form, however, it has essentially served Cuba's goal of regime stability. As Jorge Risquet, a member of the Cuban Communist Party's Central Committee, succinctly explained, "Our internationalism was aimed at defending the Cuban Revolution."[7]

Cuban foreign-policy makers believed that aiding other revolutionary movements to take power would serve Cuba's security by increasing the number of countries friendly and sympathetic to the Cuban regime. An increase in the number of leftist governments would also deflect U.S. attention away from Cuba. Furthermore, an increasingly expanded and diversified alliance network would allow for a more stable Cuban economy.

South-South Cooperation

As a counterpart to proletarian internationalism, which was aimed primarily at fledgling revolutionary movements, Cuba also attempted to develop relations with leftist and progressive governments already in power, as well as with Third World nonrevolutionary states. Such behavior made sense for many of the same reasons that Cuba engaged in internationalism. Most important, diversified dependency improved Cuban economic and strategic security.

Although Cuba did not abandon proletarian internationalism, it was eventually superseded by conventional state-to-state relations as Cuba's primary foreign-policy tool toward the Third World. Cuba's selection at the 1976 summit in Sri Lanka to chair the Nonaligned Movement (NAM) in 1979 did much to further Cuba's goal of Third World leadership. Although Cuba's chairmanship of the NAM was clouded by the island's refusal to condemn the Soviet invasion of Afghanistan, Cuba did partially regain a position of prominence in the Third World when it was elected for a seat on the UN Security Council in the late 1980s. Cuba's efforts to mediate South-South conflicts—such as the Iran-Iraq war and the Ethiopian-Somali war—also promoted itself as a Third World leader.[8] Today, more than ever, Cuba is vigorously pursuing state-to-state relations with developing countries (as well as with developed countries) the world over. In many cases, ideology is being thrown to the wind in Cuba's desperate effort to survive in the 1990s.

Western Europe and Canada

Cuba's ties to the European Community and Canada have always been of some import to the revolutionary government, and they are all the more so since the collapse of the former Soviet bloc. Canada and most Western European nations never completely cut their ties to Cuba. Trade analysis demonstrates that whenever Cuba has been able to, it has increased its trade with the West. According to the U.S. Department of Commerce, such trade rose from $678 million in 1970 to $2.2 billion in 1974 and to $3 billion in 1975.[9] This rise corresponded to the 1974 rise in world sugar prices, which considerably boosted Cuba's hard currency earnings.[10] Though the price of sugar dropped after 1974, Cuba continued to trade with the West. Cuban data indicate that between 1981 and 1986 Cuban trade with the West averaged about $1.7 billion annually. Though this number dropped to slightly below $1 billion in 1989 primarily because Cuba suspended all interest and principal payments on its hard currency debt in 1986, Cuba continues to attract Western European and Canadian trade.[11] (See Chapters 6 and 13.)

The U.S. Trade Embargo

The U.S. embargo of Cuba has profoundly influenced Cuban foreign policy and affected nearly every other country's policy toward the island. Before the Cuban Revolution of 1959, the United States was Cuba's primary trading partner—U.S. trade with Cuba topped $1 billion annually. Seventy percent of Cuban imports originated in the United States, and the United States purchased 67 percent of Cuba's exports.

The United States had three main objectives for imposing the embargo:

1. The United States hoped the embargo would promote the destabilization and ultimate overthrow of the Castro government. Because of Cuba's extensive economic ties to the United States before the embargo, the Cuban economy was an obvious point of vulnerability for the new regime. U.S. policy planners believed that economic hardship resulting from an embargo would foment enough internal dissent to lead to Castro's ouster.

Rather than inciting internal rebellion, however, the embargo proved to be a rallying point for the Cuban people against the United States. Even today, more than three decades after the embargo was first imposed, it still incites cries of nationalism on the island. "President Bush is Castro's best friend and ally," said Cesare Corti, first secretary of the Italian Embassy in Havana. "By maintaining the diplomatic and trade embargo [against Cuba], Bush allows Castro to continue saying 'no' to the U.S." Corti also noted that when the communist regimes fell across Eastern Europe, Western European borders "were all open," but by contrast, "the U.S. [was] a fortress."[12]

2. The U.S. imposed the embargo to increase the cost of and ultimately break Soviet-Cuban relations. Far from preventing the solidification of Soviet-Cuban ties, however, the embargo locked Cuba more tightly into the Soviet Union's trade and assistance sphere. The disintegration of the Soviet Union in the last two years has been the single most important catalyst for weakening relations between the two nations. The "break" between the former superpower and the island has nothing to do with the U.S. embargo. In fact, Russian officials have said that normalization of relations between the United States and Cuba would speed their complete pullout from the island. (See Chapter 8.)

3. The United States imposed the embargo to deprive the Cuban government of hard currency earnings, which, it believed, could finance Cuba's "export of revolution." The embargo, however, never prevented the Cubans from carrying out support for revolutionary movements. The early years of the embargo (1963–1968) were the most difficult for Cuba, but this was the very period during which Cuba was most active in supporting militant left-wing groups in Latin America. In fact, it may be argued that U.S. restrictions further imbued Cuba's internationalist zeal with an urgency

born from the need to compensate for the perceived threat and concrete economic disturbance that the embargo itself would produce on the island.

Ironically, not only has the economic embargo failed to achieve its goals, but it has actually been deleterious to U.S. business interests. In Chapter 14 of this volume, Michael Kaplowitz quantifies the opportunity costs of the embargo for U.S. businesses and concludes that, despite the serious economic crisis facing Cuba today, total trade turnover between the two countries could reach $1.95–3 billion in the first year after the embargo would be lifted.

Despite the thirty-year failure of the embargo policy to achieve its goals, and notwithstanding its continuing costs for U.S. businesses, some pundits argue that with the disintegration of Cuba's most important trading partners the embargo may finally have a chance to be effective. Members of the U.S. Congress and the Bush administration actively sought to tighten the embargo through legislation proposed by Congressman Robert Torricelli (D-N.J.). Torricelli's bill, which passed both houses on October 3, 1992, and was signed into law by President Bush, prohibits subsidiary trade with Cuba (permitted since 1975) and imposes further extraterritorial restrictions by punishing nations that trade with the island.

Many in the United States—and in most nations around the globe—disagree with this strategy. Jeff Bergner, former Republican staff director of the U.S. Senate Foreign Relations Committee, recently wrote: "I have favored and worked for every form of sanction and trade embargo possible. But I believe the time has come to review and to begin to reverse the policy of isolating Cuba."[13] Bergner pointed out that "it is not much of a policy to wait around until some guy dies." Even Elliott Abrams, a former assistant secretary of state for inter-American affairs in the Reagan administration—and a key architect behind that administration's increasing pressure on Cuba—has expressed an anti-Cuban-exile sentiment.[14] According to others, U.S. policy is actually counterproductive because engagement, not isolation, is what they believe the Castro government needs to continue changing in a pro-democracy, pro-free-trade direction. The embargo merely gives President Castro an excuse for the economic difficulties facing the country.

NEW CUBAN FLEXIBILITY

In 1988, 85 percent of Cuban trade was with the former Soviet Union and Eastern Europe. Cuba's purchasing power slipped 75 percent between 1989 and 1992, from $8.1 billion to $2.2 billion, according to Cuban officials. Nearly all of Cuba's imports are now in hard currency.[15] Despite the precipitous drop in Cuban global trade levels (from $13 billion in 1988 to nearly half that in 1992), a commensurate drop in Cuba's gross domestic product (GDP), and a $7 billion debt to Western countries, Cuba's trade with the West is actually increasing.[16] But the old adage "necessity is the mother of invention" is certainly true with respect to Cuba's creative yet pragmatic approach to economic (and therefore political) survival.

In Chapter 14 Michael Kaplowitz outlines several new and important Cuban trade practices, including the open interpretation of the 1982 Cuban Joint Venture Law. Over two hundred joint ventures have been signed between Cuban entities and foreign partners. The flexible interpretation and application of the old law allows foreigners 50 percent ownership, the right to hire and fire workers, tax exemptions, and the unrestrained repatriation of profits, among other things. Mr. Kaplowitz also discusses other efforts on the part of the Cubans to increase trade with the West.

If Cuban rhetoric and legislation are not convincing, recent actions by Cubans demonstrate their measured moves toward a mixed economy. In June 1992, top Cuban officials invited 125 U.S. and European business-people to an all-expense-paid whirlwind tour of Cuba's trade apparatus. The message was clear: "All foreign investment is welcome." Cuban foreign trade minister Ricardo Cabrisas told the potential investors, "We have to acknowledge . . . that there is not a Socialist world anymore."[17] And in an attempt to demonstrate Cuba's new openness, the vice president of the Cuban Chamber of Commerce told Kaplowitz during a recent trip to Havana that "Cuba is even willing to consider the possibility of mixed enterprises between foreign partners and *private* Cuban farmers."[18]

In July 1992, Cuba's parliament ratified a reformed constitution that breaks with the old concept of state ownership of property. The new constitution establishes state ownership of the "fundamental" means of production rather than *all* means of production. It also provides for the transfer of state property to individuals and enterprises. These changes allow for the establishment of autonomous enterprises operating independently, and they create the potential for ownership of small and medium-size businesses by foreigners and Cubans.[19]

Also in July 1992, Cuba replaced Foreign Minister Isidoro Malmierca with Ricardo Alarcón. Malmierca was considered an "old guard communist." Alarcon, formerly Cuba's ambassador to the United Nations, is a skillful negotiator and career diplomat with expertise on the United States.[20]

The Cuban government is clearly, albeit slowly, moving toward a mixed economy. Although its rhetoric remains fiercely independent and socialist, its actions indicate new thinking. The Cubans, self-proclaimed experts at putting all their eggs in one basket (first the United States and then the Soviet Union), are now actively seeking a diversified trade portfolio. Cuba has three principal objectives in its 1990s foreign policy: (1) to create closer ties to Asian countries, especially Japan and China; (2) to rejoin the Latin American family of nations; and (3) to improve diplomatic and economic relations with Western Europe and Canada. Cuban foreign-policy makers no doubt also hope to achieve a fourth objective: the normalization of trade relations with the United States.

THE BOOK

This book reviews Cuba's current efforts at bilateral and regional relations since the end of the Cold War. Nearly every chapter reflects the sentiment that constructive engagement, particularly in the form of trade, is the most important ingredient for promoting positive change in Cuba. Despite the economic crisis facing Cuba today, Cuban trade in international markets continues, and in some cases it is growing.

Many of the book's authors live outside the United States and have access to information not usually available to U.S. scholars. Some of the chapters focus on trade areas key to Cuba's survival that have received practically no attention to date in the literature. All of the data presented are as current as possible.[21]

The demise of Cuba's most important trade partners—the Soviet Union and Eastern Europe—has been the catalyst behind the island's move toward more pragmatic and flexible economic and foreign policy. No longer able to rely on CMEA trade subsidies, Cuba has entered the international market with creativity and vigor.

In Chapter 2, Damián Fernández reports on the ups and downs of Cuba's relations with China. For these two countries, bilateral trade has been the constant in an otherwise fluctuating political relationship. Dr. Fernández discusses the superpowers' influence on China's relations with the island over time. China is unlike other nations that are preoccupied with Cuba's debt crisis—the fall of the Soviet bloc has enhanced the Cuban-Chinese partnership on both the political and the economic level. While China will not replace the Soviet Union in Cuba's trade portfolio, joint ventures and direct trade between Cuba and Chinese provinces mark new opportunities for expanded trade between the two communist nations. Dr. Fernández also compares the two countries' increasingly similar political models of tightening political space while simultaneously expanding economic opportunities. He predicts a slow expansion of trade in the short term, unless Washington threatens to remove Beijing's most-favored-nation status if China continues to trade with Cuba.

Kanako Yamaoka's comprehensive review of Cuban-Japanese relations (Chapter 3) contributes important new data to the field. She discusses Japan's long-term stable political relationship with Cuba and its important trade component. Although Cuban-Japanese trade relations have been limited by Cuba's current economic crisis, some sectors—lobster and coffee, for example—have witnessed impressive growth. Increased opportunities for trade between the islands lie in the private sector and grassroots organizations. Ms. Yamaoka concludes that the Japanese government has been hesitant to promote trade with Cuba because of consistent U.S. pressure to prevent such trade, despite the Japanese government's belief that active engagement can help ease Cuba's difficult process of change.

Francine Marshall declares in Chapter 4 that Cuba's withdrawal from Africa (Angola and Ethiopia) marks the "end of an era." After a brief review of Cuban involvement in Africa during the 1960s through the 1980s, Ms. Marshall focuses on Cuban-African relations since the end of the Cold War. Military links that were once strong have completely disappeared. Several African nations that were staunch Cuba supporters for three decades now believe that maintaining relations with the island will create problems with the West—especially the United States. Pragmatism on Africa's part will dictate that economics (if anything), not politics, will set the future agenda with Cuba.

Chapter 5, by John Attfield, looks at Cuba's relations with the Middle East, where Cuba has sought "correct" relations even with countries with which it has had political differences. After a detailed examination of Cuba's position on the Gulf war, Mr. Attfield explores the economic potential between Cuba and the region. He concludes that while there is some opportunity for sugar-for-oil swaps and that trade relations will acquire new significance in a post–Cold War world, Cuba cannot expect to replace Soviet subsidies with Middle Eastern ones.

Wolf Grabendorff, in Chapter 6, says that Cuban-European relations have been shaped by the Atlantic Triangle—the United States, the EC, and Latin America. Although Europe has, at times, attempted to demonstrate an independent foreign policy by befriending Cuba to the consternation of the United States, today three major obstacles prevent the full blossoming of relations: Cuba's debt obligations to the EC, Cuba's human rights situation, and ideological differences. Mr. Grabendorff also examines how the breakup of the CMEA only temporarily fostered improved relations between the EC and Cuba. Despite Europe's serious concern about human rights in Cuba, most Europeans seem to agree that the U.S. strategy to isolate Cuba is counterproductive. Finally, Mr. Grabendorff includes analysis of diplomatic and trade ties with Cuba's most important European partners. His conclusion is that there is little likelihood for dramatically improved Cuban-European relations without some sort of regime change in Cuba.

In Chapter 7, Gareth Jenkins analyzes Cuban relations with Great Britain, one of Cuba's most important European trading partners. Despite U.S. efforts over the years to pressure Britain not to trade with Cuba,

Britain and Cuba have maintained a stable political and economic relationship. Mr. Jenkins writes that Britain is opposed to any attempts by the United States to impose its trade embargo on British companies. In fact, the British government is actively encouraging business with Cuba. Mr. Jenkins also carefully outlines major British business interests in Cuba and concludes that the future of British trade with Cuba is dependent upon Cuba's ability to surmount its debt crisis and reorient its trade toward Western economies.

Wayne Smith's chapter on Cuba and the Soviet Union/Russia (Chapter 8) provides a background on how Cuba aligned itself within the Soviet sphere in the early days of the Revolution and how the relationship evolved over time. Dr. Smith also looks at Cuba's relationships with the newly independent republics after the coup of August 1991. Today, Cuba has diplomatic relations with virtually all of the republics and has signed trade agreements with many of them. However, the preferential terms of trade are gone, and Cuba cannot count on diplomatic support from these new nations. Dr. Smith points out that Washington's current policy toward Cuba does not reflect that both its basic goals have been accomplished: Soviet-Cuban ties are broken, and Cuba has pledged not to intervene abroad. He posits that rather than easing tensions, the United States has raised them by tightening its trade embargo, increasing pressure on U.S. allies to stop trade with Cuba, and insisting on new preconditions before relations can be improved.

In Chapter 9, John Walton Cotman analyzes Cuba's ties to the English-speaking Caribbean community (CARICOM). This is one of the most dynamic areas of Cuban foreign policy since the end of the Cold War. Havana's increasing interest in reintegrating into the Caribbean has been reciprocated, albeit cautiously, by many Caribbean nations that fear marginalization as the world is restructured into free-trade zones. Exchanges of delegations, increased trade, joint ventures, and Cuba's admission to the Caribbean Trade Organization in June 1992 mark Cuba's new relationship with its Caribbean neighbors. Eventually, Cuba is expected to apply for and receive full membership in CARICOM.[22] Dr. Cotman reviews Cuba's bilateral relations with the most important CARICOM nations. Though CARICOM states will not be able to replace Cuba's old trade partners, they may be able to significantly improve Cuba's tourist industry and supply some oil, both essential ingredients for the survival of the current regime.

H. Michael Erisman's chapter on Cuban ties with Central America (Chapter 10) traces the roots of Cuban internationalism in the region to the early days of the Revolution. He follows the evolution of Cuban policy to the present, and he determines that proletarian internationalism as practiced in Central America has little to offer Cuba with respect to immediate or even medium-term economic gains. The costs of the old policy are high—

in economic, military, and political terms. In fact, the costs are so high that internationalism could jeopardize the Revolution's very survival—precisely what it was designed to secure. Although economic relations may not be particularly relevant because these countries export similar products, Dr. Erisman concludes that statecentric normalization is the most likely approach Havana will take to the region.

In Chapter 11, Luiz Vasconcelos reviews the step-by-step process of normalization in Cuban-Brazilian relations. Brazil, like most of Cuba's other trade partners, was not immune to Cuba's balance-of-trade problems. What once looked like a very promising new relationship now appears somewhat limited. Still, large-scale trade and scientific agreements have recently been signed between the two countries. If Cuba resolves its debt crisis, opportunity for trade between the two countries could be significant. Dr. Vasconcelos reports that, despite Brazilian government support for trade and an enthusiastic private sector, the trade embargo and accompanying U.S. pressure have greatly hindered trade between the two countries. Nevertheless, joint ventures, barter trade, and other creative trade arrangements are being negotiated regularly.

In a new analysis of Cuban-Mexican relations (Chapter 12) not previously published, Carl Migdail turns the heretofore accepted understanding of the relationship on its head. Rather than the generally accepted theory that Mexico was the renegade Latin American nation that refused to bend under U.S. pressure and break ties with revolutionary Cuba, Mr. Migdail introduces convincing evidence that, in fact, Mexico's relationship with Cuba had the tacit approval of the United States. Mr. Migdail's thesis is based on more than thirty years of reporting on Mexico. His sources include former presidents and foreign ministers of Mexico, as well as highly ranked U.S. government officials.

Despite Mexico's kowtowing to the United States, it remains to be seen whether Mexico will fold under current U.S. pressure to abandon its longstanding relationship with Havana in order to enter into the North American Free Trade Agreement. In a confidential letter showed to Donna Kaplowitz, twelve U.S. senators wrote to the president of Mexico expressing their displeasure with Mexico's $300 million line of credit to Cuba and a Mexican Commercial Advisory Office in Havana, among other things. The letter, dated April 3, 1992, concludes: "We will carefully study any subsidized trade arrangement existing between Mexico and Cuba when the North American Free Trade Agreement comes before the Senate for approval." Interestingly enough, in June 1992 the Mexican government's foreign trade bank (Banamex) said that its $300 million credit line for exports to Cuba had been used up and no further funds were available.[23]

In Chapter 13, Richard Gorham outlines Cuban-Canadian relations. Ambassador Gorham, who is a retired Canadian foreign service officer, explains that Cuban-Canadian relations have always been correct and cordial. Trade has been the main element in Canada's relations with the island; and though it had been improving until 1990, its recent decline is due to Cuba's debt problems. In 1992, Cuba's debt to Canada was (Canadian) $9 million.[24] Ambassador Gorham details Canada's opposition to U.S. legislation that prevents subsidiary trade with Cuba, and he enunciates Canadian support for Cuban readmission to the Organization of American States.

As discussed in the section "New Cuban Flexibility," Michael Kaplowitz analyzes the opportunity costs of the U.S. embargo to U.S. businesses and Cuba's pragmatic approach to trade in the 1990s in Chapter 14.

CONCLUSION

Today, Cuban economic concerns are of paramount importance, and foreign policy is shaped by economic pragmatism. Joint ventures, debt-for-equity swaps, cooperation production arrangements, and free-trade zones are some of the concrete elements that Cuba is using to reform its economy and attract foreign capital. While it is unlikely that Cuba will fully embrace capitalism under Fidel Castro's tenure (recent changes in the Cuban constitution indicate that some elements of a market system will be introduced into the domestic economy), the island has already begun to move in that direction in its international economy. On February 24, 1993, Fidel Castro announced his plans to retire as chief of state of the Republic of Cuba within the next five years. This is perhaps President Castro's most dramatic step toward reforming the Revolution, and will no doubt have tremendous impact on Cuba's foreign and economic policy.

Cuba's new economic policy has been accompanied by a new foreign policy. Fidel Castro openly admits that there is no longer a socialist world. Correct state-to-state relations are replacing Cuba's former internationalist policies. However, accusations of Cuba's human rights violations and domestic repression still inhibit some countries from taking important steps toward constructive engagement and essential trade concessions. Though Cuba's recent readmission to the Caribbean Trade Organization may foreshadow its reintegration into the Caribbean Community and Common Market, and the Organization of American States, this trend does not ensure the survival of the current system of governance on the island. It may, however, give the island enough breathing space to appropriately alter its internal political and economic course.

A time of crisis is often a time of great opportunity, and nowhere is this more true than in Cuba today. As many of the authors in this volume point out, constructive engagement will help shape the profile of Cuba's future far more than will continued isolation. Though Cuba is facing an economic crisis of monumental proportions, trade and aid can help gently nudge the island toward the economic and political reforms it so desperately needs. Proactive policies that encourage and reward positive change may stave off a violent resolution to the crisis that increased isolation may ignite. If indeed President Castro keeps his word and sets the process of transition in motion, there is little reason for President Bill Clinton to maintain an anachronistic trade embargo against the island. It still remains to be seen whether history will indeed absolve Fidel Castro.

NOTES

1. See Wayne S. Smith, *The Closest of Enemies: A Personal and Diplomatic History of the Castro Years* (New York: Norton, 1987), p. 80.

2. Castro made this statement to a group of former U.S. and Soviet diplomats during a conference on the Cuban missile crisis. See Don Oberdorfer, "Cuban Missile Crisis More Volatile than Thought," *Washington Post*, January 14, 1992, p. A1.

3. Philip Brenner, "Change and Continuity in Cuban Foreign Policy," in Philip Brenner, William LeoGrande, Donna Rich, and Daniel Siegel, eds., *The Cuba Reader: The Making of a Revolutionary Society* (New York: Grove Press, 1989), p. 259.

4. Personal interview with Cuban diplomat who wishes to remain anonymous, February 1992.

5. Andrew Zimbalist, "Economic Changes in Cuba," presented at "Cuba, the U.S. and Europe conference, Johns Hopkins University (SAIS), March 2, 1992.

6. H. Michael Erisman, *Cuba's International Relations: The Anatomy of a Nationalistic Foreign Policy* (Boulder: Westview Press, 1985), p. 7.

7. Pascal Fletcher, "Castro Ends Military Help for Revolution Abroad," Reuters, January 13, 1992.

8. For more information on Cuba's mediator role, see Donna Rich, "Cuba's Role as Mediator in International Conflicts: Formal and Informal Initiatives," in H. Michael Erisman and John Kirk, eds., *Cuban Foreign Policy Confronts a New International Order* (Boulder: Lynne Rienner, 1991).

9. Kirby Jones and Donna Rich, "Opportunities for U.S.-Cuban Trade," Latin American Studies Occasional Papers Series (Washington, D.C.: Johns Hopkins University, 1988), pp. 6–7.

10. Jorge Domínguez argues that Cuba is best at managing economic difficulty and that it manages periods of prosperity poorly. Cuba's trade deficit worsened in 1975 because of its spending spree; the island reduced its trade deficit with the industrialized capitalist countries in 1978 when world sugar prices were their lowest. "Thus," Domínguez concludes, "the U.S. government's ongoing embargo on trade with Cuba may have an effect that is the opposite of what the U.S. government intends." Jorge Domínguez, *To Make a World Safe for Revolution: Cuba's Foreign Policy* (Cambridge: Harvard University Press, 1989), pp. 194–195.

11. Economist Intelligence Unit, *Cuba Country Profile: 1991–1992* (London, 1991), p. 37; Economist Intelligence Unit, *Cuba Country Report No. 41991* (London, 1991), p. 3. Note that Cuba's hard currency debt to the West is debated.

12. William Steif, "As Conditions Worsen, Cubans Are Waiting," *Chicago Tribune*, September 16, 1992, p. C6.

13. Warren Strobel, "Castro's Foes Reassess Cuba Sanction's Value," *Washington Times*, January 16, 1992, p. A1.

14. For more information, see the *Miami Herald*, March 13, 1992, p. C1. Elliott Abrams noted that "some of the rhetoric coming out of the Cuban American community in Miami is not helping. The next president of Cuba, the next foreign minister, the next finance minister, are in Cuba today—not Dade County."

15. Personal interview with Dr. Andrew Zimbalist, professor of economics, Smith College, July 20, 1992.

16. Donna Rich Kaplowitz and Michael Kaplowitz, "New Opportunities for U.S.-Cuban Trade," (Washington, D.C.: Johns Hopkins University, Latin American Studies Occasional Papers Series, 1992), p. 3.

17. Mimi Whitefield, "Cuba is Courting Capitalists at Business, Trade Seminar," *The Miami Herald*, June 10, 1992, p. 8A; John Rice, "Cuba Talks Business with Americans, Europeans," *The Washington Times*, June 11, 1992, p. A7. See also: Damian Fraser, "Cuba Opens Doors Wide to Foreign Investment," *Financial Times*, June 11, 1992, p. 4.

18. Personal interview, Abeledo Larrinaga, vice president of the Cuban Chamber of Commerce, February 24, 1992.

19. Mimi Whitefield, "Cuba Ratifies New Constitution," *The Miami Herald*, July 13, 1992, p. 1A.

20. AP report, "Cuba Picks New Foreign Minister," *Miami Herald*, June 21, 1992, p. 12A.

21. It is important to note that data from Cuba have become very difficult to obtain since the collapse of the Soviet Union. Cuba ceased publishing its annual statistical reports in 1988.

22. Julie Vorman, "Cuba Expands Trade Links with Caribbean Neighbors," Reuters Business Report, July 3, 1992.

23. See also: *CubaINFO*, 4, No. 8, July 21, 1992, p. 7.

24. Ibid., p. 7.

PART 1

CUBA'S RELATIONS WITH ASIA, AFRICA, AND THE MIDDLE EAST

2

Cuba's Relations with China: Economic Pragmatism and Political Fluctuation

DAMIAN J. FERNANDEZ

Cuba's relations with China since 1959 can best be characterized as a see-saw. The ups and downs have been determined by ideological and practical issues, including relations with the Soviet Union and the United States; respective interpretations of the correct path to revolution and the construction of socialism; geopolitical interests, such as relations with Third World countries (Vietnam, other Southeast Asian countries, Angola, Chile); and respective political and economic needs in the face of adverse domestic and international situations.

A pivotal balance in the relationship has been maintained throughout three decades by trade policy. The most striking aspect of the relations between these two states has been their ability to sustain a healthy, albeit fluctuating, economic bond while experiencing strain in the political sphere. Economic ties facilitated a political rapprochement in the early to mid-1980s and will ensure that bilateral relations in the 1990s will stand on sure footing.

The Sino-Cuban rapprochement, the beginning of which predated the fall of communism in the Soviet Union, has been propelled mainly by pragmatism—that is, the need to secure trading partners in an attempt to deal with domestic crises and international dislocation. Although revolutionary solidarity, ideological affinity, and perceived isolation on both sides have continued to cement the bonds, the glue has been provided by imports, exports, joint ventures, and credits. However, the medium term is likely to see economic and political constraints, not the least of which might be the role of the United States in China-Cuba relations.

This chapter will focus on Sino-Cuban relations from Havana's vantage point. After a historical analysis of such relations since 1959, the article assesses the rapprochement between the two countries and the economic and political ramifications for Cuba. One of the most interesting questions is whether the rapprochement of the 1980s preceded, followed, or coincided with Mikhail Gorbachev's overtures to the Chinese after

1985. The timing of the reconciliation reveals not only the reasons behind it, but also the degree of Cuba's autonomy from the former Soviet Union. Another question concerns the political and economic nature of the rapprochement and its relationship to the changes in the socialist world. Finally, the Sino-Cuban case study illuminates the interplay between internal and external factors that shape the island's international behavior, and it reveals that Cuba continues to be highly vulnerable to the outside world because of structural, political, and economic limitations. As a consequence of global change, Cuban foreign policy since the mid-1980s has been subjected to the forces of international capitalism, forcing Havana to accommodate new demands placed on the island's domestic economy and international economic relations. To deal with the changes in the Soviet Union (on whom Cuba depended for approximately 80 percent of its foreign trade), the island has launched a program to diversify its economic links. China is a case in point.

HISTORICAL BACKGROUND

Cuba's relations with China since 1959 can be divided into five chronological stages:

1. 1959–1965: Initial Stage—Expansion of Contacts
2. 1966–1975: Political Confrontation, Continuing Trade
3. 1976–1983: Cuban-Soviet Convergence Versus China
4. 1983–1989: The Rapprochement
5. 1989–present: The Second Rapprochement—Greater Collaboration

1959–1965: Initial Stage—Expansion of Contacts

China met the triumph of the Cuban Revolution (1959) with mixed emotions. Skepticism and cautious enthusiasm gave way to interest and support after 1960 when formal diplomatic relations between the two countries were established. Beijing's initial lukewarm reaction resulted from the unorthodox approach and eclectic composition of the Cuban revolutionary forces. The Chinese wait-and-see attitude was not unique—to the Chinese as well as to the Soviets and North Americans, Fidel Castro was an unknown entity.

Several factors pushed the countries closer together after 1960. Sino-Soviet competition for influence in the Third World piqued China's interest in Cuba. In the early years of the Revolution, Cuba played both sides of the socialist world against one another to seek leverage, increase potential sources of aid, and safeguard the island's autonomy vis-à-vis the superpowers. Another factor that brought Havana and Beijing together was Ernesto ("Che") Guevara, an admirer of Mao Zedong. Guevara visited

China in November 1960 and paid tribute to the Chinese leader by tracing the origins of the Cuban *foco* strategy of guerrilla warfare (conducted by a committed group of revolutionaries in the countryside) to Maoism. Not surprisingly, some aspects of Cuban domestic revolutionary politics during this period (such as the creation of a people's militia and social mobilization for production—both Guevarist ideas) had Maoist flavor and succeeded in attracting greater interest from Chinese officials. Finally, both countries stood to gain from the promotion of bilateral trade, which consisted of the traditional exports of both nations (China sold rice, Cuba sold sugar). By 1965 China was Cuba's second trading partner (after the Soviet Union), accounting for 14 percent of the island's total trade.[1]

Although China perceived the Cuban Revolution as a blow to U.S. imperialism and a possible bridge for Beijing to Latin America, relations cooled off in 1965. By early 1966 the two countries were on a collision course. Several factors explain the confrontation. First, the Chinese believed that the Cubans were snuggling up to the Soviets, partly because of the ascendance of old-time Cuban communists associated with the Partido Socialista Popular (PSP, the pro-Soviet Popular Socialist Party), who toed the Soviet line. The Chinese also perceived that the Cubans were becoming hostile to China.

Second, bilateral relations were jarred by Beijing's announcement that it could not deliver the 1966 rice quota promised to Cuba (250,000 tons) and would not buy the 800,000 tons of sugar stipulated in 1966 protocol. The Chinese argued that the reason for their decision was that their country was suffering a severe natural calamity, a drought, which reduced agricultural output at a time when the Soviets were cutting their assistance, forcing the Chinese leaders to adjust their export of grains. Be that as it may, the decision was seen in Havana as a form of retaliation against Cuba for its growing ties with the Soviet Union. In response, Fidel Castro attacked Chinese leaders for reneging on their commitment to the Revolution and sabotaging the international socialist struggle.

A third source of irritation between the two was China's distribution of propaganda to the Cuban Revolutionary Armed Forces (FAR). The Cuban leadership saw this not only as an attempt to meddle in Cuban domestic affairs but as an orchestrated campaign by the Chinese to influence the Cuban military, the main institutional pillar of the regime. This coincided with the "microfaction affair," in which a group of former members of the PSP were allegedly planning a putsch against Castro, heightening the leadership's sensitivity to outside interference in domestic affairs.

1966–1975: Political Confrontation, Continuing Trade

During and after 1966, Cuba's relations with China deteriorated; confrontation, mutual condemnation, and distance were the hallmark of this period. By the end of 1967 China and Cuba were no longer in agreement on fundamental issues. Beijing perceived Havana's continued closeness to Moscow as an indication of anti-Chinese sentiment and Cuba's criticism of divisions within the socialist movement as an affront to Maoism.

By the end of 1967, Cuba and China did not see eye-to-eye on the appropriate revolutionary strategy for Latin America. The Chinese continued to favor the idea of peasant-led revolutions, while the Cubans reconsidered the possibility of carrying out successful struggles after the 1967 failure of Guevara's attempt in Bolivia. Moreover, Cuba opposed the establishment of pro-Chinese Marxist-Leninist parties as one of China's principal goals for Latin America.[2]

Similar disagreements had rocked Soviet-Cuban relations prior to 1968. While the Cubans had advocated guerrilla-led struggle in the countryside, the Soviets claimed that Marxist-Leninist parties should be at the vanguard of Third World revolutions. Cuba's endorsement of the Soviet invasion of Czechoslovakia in 1968 and Havana's apparent renunciation of the *foco* strategy of revolution (partly as a result of Guevara's failure in Bolivia) cleared the way for Soviet-Cuban reconciliation and, at the same time, clouded Sino-Cuban relations. In the context of Sino-Soviet rivalry, Cuba's sway to the Soviet Union dealt a heavy blow to the island's relations with China. Part of the reason that the Cubans "chose" the Soviets was that the Soviet Union could provide a bigger economic incentive than could China, and, as mentioned previously, old-time PSP members, now close to Fidel Castro, were ideologically tied to Moscow. Fifteen years of irritation would go by before Sino-Cuban relations improved.

During the 1966–1975 period, the trade situation was apparently incongruent with the political climate. Trade between Cuba and China continued to flow smoothly, although it declined significantly after 1966. Trade commissions signed annual protocols without major incident. This situation points to the pragmatic dimension of both countries' foreign policies, as well as to the operation of a group of technocrats who were capable of dealing efficiently with trade issues in a charged political climate. As Jorge Domínguez points out, "Notwithstanding their bad political relations after 1965, China still bought almost eight percent of Cuban exports in 1970. By 1970, however, the bilateral trade was balanced, so that China did not provide new trade credits."[3]

1976–1983: Cuban-Soviet Convergence Versus China

Several international issues during and after 1976 clouded the already dreary Sino-Cuban landscape. The two countries frequently found themselves on opposite sides of serious conflicts, such the Angolan civil war (1976) and the Soviet invasion of Afghanistan (1979). Cuba's growing identification with Soviet positions worldwide and Cuba's military internationalism pushed the island to head-on collision with China. A little-known fact helps explain the shift in Cuba's behavior toward China: the Soviet Union had asked Cuba to join the Moscow-led *Interkit,* the international communist body in charge of coordinating policy vis-à-vis China. After 1976, Havana's offensive against Beijing was in part a result of the country's participation in the *Interkit.*[4]

China's rapprochement with the United States in the early 1970s also served to aggravate Sino-Cuban relations. Havana accused Beijing of playing into the hands of the imperialists and undermining the common front of the Third World. China's collaboration with the Chilean government of Gen. Augusto Pinochet (which overthrew the elected government of Salvador Allende, a friend of Cuba, in a military coup in 1973) was an additional irritant. For the Cubans, the Chinese position in the Angolan and Vietnamese imbroglios (from the late 1970s to the late 1980s) was particularly worrisome and, in the case of Angola, dangerous to Cuban interests.

Cuba and China clashed over each other's policy in Africa. In 1976, Cuba, with the acquiescence and support of the Soviet Union, deployed thousands of troops in Angola at the request of that country's government. The Marxist government of Luanda was in the midst of a civil war with non-Marxist groups backed by the United States, South Africa, Zaire, and China. The Chinese had helped arm two of the rebel groups (the National Union for the Total Independence of Angola and the National Front for the Liberation of Angola) at least until 1974.[5] The Angolan operation, Cuba's first massive military commitment abroad, involved high risks for the Cuban government. Chinese assistance to the other side and Beijing's opposition to Cuba's involvement in Angola posed a serious conflict of interests.

The Chinese policy in Southeast Asia, specifically Laos and Cambodia, proved to be a relentless thorn in the side of the Cubans. Vietnam, a close ally of Cuba, clashed with China over China's support of the Pol Pot regime. Havana saw Washington and Beijing join forces against Hanoi after Vietnam sent troops into Cambodia to help topple Pol Pot. Even after the Sino-Cuban rapprochement of the early to mid-1980s, the situation in Southeast Asia continued to be a stumbling block in the way of smooth relations between the two countries. The Cuban Third Party Congress (1986) resolution on international relations highlighted that, in spite of positive changes in Sino-Cuban affairs, "the hostility and the actions of force of [China] against Vietnam constitute[d] an obstacle to a sincere improvement of the relations between Cuba and China."[6] Fidel Castro's central report to the congress echoed the Cuban Communist Party (PCC) position.[7]

In the late 1970s, Cuba continued an offensive campaign against Beijing. For instance, Havana claimed that China had justified the U.S. embargo of Cuba and the occupation of the Guantánamo base. According to Cuba, China did "not have any prestige or morality."[8] China's position on these issues was "the clearest and most blunt evidence that China [had] taken the final steps on the road towards conscious treason of Marxism-Leninism, socialism, communism, and proletarian internationalism."[9] China accused Cuba of being an "aggressive Soviet base in the Caribbean."[10] In his 1979 speech to commemorate the twentieth anniversary of the triumph of the Revolution, Fidel Castro boasted that "Cuba cannot be pressured, nor intimidated, nor bribed, nor bought. Cuba isn't China."[11] In short, during this period the Cuban position vis-à-vis China was identical to that of the Soviets.[12]

Another issue of contention between the two countries was China's opposition to Cuba's leadership role in the Nonaligned Movement (NAM). Cuba's influence in NAM could work against China's standing in the Third World, especially when the island served as host of the Sixth Nonaligned Conference in 1979. In fact, in his keynote address, Fidel Castro criticized China:

> The Yankee imperialists, their old and new allies—I am referring in this case to the Chinese government—did not want this conference to be held in Cuba.[13]

One of the last polemics during this period revolved around the Chinese experiments with neocapitalist forms of production, such as free-trade zones and joint ventures, which Cuba blasted. The official Cuban position presented Chinese reforms as flirtations with capitalism and, therefore, ideologically suspect. However, several years later the Cubans would imitate some of these policies (e.g., the 1982 Joint Venture Law) as they attempted to reform their own economy. The shift in the Cuban position— from one of condemnation to one of imitation—reminds one of the initial years of the Revolution when the pro-Chinese and the pro-Soviet paths of socialist development were debated. On both occasions, the debate manifested unsettled division between the Cuban ruling elite and the technocrats, different sides supporting different alternatives depending on ideological, bureaucratic, or personal proclivities and interests.

Even during the lowest point of Sino-Cuban relations when the war of words was reaching an all-time high, both nations signed annual trade protocols. Trade delegations continued to do their jobs without interruption or major difficulties.

1983–1989: The Rapprochement

The early 1980s brought dramatic changes in Sino-Cuban relations, opening the doors to rapprochement and, by the end of the decade, collaboration. The first turning point occurred between 1982 and 1984. In 1982 China resumed negotiations with the Soviet Union over a host of issues. In 1983 China established relations with the government of Angola, overcoming another stumbling block between the Cubans and the Chinese. By 1985 the Sino-Cuban relationship was on a new course.

The reason behind the restored friendship rests squarely on China's overtures toward the Soviet Union and Cuba. The new leaders in China after Mao's death in 1976 initiated a program reforming the country's domestic and international policies, including improved relations with the Soviet Union and Third World countries. The initiative resulted from the attempt to incorporate China into global affairs as an up-and-coming power and reinsert it into the global economy.

In the early 1980s Chinese foreign policy shifted from one of hostile opposition against Soviet "hegemonic" intentions to one of cautious tolerance and dialogue. Soviet and Cuban revolutionary internationalism in the Third World was entering a period of restraint based on a host of factors, thus helping to pave the way for improvement in trilateral relations. Guiding the rapprochement were five principles set forth by China: mutual respect for sovereignty and territorial integrity; mutual nonaggression; noninterference in each other's internal affairs; equality and mutual benefit; and peaceful coexistence. These principles helped de-ideologize relationships by introducing a general pragmatic framework into the conduct of foreign policy. The following specific goals of Chinese foreign policy in the early 1980s facilitated the application of the five principles to the Soviet Union and Cuba: (1) improvement of relations with the Soviet Union (as well as with the Third World); (2) regional and international disarmament; (3) peaceful coexistence; and (4) promotion of economic ties with the global community serving as the foundation on which to build better relations with Moscow and Havana. As Chinese relations with the Soviets improved, so did Sino-Cuban relations.[14]

In 1983 and 1984 both countries took decisive steps that indicated a new direction in bilateral relations. The pas de deux moved slowly but surely. In 1984 China made a book donation to the José Martí National Library; the Chinese women's Olympic basketball team visited Cuba (a new version of ping-pong diplomacy); Flavio Bravo, a high PCC official, met with the Chinese ambassador to Cuba; both countries signed several economic and social agreements, including a shipping agreement; and a new Cuban ambassador to China, Rolando López, replaced Ladislao Gonzalez.

A new spirit imbued Sino-Cuban relations. The Chinese, rather than the Cubans, took the initiative to repair the rift. Cuba not only responded positively but, in the late 1980s, became the pursuer in the relationship. After 1983 the two countries expanded their diplomatic and commercial contacts. From then on, Cuba became increasingly interested in China as relations with the Soviet Union and Eastern Europe soured because of perestroika and the demise of communism in that area of the world. For example, the Cuban Ministry of Foreign Relations (MINREX) paid more attention to China; Cubans of Chinese descent were brought in to work with Chinese affairs in MINREX, as were Asian specialists.[15]

The rapprochement between Havana and Beijing preceded the rise to power of Mikhail Gorbachev (1985) in the Soviet Union and responded to a logic of its own. Two main factors helped improve bilateral relations: (1) China became interested in improving political and economic relations with Latin America and the Third World, and (2) Cuban military involvement in Third World conflicts declined. The rapprochement was consolidated and Chinese officials declared that Cuba and China held "identical positions" on a number of international issues. Sensitive issues, however, such as divergent positions vis-à-vis Vietnam and Kampuchea, did not disappear.[16]

China's renewed interest in Cuba must be seen in the broader context of domestic and international Chinese politics. After Mao's death, his successors brought in a new agenda. After the Chinese made the first efforts to mend fences with the island, Cuba reacted positively but with caution. The Cuban Communist Party newspaper, *Granma,* reported: "A new generation of Chinese leaders chosen for their reformist projections, technocratic education, and their effectiveness in implementing the official program of modernization through large-scale cooperation with the West" will move the country forward.[17]

Havana seemed to endorse the economic reforms sponsored by Deng Xiaoping, partly because at that time the island was also experimenting with new economic mechanisms, such as the Free Peasant Markets and the Joint Venture Law of 1982, to revitalize the national economy. By 1986, however, the top Cuban leadership was less enthusiastic about free-market policies. In response to a Mexican journalist's questions regarding China's opening toward capitalism, Fidel Castro responded:

> The Chinese first went to an extremism of the left, and when errors are made due to extremism of the left, by and large, oscillations to the right follow. . . . I think that the errors of the extremism the Chinese committed pushed them also to pursue a way too broad opening to the West. . . . We must allow Chinese to continue their experience and see what results it will produce, we shouldn't be pessimists.[18]

Months later, the Campaign to Rectify Errors and Negative Tendencies (Rectification Campaign) was in full swing in Cuba, undoing many of the liberal reforms that the island, like China, had been pursuing. Although after 1986 Castro did not mince words against neocapitalist experiments and socialist countries that flirted with capitalism, the Fourth Party Congress (1991) endorsed joint ventures with multinationals as a way to generate economic growth in Cuba. These mixed enterprises are similar to Chinese free zones. Relations with China, including joint ventures, fit into the development plans of the Cuban government.

1989–Present: The Second Rapprochement—Greater Collaboration

Changes in the Soviet Union and Eastern Europe, symbolized by the crumbling of the Berlin Wall in 1989, have pushed China and Cuba closer together. Faced with international and domestic crises, both countries have strengthened their ties. In short, the second rapprochement was important for Cuba. China gained importance as one option (among others) for trade diversification, with the added benefit of political solidarity.

Since the mid- to late 1980s, the island has tried to find alternatives to its economic reliance on old-time socialist allies by reaching out to new commercial partners in Latin America specifically and to a lesser extent elsewhere, including Asia. The second Sino-Cuban rapprochement must be seen in the context of dramatic cuts in Cuban trade with and aid from the former communist countries. Although no one country will replace the Soviet Union's role in the Cuban economy, in this period of crisis every new trade accord and every concession helps the national economy. Visits by Chinese and Cuban officials to each other's countries have become frequent. Closer economic and political collaboration has been institutionalized by the establishment of joint commissions and a Sino-Cuban Friendship Society.

Trade between Cuba and China has fluctuated since the 1960s because of both economic and political factors. In the 1980s, the characteristic peaks and valleys were evident in the trade figures. In 1984 total trade turnover between the two countries reached almost 448 million pesos (pesos are equivalent to dollars). After a slight decline in 1985, trade dipped to 180 million pesos in 1986 and slightly over 186 million in 1987. There was a 100 percent increase in trade in 1988, and by 1989 total trade turnover between the two countries superseded the 1984 level.[19] According to Gillian Gunn, Cuban-Chinese trade was important for both countries:

> Bilateral trade for 1990 [was] almost $500 million, representing an 11 percent increase from 1989. In the first quarter of 1989 Cuba sold China 67 percent more than what it purchased, signalling a positive trade balance for the Cubans. By the beginning of the 1990s, China was Cuba's third largest supplier of consumer goods.[20]

Yet by the late 1980s the island's trade with China accounted for less than 5 percent of the total value of Cuba's merchandise trade.[21]

Although Cuba has become China's principal economic partner in Latin America, the total Sino-Cuban trade is in no way comparable with Sino-Cuban trade between the 1960s and 1980s or Cuban-U.S. trade before 1959. Since 1986, the dollar has been the unit of payment in trade between China and Cuba. Both partners cover trade deficits via credit in convertible currency. Prices are usually determined based on world prices and finalized in annual trade protocols. However, Cuba and China signed a five-year trade agreement for 1991–1995.[22]

Although the trade basket has diversified, sugar has continued to be Cuba's principal export to China. (China is Cuba's second largest sugar buyer.) Total sugar exports increased after the mid-1980s, reaching their highest level in 1988 at a total of 1.3 million tons (raw value). In 1990 sugar exports totaled 892,000 tons (raw value). Cuba's sugar sales to China, unlike those to the Soviet Union until the late 1980s, are not at a subsidized price. In fact, in 1988 China paid Cuba 7.7 cents per pound of sugar, while the world market price for sugar was about 10.2 cents per pound.[23]

The diversification of the trade basket is impressive, both quantitatively and qualitatively (see Tables 2.1 and 2.2). Bilateral scientific-technical cooperation covers a wide spectrum, from food production to the environment, from genetic engineering to urbanization. Cuban officials expect that biotechnology and its derivatives will become another significant item in the bilateral trade. In 1991, Cuba sold $15 million in medicine (particularly interferon) to China, in addition to nickel, citrus fruits, and furniture.

Table 2.1   Cuban-Chinese Trade

Cuban Exports to China	Cuban Imports from China
Books, records, and publications	Bicycles
Cassettes	Bulldozers
Citrus	Clothing
Electronics	Container ships
Hermetically sealed juices	Cosmetic items
Nickel	Fans
Nickel concentrate	Ferrochrome
Pine seeds	Food items (rice, soybeans, canned meat)
Rum	Handicrafts
Steel bars	Industrial products, machinery, and equipment
Sugar	Medical equipment
Textiles	Plastic articles
Tobacco	Rubber
	Shoes
	Spare parts
	Textiles
	Tools
	Toys

China, in turn, exports a wide range of agricultural, manufactured, and, increasingly, industrial goods to Cuba. Rice constitutes 30–40 percent of Cuba's imports from China. Cuba also imports meats, beans, peanuts, and soybeans. Another important import from China is textiles, constituting 10–20 percent of the total imports from that country between 1986 and 1990. Commerce and cooperation in electronic goods is expected to

**Table 2.2   Cuban-Chinese Scientific-Technical Cooperation
(joint commission established in 1989)**

General Forms of Scientific-Technical Cooperation

Exchange of specialists
Exchange of technology
Joint research projects
Exchange of information

Specific Areas of Cooperation

Fisheries (freshwater shrimp breeding)
Sugar industry technology
Agriculture, horticulture
Livestock
Public health, hygiene, traditional medicine, acupuncture
Food production
Genetic engineering
Biotechnology
Population control
Forest preservation
Steel production
Light industry
Environment
Construction equipment
Shipyards
Prevention and control of cattle diseases
Rice and soybean cultivation

increase.[24] For Cuba, Chinese consumer goods (relatively inexpensive and of good quality) help satisfy high consumer demand on the island. The political benefits of this sort of trade are probably higher than the economic benefits.

According to a report written by Soviet experts, "In 1990 the Cuban government started to establish direct lines with some of China's provinces. An accord was signed with the authorities of Hainan. Cuban organizations will participate in the modernization of two sugar factories in that province and in the construction of a yeast factory."[25] The report also indicates that Cuba is studying the experience of China's free-trade zones and joint ventures, especially in Shanghai, and that there is a possibility of Sino-Cuban joint ventures in light industries on the island. China and Cuba have already built a bicycle factory and a fan factory jointly in Cuba. Other joint ventures in the sugar industry and in the production of processed foodstuffs have been discussed.[26]

Attempts to improve the trade profiles of Cuba and China are related to the domestic needs of each nation. Both countries are pursuing new trade partners and opportunities wherever they are found. (China has been the most noticeable, but in no way the only, trade outlet Cuba has found.) Cuba and China's economic difficulties on the one hand and the countries' development plans on the other make this pursuit vital. Trade relations between the two survived the turmoil of the 1960s and 1970s, and this survival helped strengthen commercial ties in the 1980s. Domestic and international factors coincided to thrust their bilateral commercial relations into full speed by the late 1980s, with ideology facilitating what is basically a pragmatic relationship.

The second rapprochement has been associated with Cuba's endorsement of China's political model as well as its economic goals. Although Cuba did not condone the massacre of the students in Tiananmen Square in June 1989, the Cuban government failed to criticize the action. Cuba's position on the June events defended China's rights to act according to its national interest and, at the same time, defended Cuba's own human rights policy. The official Cuban position was that the Tiananmen situation was a domestic affair and that China had the sovereign right to address it in any way it saw necessary, without international meddling. Based on this experience, Cuba and China have claimed that they share similar positions on human rights. The policy has had costs, though. Havana's support of Beijing drew criticism from old friends, especially from Latin American leftists.[27]

Since the events at Tiananmen, Cuba has seemed to follow the Chinese method of dealing with internal dissent by increasing repression and ignoring international condemnation. During the last months of 1989 the Cuban government launched a campaign to arrest and harass human rights activists, reversing a short-lived policy of greater tolerance. But the Chinese model, if one indeed exists, is not a foreign import to Cuba. It has deep roots in Cuban soil. It is argued that the effect of the Chinese way of dealing with difficulties has underscored Cuba's propensity to act in an orthodox and isolationist manner. Those within the Cuban apparatus who defend orthodoxy can use China as an example of the benefits (short-term or otherwise) of strong-arm tactics to avoid losing political control.

However, unlike China, the international community will not sweep Cuba's human rights misdeeds under the carpet. Despite China's egregious human rights record, the United States offered China most-favored-nation status; Fidel Castro, however, cannot expect the same treatment. Simply put, Cuba does not command the same level of international respect that China does. Havana cannot act as if it were Beijing without paying a price for its behavior.

CONSTRAINTS ON THE RELATIONSHIP

In spite of the broad spectrum of Sino-Cuban cooperation in place since the mid-1980s, the relationship has encountered constraints that will limit its possibilities in the future. The geographic, linguistic, and cultural distances that separate both countries, although not insurmountable, present some obstacles. More serious constraints, however, are of an economic and political nature.

Economic possibilities are limited. China is not the Soviet Union and will not adopt Cuba at a cost of billions of dollars per year. In short, the Chinese have no intention of replacing the Soviets as the benefactor of the Cuban economy. Economic prospects are handicapped by both nations' structural deficiencies as well as by a lack of foreign reserves. For example, sugar continues to be Cuba's principal export to China. Yet Cuban sugar production is in decline, forcing China to turn to other producers. Low world prices and demand inelasticity for the commodity are additional sobering factors. Cuba will have to rely on nontraditional exports if it wants to expand commerce with China. The list of exports mentioned earlier indicates that this has been taking place, but it is not clear if the Cuban economy can produce these items efficiently and in sufficient quantity (particularly given the present economic dislocations) to satisfy the Chinese, were that demand to increase.

In the short term, trade will continue to expand slowly. However, in a surprising declaration in mid-1992, Carlos Lage, a member of the Cuban Politburo, denied that Cuba had increased its commerce with China. As Cuban foreign reserves dwindle, imports will be cut and the available reserves will be used for top-priority items (e.g., oil and food). This situation will affect trade with China, which had been on the upsurge at least through 1990.[28]

Certain constraints are presented by geographic, linguistic, and cultural distances. China realizes that its future in Latin America rests not only on Cuba but on the larger countries of the region: Brazil (until recently China's number one trading partner in Latin America), Mexico, Chile, Argentina, and Uruguay, among others. In May 1990 the Chinese president, Yang Shang-Kun, visited those five countries, flying over Cuba. Chinese officials declared that they will seek to build cooperative relations with these big countries, and with Latin America in general, based on peaceful coexistence, mutual respect, and the expansion of bilateral trade, technical cooperation, and joint ventures.[29]

A *Beijing Review* article on Latin America reviewed the economic potential of the area—specifically, Mexico, Venezuela, Uruguay, Bolivia, Chile, Brazil, Peru, and Colombia—while it failed to mention Cuba.[30] Political rhetoric notwithstanding, China's economic pragmatism will lead it to concentrate on strengthening ties with the larger and more dynamic economies of Latin America, possibly to the detriment of Cuba. Countries with larger industrial capacity, greater efficiency, and broader markets might command China's attention.

Ideological affinity, while not the main pillar of the relationship, is a precarious base on which to build strong Sino-Cuban bilateral ties. If the history of Sino-Cuban relations since 1959 is any indication of what the future holds, one can expect snags as divergent ideological positions emerge between Beijing and Havana. This is a particularly likely outcome considering the presence of reformist groups within the Chinese state bureaucracy and the party.[31]

An additional constraint may be posed by the United States. The U.S. policy toward Cuba was toughened through the approval of the Torricelli Bill, which gives the U.S. president the option of taking action against any most-favored-nation trading partner that gives Cuba trade concessions. Washington may pressure Beijing to curtail favorable and sensitive trade with Havana. Such is the case not only with Chinese loans and subsidies but also with any assistance China might extend for Cuba's nuclear projects (which are of particular concern to Washington). Therefore, Sino-Cuban relations might become once again, to some extent, triangular— U.S.-Sino-Cuban—which will result in bilateral relations tending to become more difficult to manage.

CONCLUSION

Sino-Cuban relations since 1959 have been unstable because of a host of ideological and practical factors but largely because after 1968 such relations became triangular—Sino-Soviet-Cuban. The rapprochement, initiated by Beijing as part of a new global strategy in the early 1980s, and in part a response to the decline of Cuba's revolutionary internationalism, which China opposed, blossomed into close diplomatic contacts and strengthened economic ties by the end of the decade and the beginning of the 1990s. Both governments, faced with domestic pressures and rapid changes in the socialist world, found themselves in need of, above all, economic partners and political allies. In response to domestic and external pressures, they have sought business and solidarity with one another. The pragmatic, or nonideological, dimension of trade has become the most important aspect of Sino-Cuban relations.

In spite of an increase in the volume of trade, the economic future of the relationship is limited because of domestic and global economic constraints. Moreover, Cuba is less attractive to China than China is to Cuba, a situation that underscores the vulnerability of a small, poor country. The potential triangular relationship—United States–China–Cuba—will tend to complicate Sino-Cuban affairs by imposing additional constraints on them.

NOTES

The author acknowledges the support of a Mellon Grant, awarded by the Latin American and Caribbean Center at Florida International University, which helped completion of this chapter.

1. Jorge I. Domínguez, *To Make a World Safe for Revolution: Cuba's Foreign Policy* (Cambridge: Harvard University Press, 1989), p. 69.

2. Cecil Johnson, *Communist China and Latin America: 1959–1967* (New York: Columbia University Press, 1970), pp. 129–130.

3. Domínguez, *To Make a World Safe*, p. 69.

4. Personal interview with former Cuban official, September 10, 1990.

5. Pamela Falk, *Cuban Foreign Policy: Caribbean Tempest* (Lexington, Mass.: Lexington Books, 1985), p. 85.

6. *Granma*, February 8, 1986, p. 4.

7. *Granma*, February 7, 1986, pp. 2–4.

8. *Granma*, September 4, 1979, p. 3.

9. *Granma*, June 1, 1978, p. 1.

10. *Granma*, June 2, 1978, p. 1.

11. *Granma*, January 1, 1979, p. 2.

12. *Granma*, June 1, 1978, p. 1.

13. *Granma*, September 4, 1979, p. 2.

14. See Samuel S. Kim, *China and the World: New Direction in Chinese Foreign Policy* (Boulder, Colo.: Westview Press, 1989).

15. Personal interview with former Cuban official, Miami, June 1990.

16. *Granma*, February 8, 1986, p. 4.

17. *Granma*, September 18, 1985, p. 7.

18. *Granma*, June 15, 1986, p. 2.

19. *Anuario Estadística de Cuba, 1989* (Havana, 1990).

20. Gillian Gunn, "Will Castro Fall," *Foreign Policy* 79 (Summer 1990), p. 142.

21. For additional discussion see Jorge Pérez-López, "Swimming Against the Tide," *Journal of Interamerican Studies* 33, no. 2 (1991).

22. G. Zuikov et al., "Informe Sobre la Economía de Cuba," mimeo (Fundación Liberal José Martí, 1992), p. 129.

23. Pérez-Lopéz, "Swimming Against the Tide," p. 113.

24. Zuikov, "Informe Sobre," p. 131.

25. Ibid., p. 134.

26. Ibid.

27. Carlos Monsivais, "Cuba: Todos Somos Ortodoxos," *Proceso* (Mexico), July 24, 1989, p. 36.

28. *El Nuevo Herald*, May 6, 1990, p. 3A.

29. *Beijing Review* 33, no. 22 (May 28–June 3, 1990), pp. 7, 9.

30. *Beijing Review* 33, nos. 5–6 (January 29–February 11, 1990), p. 14.

31. *New York Times*, July 30, 1990, p. 1.

3

Cuban-Japanese Relations in Japanese Perspective: Economic Pragmatism and Political Distance

KANAKO YAMAOKA

The relationship between Cuba and Japan has been relatively stable for most of the years of their diplomatic history. Japan, like the majority of developed countries, has had continuous diplomatic and economic relations with Cuba since the Cuban Revolution, in spite of U.S. influence.

One important factor that makes this stability possible is geographic distance, which explains in part Japan's relative indifference to its relationship with Cuba compared with its relations with other Asian countries. Another important factor is the Japanese diplomatic tradition of concentration on its own economic interests. Since the end of World War II, because Japan has been interested almost solely in the economic aspects of its foreign relations, it has avoided political involvement in other countries' domestic affairs. However, at times, international organizations or Japan's relations with its allies (principally the United States) have prevented Japan from maintaining this focus.

The primacy of economic affairs started to undergo gradual change in the 1980s, and Japan has increasingly assumed greater political and military responsibility.[1] This is due in part to the decline of U.S. economic dominance and Japan's commensurate economic growth. Despite Japan's hesitancy in assuming greater responsibility, many countries, primarily the United States, no longer allow Japan to "shirk political involvement."[2] Today Japan has reached a turning point in its diplomatic history, and it is reevaluating its foreign policy.

Accordingly, Japan's relations with Cuba are also changing. Since the collapse of the Soviet Union and the Eastern bloc, Cuba has been forced to seek new survival methods. There is now far more a possibility of interaction between Japan and Cuba, and greater Japanese influence in Cuba as well.

This chapter reviews the history of Cuban-Japanese relations within a global and regional context and analyzes the factors that affect their relations. The chapter also examines future perspectives for the two countries.

CUBAN-JAPANESE DIPLOMATIC RELATIONS

Until the beginning of the 1960s, Japan's main interest in Latin America, including Cuba, was emigration to the region rather than economic affairs. Because of the underdeveloped Japanese economy and continuous increase of the country's population, the Japanese government strongly backed Japanese emigration; emigration programs were the center of the government's foreign policy toward Latin America. There are currently about one million Japanese immigrants in Latin America, about 80 percent of whom reside in Brazil. About seven hundred Japanese immigrants and their offspring reside in Cuba, almost all of them having immigrated before the Revolution.

The Cuban Revolution attracted a lot of attention from the Japanese people, especially the leftists and intellectuals. Although much of the Japanese leftist enthusiasm for the Revolution disappeared at the end of the 1960s when Castro expressed his clear support for the Soviet Union, Japanese interest has generally remained strong relative to Cuba's size. Since the 1960s, as the Japanese economy has developed, Japan's interest in Cuba has gradually shifted to economic affairs: first to trade and later (since the middle of the 1980s) also to economic assistance.

Diplomatic relations between Cuba and Japan started on December 21, 1929. In 1930 Japan established its legation in Havana; in the following year, Cuba did so in Tokyo. As did all the other Latin American countries, Cuba suspended its relations with Japan during World War II, having sided with the Allied countries. In 1952, after Japan signed the San Francisco Peace Treaty with most of the Allied nations, Japan reestablished relations with Cuba, as well as with other Latin American countries. Embassies were established in both Havana and Tokyo in 1957.

There have been no interruptions in Cuban-Japanese relations since the 1952 reconciliation. Even after the United States suspended diplomatic relations and imposed the economic embargo against Cuba, Japan, along with most other Western countries, maintained diplomatic and commercial relations with Havana. In April 1960, the Japanese Diet unanimously supported the conclusion of a friendship and commercial treaty with Cuba and has maintained it to the present. Japan's policy stands out as an extreme example of nonintervention and the primacy of economic relations.[3] Two main reasons for this attitude are (1) the geographic and therefore political distance between Japan and Cuba and (2) Japan's diplomatic tradition and trade policy toward not only Cuba but all countries.

Historically, Japan has not maintained close relations with Latin America compared with its relations with Asia, the United States, and Europe. On the one hand, this nonintimacy has allowed a situation in which neither enmity nor serious conflict has existed between Cuba and Japan. On the other hand, Japan lacks interest in and knowledge of Latin America, a situation that has left Japan with no political interest in Cuba.

The second reason for Japan's policy more fully explains the country's attitude toward Cuba. Japan's foreign policy since World War II has been based on (1) its general support of U.S. foreign policy and (2) its concentration on its own economic development and efforts to avoid political involvement in international affairs.

Japanese support of the United States is an important factor in Japan's foreign policy, especially in its policy toward Latin America. Japanese decisionmakers have believed that Latin America lies in the "backyard of the United States."[4] Japan has basically chosen to follow U.S. policy in order to avoid unnecessary conflicts with the United States, which Japan views as its military patron and most important economic partner.

Japan's geography prevents economic self-sufficiency—therefore, foreign trade is essential to the country's survival. Because Japan lacks raw materials, economic development depends on imports of such materials and exports of manufactured goods. Therefore, Japan does not wish to lose good relations with any country, because all are viewed as potential markets for Japanese products and, in many cases, crucial suppliers of raw materials. When Japan sees two parties clash, it tries to choose a policy that befriends both sides. This is a fundamental policy that takes precedence over even U.S. opposition.

This attitude is reflected in Japanese policy toward Cuba. One of the most significant examples of this policy was Japan's reaction to the Cuban missile crisis of 1962. In contrast to the U.S. blockade of the island, Japan (as well as Canada, Mexico, and the Western European countries) neither cut diplomatic relations nor stopped trade with Cuba.[5] In the UN Security Council, Japan has supported the U.S. policy of the economic embargo, though it has simultaneously maintained economic relations with Cuba.

CUBAN-JAPANESE ECONOMIC RELATIONS

Trade

Trade is the most important component of Cuban-Japanese economic relations. However, though Japan has been one of Cuba's main hard currency trading partners since the 1970s,[6] Cuba's share in Japan's trade is small (see Table 3.1). In 1989, for example, Cuba's share of Japan's total imports amounted to merely 0.06 percent ($133 million); the island's share of Japan's total exports was only 0.02 percent ($54 million). Latin America in general plays a minor role in Japan's trade. In 1989, Latin America's share of Japan's total imports amounted to 4.2 percent ($8.8 billion); its share of Japan's total exports was 3.0 percent ($8.5 billion).

**Table 3.1 Japan's Trade with Cuba, 1962–1991
(in thousands of U.S. $)**

Year	Imports	% of Japan's Total Imports	Exports	% of Japan's Total Exports
1962	35,809	0.64	10,597	0.22
1963	22,948	0.34	2,773	0.05
1964	53,444	0.67	34,393	0.52
1965	29,201	0.36	3,469	0.04
1966	22,227	0.23	6,497	0.07
1967	26,117	0.22	7,404	0.07
1968	33,268	0.26	2,448	0.02
1969	68,039	0.45	9,796	0.06
1970	110,674	0.59	39,213	0.20
1971	129,060	0.65	53,821	0.22
1972	145,373	0.62	50,742	0.18
1973	181,639	0.48	106,714	0.29
1974	441,643	0.71	203,181	0.37
1975	340,523	0.59	438,367	0.79
1976	50,297	0.08	199,542	0.30
1977	63,087	0.09	361,376	0.45
1978	106,195	0.13	211,814	0.22
1979	123,796	0.11	140,656	0.14
1980	187,411	0.13	238,740	0.18
1981	154,250	0.11	266,824	0.18
1982	114,832	0.09	125,682	0.09
1983	92,120	0.07	104,724	0.07
1984	77,987	0.06	250,310	0.15
1985	92,292	0.07	300,901	0.17
1986	131,117	0.11	292,681	0.14
1987	116,138	0.08	113,914	0.05
1988	138,118	0.08	116,316	0.04
1989	133,362	0.06	54,461	0.02
1990	94,926	0.04	72,657	0.03
1991	141,800	n.a.	35,600	n.a.

Source: United Nations International Trade Statistics Yearbook, 1962–1990.
Note: 1991 data were drawn from the trade statistics of the Japanese government.

Japan's exports to Cuba are varied, ranging from chemical products to machinery; its imports from Cuba are composed primarily of sugar and seafood products (mainly lobster). Japanese exports to Cuba grew between 1973 and 1988; though total trade turnover slowed in the late 1980s, Japan's imports from Cuba have increased since 1990.

Each year from 1962 to 1975, sugar constituted more than 90 percent of Japan's imports from Cuba (see Table 3.2). In 1962, Japan's sugar imports from Cuba amounted to $35.7 million; in 1970, $106.4 million; and in 1974, $419.9 million. Since 1976, sugar has made up about 50 percent of Japan's total imports from Cuba, and seafood products account for about 30 percent.

Table 3.2 Japan's Imports from Cuba: Sugar and Seafood Products, 1962–1991 (in thousands of U.S. $)

Year	Sugar	% of Total Imports[a]	Seafood	% of Total Imports[b]
1962	35,748	99.8	0	0.0
1963	22,909	99.8	0	0.0
1964	53,259	99.7	0	0.0
1965	29,019	99.4	0	0.0
1966	22,090	99.4	0	0.0
1967	26,001	99.6	0	0.0
1968	32,976	99.1	0	0.0
1969	65,873	96.8	1,897	2.8
1970	106,449	96.2	3,924	3.5
1971	124,603	96.5	3,788	2.9
1972	135,819	93.4	5,104	3.5
1973	168,052	92.5	7,759	4.3
1974	419,884	95.1	14,173	3.2
1975	322,266	94.6	13,749	4.0
1976	28,125	55.9	19,109	38.0
1977	34,186	54.2	20,514	32.5
1978	70,046	66.0	29,510	27.8
1979	84,581	68.3	26,188	21.2
1980	146,101	78.0	27,387	14.6
1981	130,070	84.3	12,590	8.2
1982	76,405	66.5	23,933	20.8
1983	57,339	62.2	25,996	28.2
1984	43,738	56.1	26,774	34.3
1985	49,879	54.0	34,383	37.3
1986	81,345	62.0	37,244	28.4
1987	48,217	41.5	38,339	33.0
1988	68,853	49.9	42,504	30.8
1989	57,584	43.2	44,405	33.3
1990	38,606	40.7	34,386	36.2
1991[c]	88,090	62.1	34,713	24.5

Source: United Nations International Trade Statistics Yearbook, 1962–1990.
Notes: a. Percentage of Japan's total sugar imports from Cuba.
b. Percentage of Japan's total seafood imports from Cuba.
c. 1991 data were drawn from the trade statistics of the Japanese government.

Cuba's share of Japanese sugar imports was about 22 percent in the 1960s, 28 percent (a postrevolutionary high) from 1970 to 1976, and 12 percent in the 1980s. In 1990, its share dropped to 6 percent, though it recovered to nearly 15 percent in 1991. Cuba's share of Japan's total sugar imports is relatively high, considering that Japan has alternative sugar suppliers. In 1991, the four largest sugar exporters to Japan were Australia, Thailand, South Africa, and Cuba (see Table 3.3). Unit prices (in c.i.f.) are lowest in Thailand and highest in Cuba;[7] freight costs to transport sugar to Japan from Thailand and Australia (sometimes from South Africa) are lower than Cuban transport costs. Yet, despite economic

Table 3.3   Japan's Sugar Imports from Its Main Suppliers (1991)

Country	Quantity (million tons)	Value (in millions of U.S. $)	Unit Value ($)
Australia	578,771	151.0	261.0
Thailand	483,141	122.8	254.3
South Africa	358,442	95.6	266.6
Cuba	351,211	93.7	266.7

Source: Trade statistics of the Japanese government.

costs, Japan has continued to purchase Cuban sugar for the following reasons:

• The quality of Cuban sugar is very good.
• Japan imports all its sugar through the international free sugar markets and has a yearly contract with each sugar-producing country. Market theory dictates that it is better for Japan to buy from Cuba if Cuba offers a low price or if Japan is unable to purchase enough sugar from other countries.
• Generally, transactions are in the form of barter trade. Therefore, in order to sell Japanese products to Cuba, Japan must buy Cuban products. This is especially true for firms that have extended credits to Cuba to obtain some return on their credits through new trade.

Japan's imports of seafood products from Cuba were zero until 1969, when Japan imported $1.9 million worth of such products. This number jumped to $7.8 million in 1973 and to $14.2 million in 1974. The main reason for this increase was that one of the largest Japanese fishery companies, Taiyo Fishery, launched a large project to purchase Cuban lobsters. Though Japan imports a large quantity of lobsters from temperate zones—Australia and the United States—it prefers Cuban rock lobsters, which are natural, not cultured, and larger in size than the temperate types.

Another important item that Japan imports from Cuba is coffee beans. Cuba's share of Japan's total coffee imports increased from 0.7 percent in 1985 to 0.9 percent in 1986, 2.6 percent in 1987, and 3.2 percent in 1990. It reached a high of $22.9 million in 1989 (though it fell to $13.2 million in 1991). This growth is due partly to a drastic increase in Japan's consumption of coffee in the last half of the 1980s. Yet the share of Cuban coffee to Japan's total coffee imports has increased more than the growth of Japan's total imports; this is because Cuba produces coffee of excellent quality, and the Japanese market demands such high-quality products. Until the mid-1980s, Cuban coffee was not widely known in Japan. It had been sold as a part of Jamaican "Blue Mountain" coffee. Yet Cuban coffee exporters wanted to develop their own market and believed that their product's quality was equivalent to, or better than, Blue Mountain coffee. Since the mid-1980s Cuba has exported its coffee with the special brand name "Crystal Mountain." Crystal Mountain coffee beans are specially selected for export to Japan.

Although nickel is one of Cuba's main exports, it is not an important item in its trade with Japan. Between 1962 and 1989, Japan imported Cuban nickel only in 1973, 1975–1984, and 1986. Cuba's share of total Japanese nickel imports reached a high of 2.1 percent in 1982. Strict U.S. control on imports of Cuban nickel and products containing Cuban nickel is the main reason Japan does not import much of this material. Firms that plan to import Cuban nickel or produce goods containing Cuban nickel must register annually with the Japanese government; then the government must license an oversight program verifying that the firms' products destined for the United States do not contain Cuban nickel.

Although Japan imports a large amount of tobacco every year, Cuba's share is small, reaching a high of only 0.1 percent in 1974. Cuban tobacco is expensive compared with tobacco from other countries, such as the United States, and Cuban tobacco is used solely for cigars; Japan's demand for cigars is very low.

Cuba's imports from Japan are much more diversified than Japan's imports from Cuba. Most of the items, including intermediate goods, are manufactured goods, though none of these items constitute a large percentage of total Cuban imports from Japan. Cuban imports from Japan include chemical products, dyeing and color materials, pharmaceutical products, plastics, rubber, paper, iron and steel, other metals, and miscellaneous machinery. Rubber (mostly automobile tires), iron and steel, and machinery are especially important in Japan's exports to Cuba (see Table 3.4). Japanese trucks are used in the sugar industry, and pharmaceutical products imported from Japan are used to make medicines.

Cuba's imports from Japan are influenced by Cuba's economic situation. In the 1970s, when it had high foreign reserves due to high sugar prices, Cuba increased its imports, including those from Japan. In the 1980s, according to the Cuban government's economic policy to increase its imports, Cuba imported a large quantity of manufactured goods from Japan, despite low sugar prices and high interest rates. The 1980s policy caused Cuba to experience serious foreign reserve shortages and a debt problem, and thus the government implemented an austerity policy. In 1987, Cuban imports from Japan, as well as from other countries, dropped drastically, and they continued to decrease until at least 1991 (with the exception of 1990).

In 1990, seventeen Japanese firms had branch offices in Cuba for sales of their products or for trading; this number has dropped to eleven, a decrease

Table 3.4 Japan's Major Exports to Cuba, 1962–1990
(in thousands of U.S. $)

Year	Rubber	Iron and Steel	Machinery
1962	13	3,179	3,682
1963	0	1,673	293
1964	2,108	1,730	7,323
1965	450	209	1,251
1966	267	2,064	1,908
1967	474	2,906	2,347
1968	154	957	853
1969	1,199	2,385	2,859
1970	2,745	3,754	15,287
1971	5,514	3,685	27,053
1972	2,115	9,039	23,055
1973	5,405	20,563	53,430
1974	12,071	29,560	96,074
1975	21,920	55,095	190,668
1976	8,933	10,070	92,568
1977	8,044	14,923	230,063
1978	6,717	10,912	122,651
1979	3,399	7,070	71,092
1980	9,811	13,569	62,804
1981	13,464	16,114	137,922
1982	3,539	5,367	72,363
1983	5,239	6,374	48,359
1984	11,983	21,752	139,269
1985	17,663	27,991	152,429
1986	12,422	12,466	150,276
1987	4,857	6,066	70,944
1988	6,419	4,606	71,531
1989	2,223	1,630	34,635
1990	12,935	2,447	40,998

Source: United Nations International Trade Statistics Yearbook, 1962–1990.

that is due mainly to Cuba's declining economic situation. A majority of these firms are trading companies. In accordance with Japanese business customs, nearly all trade contracts are made through such trading companies, and thus many Japanese firms indirectly buy and sell goods and services in Cuba using these companies. Major Japanese trading firms in Cuba include Marubeni, C. Itoh, Nissho Iwai, Meiwa (a subsidiary of Mitsubishi), Kanematsu, and Mitsui. Hino Automobiles (supplying trucks and buses) and Komatsu (providing agricultural and construction machinery) also have offices in Havana. In addition, there are several small trading companies specializing in the Cuban market.

There are three major limitations in trade between Cuba and Japan. One is the application of the COCOM (Coordinating Committee for

Export Control) agreement, which prohibits exports of goods and services that are potentially strategic items to communist countries. This is a serious impediment to Japan's exports to Cuba. The standards of the application of the COCOM agreement are not open to the public, but individual governments can decide whether an item is applicable for regulation. Therefore, when Cuba attempts to import items of new technology, such as computers, the COCOM agreement has prevented it.

The Japanese government also restricts trade between the islands.[8] The government has directed the private sector to refrain voluntarily from going "too far" in conducting trade with Cuba, in order not to offend the United States. For example, because the United States has not permitted vessels used in trade with Cuba to dock at U.S. ports, Japan uses Cuban or a third country's vessels, rather than its own, in its trade with the island. Third-country ships also carry goods from Japan to a neighboring port, such as Jamaica, and then the cargo is transshipped to Cuban flag carriers.

Cuba's debt to the Japanese private sector and to the government also constrains trade. Since Cuba's debt crisis of 1985, Japanese business in Cuba has been slow to develop. From 1974 to 1991, the trade balance between Cuba and Japan favored Japan. Cuba's deficit accumulated in the form of export credits and delayed payment and has now reached 190 billion Japanese yen (about $1.5 billion). It is not clear when or if these credits will be returned. Furthermore, Japanese firms can no longer receive export credits from the Japanese government when they export goods to Cuba. Since 1989, all trade between Cuba and Japan has been done by barter or advance payment of cash or check, and not by credits.

Investment

Cuba is currently trying to attract foreign capital by promoting investment and joint venture programs, and it has been successful in some cases (see Chapter 14). But no Japanese firm has yet reached an agreement with Cuba for such an investment program. Cuba's debt problem presents the greatest obstacle to the development of Japanese business in Cuba. Currently, most Japanese firms' principal goal is to obtain the return of their credits, not to start or develop new projects. However, Cuba has been suffering from a foreign reserve shortage, and Japanese firms, like firms from other countries, cannot expect their credits to be paid back in the near future.

Cuba has offered several programs to escape its debt and capital shortage dilemma. For example, if a Japanese firm invests tourism, the amount of debt that Cuba owes that firm is to be considered as a part of the firm's investment. In another proposal, if a firm participates in a joint venture program that utilizes idle factories to promote an export, part of the profit goes to pay off the debt to the firm. However, to date the Japanese private sector has refused to invest new capital in Cuba until Cuba repays its debt. Furthermore, the general economic situation and Cuba's bureaucratic system discourage further business investment.

Government Aid

Another factor influencing economic relations between the islands is the Japanese government's aid to Cuba, which is affected by Japan's political and economic interests. The Japanese government has based its assistance on "a developing country's self-reliance in its development."[9] In other words, the country must rely primarily on its own internal resources for economic development. Furthermore, U.S. government opposition to Japanese aid to Cuba has also been an inhibiting factor.

Since 1986, Japan has greatly increased its grant and aid programs around the world. Between 1985 and 1987, the amount of Japan's Official Development Assistance (ODA) doubled, from $3.8 billion to $7.5 billion. In 1989, Japan's ODA reached nearly $9 billion and was the world's largest government aid program. In 1990 and 1991 Japan's ODA was the second largest (after the United States) in the world, and it is expected to become the largest again in 1992. Japan's ODA program includes grants, loans, and technical assistance.

Table 3.5   Japan's ODA to Latin America and Cuba, 1985–1990 (in millions of U.S. $)

Year	To Latin America		To Cuba
1985	224.93	(5.9%)	0.09
1986	316.54	(5.6%)	0.23
1987	417.99	(5.6%)	0.21
1988	399.29	(4.4%)	0.48
1989	563.33	(6.3%)	0.35
1990	561.20	(6.2%)	0.55

Source: Japan's ODA Yearbook, Ministry of Foreign Affairs, 1990 and 1991.
Notes: Japan's ODA to Cuba contains only grants, no loans. In its grant, Japan has given only technical assistance. The numbers in parentheses indicate the percentage of Japan's total aid worldwide.

Although Japan has granted ODA funds to Cuba, the amount has been insignificant. However, as shown in Table 3.5, Japan's aid to Cuba grew from $90,000 in 1985 to $550,000 in 1990.[10] This growth reflects Japan's overall increase in aid to developing countries since 1986. In 1989, Japan was the fourth largest donor of aid to Cuba after Italy, Sweden, and France (but excluding the Soviet Union), and Japan's share of the total bilateral aid to Cuba that year was 3.32 percent. The increase in 1990 is probably consistent with the general increase of Japanese aid to Latin America.

Most (57 percent in 1989) of Japan's ODA is spent on bilateral aid to Asian countries; Latin America's share of Japan's total ODA was only 6.6 percent in 1989. Therefore, the small amount given to Cuba appears to be due less to Cuba's status in Latin America than to Latin America's political distance from Japan.

Government loans have never been part of Japan's ODA program in Cuba, but grants are given in the form of technical assistance. To date, such aid has consisted of (1) a Japanese training program for Cubans and (2) a transfer of Japanese specialists to Cuba.

The training program started in 1960 when Japan received two Cuban trainees. The program was discontinued between 1961 and 1969, but in 1970 one Cuban trainee was sent to Japan. Since 1973, Cubans have been received every year, and Japan has accepted between five and ten trainees from Cuba since 1985. Most trainees participate in courses held by the Japan International Cooperation Agency (JICA), which implements the government's technical assistance programs. In 1990 and 1991, five Cuban trainees participated in courses in telecommunications, health and medicine, livestock industry, metal industry, and tourism, among others.

Based on requests from a recipient country's government or from international organizations, the Japanese government sends specialists from the appropriate field(s) for teaching or training abroad. Japan sent specialists to Cuba for the first time in 1990; three specialists, in the fields of hotel management, flower cultivation, and Japanese language training, were sent. In 1991, however, no government specialists were sent to Cuba because of the deterioration of living conditions there.

Japanese aid is based not on ideology but on the stability of the receiving government and Japan's aid policy, which is closely linked to Japan's economic interests. Japan believes that the Castro regime is a factor of instability in the region, and thus increasing aid to Cuba would be tantamount to increasing the degree of instability. For example, the Japanese government is concerned that its aid will be used for military assistance such as aiding insurgencies in other countries. Thus, Japan does not provide assistance in areas of "dual-use fields" of expertise, such as architecture. It is likely that the Japanese government plans to increase its ODA to Cuba, but Cuban "democratization" is an important prerequisite before this increase can occur.

PERSPECTIVE ON THE FUTURE

Japanese public and private interest in Cuba is not as high as it is in, for example, Asian countries, and it is unlikely that Japan will make any major change in its long-standing policy toward Cuba in the near future.

Possible improvements in the relations between Cuba and Japan will depend on external factors, to which Japan is reactive. Such factors include changes in other powerful countries' attitudes toward, for instance, increased aid to Cuba; change in U.S. policy toward Cuba; and political change in Cuba.

Given the severity of the economic crisis in Cuba today, there is little room for maneuver by either Japanese firms or the Japanese government. As for Japan's private investment, the serious shortage of resources and infrastructure, as well as Cuba's bureaucratic system, are significant obstacles to Japanese firms interested in increasing investment in Cuba. Cuba will inevitably have to adjust to a market-oriented economy if it wishes to obtain more foreign investment to reconstruct its economy.

For the present, the Japanese private sector seems more willing than the Japanese government to participate in activities with Cuba. While the government hesitates to provide more economic assistance to Cuba, the Japan Silver Volunteers, a leading nongovernmental organization in Japan, started sending its staff to Cuba in 1990. In spite of the serious economic conditions in Cuba, three staff members currently live there and teach the Japanese language.

At the grassroots level, Cuban-Japanese relations are improving. For example, although the number of Japanese visiting Cuba is small compared with the total number of Japanese tourists, the number of Japanese tourists in Cuba has been increasing for the last two years. Until 1989 only about one hundred Japanese tourists visited Cuba every year. In 1990, however, this number jumped to 972; most of this increase was a result of the Peace Boat program.[11] In 1991, 1,168 tourists visited Cuba, and more tourists were expected to visit in 1992. Since 1986, the depreciation of the dollar against the Japanese yen has made it easier for Japanese to travel abroad, and the number of Japanese tourists traveling overseas has dramatically increased. In addition, the Cuban government's efforts to attract Japanese tourists since 1990 have been successful.

In recent years, Latin American expectations of aid from Japan have increased, and it is imperative for the two regions to establish closer relations. Japan's positive image in Latin America is a result, in part, of Japan's political distance and economic prosperity. Japan is one of Cuba's main trading partners, and the relationship between the two countries has developed into one of mutual trust, especially compared with Cuban-U.S. relations.

Because Japan's economic-based foreign policy is changing and the country is emerging as a political power, it is all the more important for Japan to encourage the Cuban government to begin the process of adjustment. Japan can help Cuba make moderate reforms. In its new role as a world leader, Japan can support and encourage other countries to assist Cuba through its difficult process of change. Japan could also cooperate with the European Community and other developed countries such as Canada to improve relations between Cuba and the United States. Japanese foreign policy toward Cuba will be a test case in Japan's pursuit of a new course in the development of its post–Cold War objectives.

NOTES

1. For example, in 1991 when the prime minister of Malaysia initiated the East Asian Economic Grouping (EAEG), which was planned to promote economic cooperation among Asian countries, he asked Japan to be the leading country of the group. Although Dr. Mahatir's initiative was not accepted by the Japanese government because of (1) Japan's opposition to forming an economic bloc, (2) U.S. pressure to prevent Japan from participating in the initiative, and (3) the lack of a consensus among all other Asian countries, this action was important because for the first time Asian countries asked Japan to take a leadership role in the international arena. Another example is that the U.S. government has asked Japan (and also Germany) to take additional military responsibility for each country's security.

2. There are four factors related to greater Japanese involvement: (1) It is no longer possible for the United States to support its global policy in financial terms. (2) The world is becoming multipolar, and Japan and the European Community have gained more power as important actors in world affairs. (3) With the end of the Cold War, both the United States and Japan lost the strongest incentive to maintain powerful armed forces. Instead of military force, economic strength has appeared to be the decisive element in the degree of power that a country possesses. (4) Because of technological progress, the world is becoming more and more interdependent in economic terms, and borders between politics and economics are becoming ambiguous; thus it is necessary for Japan to cooperate with other countries more closely, even when Japan is mainly interested in economic affairs.

3. Jorge Domínguez, *To Make a World Safe for Revolution: Cuba's Foreign Policy* (Cambridge: Harvard University Press, 1989, p. 195), Domínguez admits that, among Western countries, Japan acts almost solely according to the market mechanism.

4. Peter Smith, *Japan, Latin America, and the New International Order*, mimeo (Tokyo: Institute of Developing Economies, 1990), p. 30. Based on his interviews with some members of the Japanese Diet, the author points out "the subordination of Japan's relationship with Latin America to the United States."

5. In a discussion at the Japanese Diet on October 15, 1962, Kei Hoashi, a Diet member from the Socialist Party, stated that Japan's sugar consumption depended considerably on Cuba and that Japan should maintain its trade with the island. Before the Cuban Revolution, Japan imported a large amount of sugar from Cuba; in 1957, Cuba exported 513,823 metric tons to Japan. This amount was approximately 1.5 times as much as the sugar trade between the islands in 1991, which was 351,211 tons.

6. In 1991 Japan was the second largest trading partner of Cuba (next to Canada) among capitalist countries for imports and eighth largest for exports. Economist Intelligence Unit, *Country Profile, 1992* (London, 1991).

7. Japan imports about 65 percent of its total domestic sugar consumption, and all of its imports are through the international sugar market, with no quota system or other trade regulations.

8. Although in general, as previously described, the Japanese government lets the private sector act according to market economy theory, it sometimes guides Japanese firms in a certain direction for political reasons.

9. Japan's leading sociologist, Chie Nakane, points out in her book *Japanese Potentiality and Limits* (in Japanese) (Tokyo: Kodansha, 1978), that this stance is based on Japanese traditional philosophy, by which people believe that everyone is able to enjoy a sensible life if they are willing to make the effort (p. 9). Therefore, Japanese people do not believe that it is a richer country's obligation to help poorer countries. The government, therefore, must prove to the Japanese people that helping developing countries is a long-term economic and political interest for Japan (p. 11).

10. This amount represents all the expenditures of Japanese ODA to Cuba, and it is still small compared with the cases of Mexico and Brazil. In 1988 Mexico obtained $38.8 million from Japan, and Brazil received $66.4 million. Yet, Japan's aid to Cuba is larger than the other Caribbean countries, except Trinidad and Tobago.

11. Peace Boat is a private organization that conducts tours, not only for sightseeing but for the study of society and culture of foreign countries. In 1990, as part of their around-the-world cruising tour, about 450 participants visited Cuba for two days. Among other programs, they visited Russian children receiving treatments for radioactive contamination from the Chernobyl disaster.

4

Cuba's Relations with Africa: The End of an Era

Francine Marshall

A great deal of scholarly attention has been focused on Cuba's policy toward Africa.[1] Therefore, this chapter will concentrate on the most recent post–Cold War period and will begin with only a brief history of Cuban-African relations. It then takes a closer look at Cuba's relations in the African countries where it has been most active—Angola, the Horn of Africa, and Mozambique. The third section of the chapter describes Cuba's civilian assistance to Africa, and the final section briefly describes Cuba's current diplomatic and trade ties to the region.

CHANGING ROLE OF CUBA'S INVOLVEMENT IN AFRICA

Cuba's relationship with the African continent can be broadly defined by three distinct periods. In the first period, Cuba assisted Africa's fledgling independence movements. In most cases, that assistance took the form of military ties, with Cuba providing organizational advice and, occasionally, soldiers. During the second period, the Cold War intensified and the extent of Cuban military involvement expanded along ideological and geopolitical lines. During this period, Cuban civilian assistance increased in countries expressing socialist sympathies. In the post–Cold War period, economic difficulties in Cuba and on the African continent have forced both the Cubans and the Africans to adopt pragmatic policies based on expanding trade and technical cooperation.

The Early Days

Cuban-African relations intensified shortly after the Cuban Revolution. The new Cuban government expressed a strong affinity for the poor, the majority of whom were Afro-Cubans. Pres. Fidel Castro referred to Cuba as an "African nation," expanding upon the notion of Cuba's natural solidarity with Africa. The Castro government was also committed to assisting progressive groups fighting against colonial and racist powers, many of which were in Africa. Furthermore, the U.S.-imposed Organization of American States (OAS) embargo against the island forced Cuba to seek relations with nations outside of its hemisphere.

The first ties with Africa began in 1960 when Cuba provided military and medical supplies to the Algerian Liberation Front (FLN).[2] The Cubans founded their first military mission in Ghana in 1961 and maintained it until Ghana's Kwame Nkrumah was ousted in 1966.[3] The Cuban presence was solidified with Che Guevara's extended trip to the Congo from December 1964 to March 1965. Though Guevara's goals of forming a union of Third World and pro-independence movements aimed at combating imperialism failed, the Cubans trained insurgents from around the continent in Congo-Brazzaville, Tanzania, and Algeria. The Cubans assisted in the training of insurgents from Namibia, Rhodesia, Zanzibar, Senegal, Cameroon, Nigeria, South Africa, the Belgian Congo, and other countries.[4]

From Ideology to Pragmatism

By the 1970s, it was becoming clear that the guerrilla offensives had, to a large extent, failed in Africa and Latin America. Cuba's promotion of armed struggle clashed with the Soviet Union's desire to expand diplomatic and trade ties to countries following peaceful routes to power, and Cuba began to sacrifice some revolutionary ideals as it sought Cold War allies. For example, in order to benefit from Ethiopia's geographic and mineral importance, Cuba and the Soviet Union supported the newly empowered Marxist-Leninist president of Ethiopia, Mengistu Haile-Mariam, over their traditional allies, the Eritrean rebels and Somalia. Assistance continued to be given to revolutionary governments espousing Marxism-Leninism, but state-to-state relations expanded as well.

By the mid-1980s Cuba had relations with over forty countries in Africa, including some that supported forces fighting against Cuba's socialist allies in Angola (e.g., Zaire and the Ivory Coast).[5] The Cubans even cultivated relations with some of Africa's most brutal and tyrannical regimes—including those of Nguema Macias in Equatorial Guinea and Idi Amin in Uganda—when they believed those relations were to their advantage.[6] The Cubans limited their support of liberation movements to the African National Congress, the Southwest African People's Organization, the Polisario Front, the Zimbabwe African People's Union, and, later, the Zimbabwe African National Union.[7]

Current Relations

In the post–Cold War era, many of the reasons for Cuba's active involvement in Africa have eroded. The African continent has been decolonized, and South Africa is the only minority-ruled country remaining there. In addition, the increasingly impoverished African countries have turned to the West for economic assistance, forcing them to abandon socialist economic policies and move toward market-oriented economies and stabilization programs. But perhaps the most important change in Cuba's policy has been prompted by its own domestic economic crisis. Without the logistical and financial support from the former Soviet Union and Eastern Europe, Cuba cannot maintain an activist international policy in Africa.

In a major announcement during a conference on the Cuban missile crisis in January 1992, President Castro stated that Cuba's international policy would change. "We have problems at home and internationalism begins at home," he declared, and he said that Cuba would no longer provide military assistance to revolutionary movements abroad.[8] Because the Cubans' first priority is the survival of their own revolution, they are promoting diplomatic ties and trade relations that will alleviate the sudden financial vacuum left by the Soviet Union. According to the Cubans, they no longer have any troops or military advisers in Africa. President Castro said that Cubans have not abandoned their humanitarian aid programs and will continue such programs to the extent that it is economically feasible to do so.

With the end of the Cold War, and with economic problems paramount in Cuba and the African countries, Cuban-African relationships are no longer based primarily upon ideology or geopolitical concerns but rather on more pragmatic and immediate economic needs. Ironically, even though the Cubans' military and civilian presence on the continent is at an all-time low, Cuba has diplomatic relations with more African countries than ever before.

CUBAN MILITARY INVOLVEMENT IN AFRICA

At the height of Cuba's involvement in Africa, Cuban military and civilian personnel were in seventeen nations (see Map 4.1), and as many as six hundred thousand Cuban troops may have served in Africa. Militarily, Cuba was most heavily committed in three countries: Angola, Ethiopia, and Mozambique.

Angola

Background. The history of Cuban involvement in Angola has been well documented, but a few major points bear repeating. First, Cuba initiated its support for the Popular Movement for the Liberation of Angola (MPLA) in 1966 during its first period of focusing assistance to Marxist-Leninist guerrillas fighting imperialist powers.

Map 4.1   Cuban Military and Civilian Presence in Africa, 1978

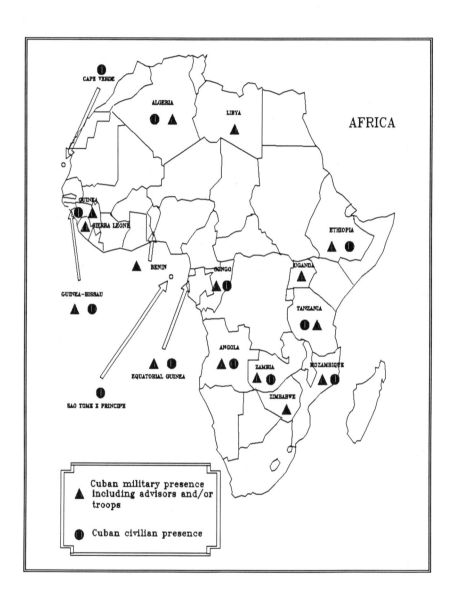

Sources: Sergio Díaz-Briquets and Jorge Pérez-López (1989) and William M. LeoGrande (1982).

Second, Cuban military intervention in support of the MPLA was initiated at the request of the MPLA following the incursion of South African troops into Angolan territory in October 1975, almost a month before the Portuguese were scheduled to withdraw.

Third, the Cuban decision to commit large-scale military assistance in Angola was made independently of the USSR and was supported by the Organization of African Unity. Cuba boosted its prestige as an underdeveloped country willing to shed blood for an anti-imperialist and anti-apartheid cause without asking for military or economic concessions in return. The support of the African countries helped President Castro to obtain chairmanship of the Nonaligned Movement in 1979.[9]

Fourth, after the Portuguese completed their withdrawal in November 1975, the civil war among the MPLA (led by Agostinho Neto and then by José Eduardo dos Santos following Neto's death in 1979), UNITA (the National Union for the Total Independence of Angola), and the FNLA (the National Front for the Liberation of Angola) quickly turned into a Cold War battle. The United States and South Africa provided assistance to UNITA and the FNLA, while the Soviets and the Cubans aided the MPLA. Thus, Cuban relations with Angola entered the second period of escalated assistance during the Cold War. At the period's height, the Cuban government had fifty thousand troops and five thousand to ten thousand civilian advisers in Angola.[10] Several attempts to negotiate the conflict failed. While blame for some of the failures can be placed on each of the participants, it is widely acknowledged (even by the Americans) that repeated South African incursions into Angola prolonged the conflict.[11]

The late 1980s. By 1987, it became clear that the military intervention in Angola was not worth the cost to any of the participants. For the Cubans, the international prestige they had gained when they had first come to the aid of the Angolans had dissipated. Domestically, the Cuban people were dissatisfied with the length of the war effort and the loss of lives. Cuban troops had been attacked several times in 1983 and 1984 while in logistical positions and several thousand Cubans died. (Estimates of Cuban casualties during the Angolan war range from a few thousand to twelve thousand. Cuban official statistics acknowledge more than two thousand deaths in Angola.)[12] This increasing loss of Cuban life can be attributed to Angolan troops not being trained to use more technical military equipment, forcing Cuban troops to fight on the front line as the conflict continued. Furthermore, the sophisticated Soviet weaponry was balanced by U.S. arms and led to a military stalemate. In addition, the economic cost of the war mounted as the price of oil fell from $45 to $13 per barrel in the mid-1980s, restricting Angola's export revenue and its ability to pay the Cubans for their presence.[13]

The war in Angola had become a blot in the détente agenda and a drain on military resources for the United States and the Soviets. Likewise, almost twenty years of military involvement in Angola had strained South African resources and helped destroy its international image. It is widely viewed that the war reached a climax with the defeat of the South Africans at the strategic town of Cuito Cuanavale in the fall of 1987. There, Cuban aid was decisive in the MPLA victory over South African troops and UNITA, convincing all parties that it was time to negotiate.

The United States finally succeeded in brokering an agreement among Angola, South Africa, and Cuba in December 1988. The Tripartite Agreement called for the implementation of UN Resolution 435 (providing for the independence of Namibia through free and fair elections); the departure of all South African forces from Namibia; the staged withdrawal of Cuban troops from Angola with on-site verification by the UN; and the respect by all parties of the principle of noninterference in the internal affairs of the states of southwestern Africa.[14] Angola and Cuba viewed Namibia as an integral part of the resolution to the conflict because of their desires to advance the cause of anticolonialism and to prevent South Africa from using Namibia as a base from which to invade Angola.

A joint commission composed of Angola, Cuba, and South Africa was established to oversee the implementation of the agreement. Namibia became a member of the commission after its independence on March 21, 1990, and the United States and the Soviet Union were observers.

Under the supervision of the UN Angolan verification mission, Cuba began withdrawing troops from Angola in January 1989 and completed the withdrawal on May 25, 1991—thirty-six days ahead of the July 1 deadline. Although the accord did not include the Cubans' earlier demands that apartheid be abolished and Namibia receive independence before they pulled out of Angola, Castro was publicly pleased with the accord. He said that the signing of the Tripartite Agreement "successfully ends one of the most glorious pages" of Cuban history.[15] The Cubans were privately unhappy that while the agreement removed South African troops as a direct threat to the MPLA, it did not specifically require that either South Africa or the United States refrain from aiding UNITA. Indeed, their fears were justified when both the United States and South Africa continued to provide assistance to UNITA and fighting between UNITA and the MPLA continued after the Cuban withdrawal.

On May 31, 1991, almost three years after the signing of the Tripartite Agreement, the MPLA and UNITA finally signed a peace accord. The process of registering an estimated four million eligible voters out of a population of eight million began in May 1992. Progress was slow on the implementation of the military aspects of the accord and only a small percentage of the existing forces had been demobilized before the elections were held on September 29 and 30, 1992. Official election results stated that in the presidential race, Dos Santos won 49.57 percent of the vote to Savimbi's 40.07 percent. Because neither candidate won a majority of the valid votes, regulations required that a runoff election be held. In the legislative contest, the MPLA won 53.74 percent of the votes to UNITA's 34.1 percent. Although international observers certified the elections to be free of major irregularities, Savimbi charged that there had been major fraud. He did not provide evidence to validate his claims, however, and tensions between the MPLA and UNITA escalated. Then at the end of October, UNITA launched a series of attacks in Luanda. The fighting has since escalated, and diplomats there are not hopeful of a resolution to the conflict in the short term.[16]

Relations today. Pres. José Eduardo dos Santos discarded Angola's Marxist-Leninist ideology in the fall of 1990 and Angola began to court the West. While personal relations between dos Santos and Castro have remained friendly, the Cubans are discouraged by some of the changes taking place in Angola. State-owned farms and nationalized industries are being referred to as "mistakes" by MPLA members.[17] The government recently surrendered its monopoly on all mineral rights and introduced a new mining law that makes it possible for private foreign and local companies to invest in prospecting and mining.

When asked in 1991 how the Cubans felt about the MPLA's abandonment of Marxist-Leninist ideology, Cuba's former ambassador to Angola replied, "We did not come here to defend Marxism-Leninism: We are here to help the Angolan people defend their sovereignty."[18] Cuba's current ambassador to Angola, Reinaldo Lefferte, said in April 1992 that future Cuban-Angolan relations will depend upon the outcome of the general elections in September. He said, "Should the winning political party wish to maintain official relations with Cuba, we will be willing to maintain such relations with the future Angolan government."[19]

Dos Santos calculated material losses due to the war at $12 billion; 10 percent of the population was displaced, and over five hundred thousand Angolans were crippled. Given such grim statistics, the Angolans' main goals are to breathe life back into the war-torn economy (which means courting the West). An attempt to prevent the United States and the South Africans from providing military funding for UNITA has also meant that the MPLA has moved closer to the West. Both goals necessitate that relations between the MPLA and the Cubans not be as close as they once were.

Pros and cons of Cuban involvement. Cuba's involvement was fundamental in securing the presence of the MPLA in Angola, gaining independence for Namibia, and freeing both countries from South African aggression. Cuba's prestige from this involvement in Angola catapulted the island into its leadership role in the Nonaligned Movement. Cuba did, however, pay dearly for its involvement in Angola. In addition to the decline in domestic and international support as the conflict continued, the Cubans' early support of the MPLA sabotaged the potential warming of relations between Cuba and the United States that were initiated during the Ford administration.

The Horn of Africa

Background. Cuba's second largest military involvement in Africa was in Ethiopia. Again, the history of Cuba's involvement there is well documented; what follows are the most important developments. First, the circumstances under which Cuba became involved in the Horn of Africa differ significantly from those in the Angolan situation. Cuba had supported the MPLA in Angola for a decade prior to Angolan independence and sent in troops only after Angola faced external aggression. However, in the Horn, the Cubans had supported Ethiopia's traditional enemies—Somalia and Eritrea. They supported Somalia because its postindependence government proclaimed itself socialist. The Cubans' support for Eritrea stemmed from the Eritreans' struggle for national independence and liberation from Ethiopian colonialism. In 1977, Ethiopia requested political and military support to fight against Somalia's Siad Barre and the Western Somali Liberation Front (WSLF) guerrillas, who were fighting in the Ogaden for cessation. The Cubans knew that although the new Ethiopian government—led by Mengistu Haile-Mariam—espoused Marxist-Leninist ideology, the establishment of relations with the Ethiopians would cause problems with the Somalis and the Eritrean rebels. Thus, when the Cubans responded favorably toward the Ethiopians, geopolitical rather than ideological reasons seemed paramount. Unlike in Angola, where the Cubans took the lead and acted somewhat independently of the Soviets, in Ethiopia Cuban-Soviet strategy was coordinated from the outset.[20] Because of Ethiopia's geopolitical value (e.g., its Red Sea access and its location within missile range of the Arab peninsula), the USSR was quick to take advantage of the change in government there and was eager to bring the Cubans along—leaving Cuba more open to the charge of acting as a Soviet proxy.

The second point to make here is that the Cubans felt uncomfortably drawn between their historical ideological allies and their new Cold War ally; thus they attempted to mediate Ethiopia's conflicts with both the Somalis and the Eritreans.[21] The separate mediation attempts failed. The Somalis entered the Ogaden in July 1977 and severed relations with the Cubans and the Soviets in November 1977. The Cubans began providing substantial amounts of military aid to the Ethiopians in January 1978.[22] During the peak of the fighting in 1977–1979, some twenty-four thousand

Cuban troops were in Ethiopia.[23] This military support enabled the Ethiopians to drive the Somali forces out of Ethiopia by March 1978. Following that victory, Cuban troops began to withdraw immediately from Ethiopia, reducing their numbers to sixteen thousand by January 1979.[24] In addition, the French press indicated that despite reports of renewed fighting in the Ogaden and the neighboring Bale Province in 1980, the Ethiopians appeared to be fighting without the assistance of Cuban troops.[25]

Third, the Cuban assistance in the Ogaden freed Mengistu to turn his attention to the northern rebels of Eritrea and Tigray. The Marxist-Leninist faction of the Eritrean rebels, the Eritrean People's Liberation Forces (EPLF), whom the Cubans had supported since 1970, felt abandoned by the Cubans. Although the Cubans maintain that they never became directly involved in the fighting, some of the rebel Eritrean factions claimed that Cuban soldiers fought on the Ethiopian front lines. Castro himself made a public statement to Mengistu that the Cubans did not want to become directly involved in the fighting in Eritrea and urged a negotiated settlement.[26] The Cubans may have at least provided some military advice during the fighting, since the last Cuban military personnel did not leave Ethiopia until September 1989.[27]

Relations today. In May 1991, Mengistu fled Ethiopia. His departure was the result of a combination of forces—the end of the Cold War and Soviet support, loss of his Eastern-bloc bodyguards, breakup of the military, the increasing costs of civil war, and the successes of the Eritrean and Tigray guerrillas. He was replaced by a transitional government whose mandate is to "pave the way toward democracy and elections to take place by the end of 1993."[28] That process began with elections for fourteen regional assemblies on June 6, 1992.[29]

Ethiopia's transitional government has completely altered relations with its former allies. Diplomatic relations between Cuba and Ethiopia have been reduced to the level of chargé d'affaires and are considered "cordial." In addition, the Ethiopians are seriously considering closing their embassy in Cuba because of economic difficulties and political priorities, even though it is the only embassy they have in the Western Hemisphere. But according to Fisseha Adugna, counselor for political affairs at the Ethiopian Embassy in Washington, D.C., they are considering moving it "to a position of more strategic interest—like Brazil."[30] There are no Cuban military advisers or troops left in Ethiopia.[31]

Fisseha said that while there is no reason for the Ethiopian government to sever relations with Cuba, Cuba is no longer a priority in terms of foreign policy. Communication received from Addis Ababa stated that barter-trade relations initiated during the Mengistu regime have not materialized, and there are no plans for any new initiatives in that area.[32] The current Ethiopian government views the entire Cold War period—in which thousands of

Ethiopians died fighting against Somalia and amongst themselves—as having been a disastrous era for the country.

Pros and cons of Cuban involvement. Cuba's assistance to Ethiopia was more costly than its involvement in Angola. First, the Carter administration, which had hoped to normalize relations with Cuba, had been willing to accept Cuban involvement in Angola but was not willing to do so with Ethiopia. One of the preconditions for normalization of relations became Cuba's withdrawal from Ethiopia.[33] Second, the Soviets and the Cubans had hoped to maintain relations with Somalia while building new ones with Ethiopia—that goal was not attained.[34] Third, the tactics that Mengistu used to quell his critics (including frequent executions of dissident members and other repressive internal policies) made the Ethiopian government unpopular internationally, and Cuba was tainted by association. Fourth, Cuba's willingness to forsake Somalia and turn a blind eye in the case of the Eritreans gave credence to the argument that Cuba's policy in the Horn was closely coordinated with Moscow. And finally, because of Cuba's abandonment of the EPLF, other nationalist movements learned that they could not necessarily rely on Cuban support.[35]

Mozambique

Background. Cuba's involvement in Mozambique is perhaps the most interesting facet of the island's foreign policy in Africa. First, as in the case of Angola, communication between the two countries was initiated because of Cuba's desire to assist the Mozambican rebels in overthrowing colonialism. Yet, the Mozambican rebels—the Front for the Liberation of Mozambique (FRELIMO)—were as politically independent as Castro had been, and strategic differences of opinion made initial contact difficult.

The first leader of FRELIMO, U.S.-educated former UN official Eduardo Mondlane, disagreed with the viability of the *foco* theory in Africa. He believed that a Maoist-style long-term peasant mobilization was better suited to the indigenous conditions in Mozambique. Samora Machel, who took over the leadership of FRELIMO after Mondlane was assassinated in 1969, was equally outspoken against the Cuban *foco* theory. Thus, when the Cubans first offered military assistance to FRELIMO in 1965 and 1967, FRELIMO declined. Finally, in 1968, FRELIMO did accept modest amounts of Cuban "medicines, war material and training."[36] Nevertheless, when FRELIMO came to power after the country's independence from Portugal in 1975, it had been with predominantly Chinese and not Cuban or Soviet aid. It was not until Machel personally met Castro in 1977 that relations substantially improved. It was during this time that incursions from the South Africa–backed Mozambique National Resistance (RENAMO), a right-wing faction opposed to the socialist government, rapidly increased. Machel needed heavier weapons and better military training in order to counter the continuous bombing of Mozambican ports and oil pipelines.[37] The Cubans responded, and at the height of its military involvement in 1976, Cuba had an estimated twelve hundred military personnel in Mozambique.[38]

A second unique aspect to Cuba's presence in Mozambique involves the reaction of the U.S. government, which was not like its reaction to Cuba's involvement in Angola or Ethiopia. There are several reasons for this: (1) the Soviet Union was not heavily involved; (2) the Cuban troop involvement was not as high; (3) the United States did not see a viable alternative in RENAMO, whose ideology was unclear and whose brutal human rights abuses were well documented; and (4) Samora Machel had not been close to Castro, like Neto in Angola had been, and Machel had shown a great deal of independent thought and movement.[39]

Third, the Mozambicans were cautious about their relations with the Cubans because of a desire to remain uncommitted during the Cold War. For example, when Cuba supported the USSR after the Afghan invasion in 1979, Machel objected to what he viewed as Cuban efforts to turn the Nonaligned Movement into support for Soviet policies in the Third World.[40] Also, in the mid-1980s, Mozambique's own regional realities encouraged FRELIMO to become less hostile toward UNITA in Angola and to sign the 1984 Nkomati (nonaggression) Accord with South Africa, in which Mozambique pledged not to provide logistical facilities to the military arm of the African National Congress and South Africa promised to suspend support for RENAMO. The Mozambicans seem to have lived up to the accord, while the South Africans continued supporting RENAMO.

Machel died under suspicious circumstances in 1986. His successor, Joaquim Chissano, sought to improve Mozambique's economic situation, thinking that the only way to do so was by reaching out to the West. During the summer of 1989, Chissano dropped the Marxist-Leninist credo and transformed FRELIMO from a "vanguard of the worker and peasant alliance" to "a party of all the Mozambican people."[41] Despite the political differences between Cuba and Mozambique, relations between the two countries remained friendly, and by the end of the decade four hundred to six hundred Cuban military advisers still remained in Mozambique.[42] There is no firm evidence that "Cuban troops" were in Mozambique—there were simply military advisers, and as of the late 1980s their role had been increasingly restricted to militia training.[43]

Relations today. Diplomats from the Mozambican and Cuban embassies in Washington say that no Cuban military personnel remain in the country.[44] Most scholars say that if any military advisers remain in Cuba, they would number less than 50.[45]

Chissano has moved closer to the West. In January 1990 he introduced a draft constitution that called for universal suffrage, a secret ballot, direct elections for both the president and the parliament, and the reintroduction of private ownership of land.[46] Since Chissano adopted a pro-West diplomatic stance in the late 1980s, the United States has sent increasing amounts of aid to his government. In fiscal year 1992, Mozambique received the largest amount of U.S. assistance (including a modest amount of military training) of any country in sub-Saharan Africa.[47] Likewise, State Department Officials expect Mozambique to be among the top aid recipients for fiscal year 1993.

Peace talks with RENAMO, mediated by the Roman Catholic Church, have been under way since July 1990. The Mozambicans are now looking to the United States to assist in the mediation efforts. Chissano said that it was the seven-point "American position" that provided the basis for the first round of talks in 1990.[48] In May 1992, the State Department agreed to become a formal observer in the peace talks. The Cubans, on the other hand, are not involved in the negotiations, nor have the Mozambicans asked them to become involved.

Pros and cons of Cuban involvement. Cuban involvement in Mozambique was beneficial for both countries during 1977–1979, but today Mozambique considers close relations with Cuba to be an impediment to its goals of increased economic growth and peace within the country. While a small number of civilian programs still remain (see "Civilian Assistance" section), in general the Mozambicans have distanced themselves from the Cubans while drawing closer to the West, the United States in particular. Because there was no Cold War conflict there, relations between the United States and Cuba were unaffected by Cuba's involvement in Mozambique and the smaller scale of the military involvement was less economically costly for the Cubans.

CIVILIAN ASSISTANCE

Cuba provides civilian assistance for two main reasons: (1) to assist developing countries with desperately needed technical, medical, and educational assistance and (2) to spread information about the Cuban Revolution to people in developing nations. Civilian assistance also plays a fundamental role in developing Cuba's international image and influence in various countries. A significant number of African decisionmakers have had a prolonged exposure to the Cuban view of the world via Cuban civilians in their countries and via opportunities to study in Cuba.[49] In recent years, the Cubans have also reaped economic benefits by charging richer countries for their expertise.

Cuban civilian assistance to Africa began in the early 1960s. The Cubans sent fifty-three public health workers to Algeria in 1963, and Cuban medical teams worked in the Pemba island in Tanzania in 1965. However, significant numbers of Cuban civilian personnel did not begin working in Africa until 1976.[50] Over four thousand Cubans served in Africa in that year. Estimates of Cuban civilian personnel in sub-Saharan Africa reached as high as eleven thousand in 1978, with eighty-five hundred of those in Angola alone.[51] (See Map 4.2.)

Cuban sources say that until 1977 all civilian assistance to developing countries was free. In 1978 Cuba began to offer "for pay" services in the areas of construction and public health to countries that were in a position to afford them.[52] Currently, there is a two-tier program for civilian aid. Those that cannot afford to pay are responsible only for the living expenses of Cuban personnel; in such cases Cuba continues to pay the salaries of its workers. The majority of assistance is provided on this basis. The second tier is for richer countries that can pay all the expenses of the Cuban civilian workers, including salary. The exact terms are negotiated by Cuba and the respective foreign government.[53] Cuba also provides emergency assistance free of charge in times of natural disaster.

As of June 1992, Cuban civilian personnel were working in twenty-one African countries in the fields of public health; education; sports; technical expertise in producing sugar; fishing; animal genetics, and construction.

Education

Cuba prides itself on providing free education to students from around the world. In June 1992, there were some twenty-two thousand foreign students from 101 countries studying in Cuba;[54] three-quarters of them, or about seventeen thousand, were from African countries.[55] (See Table 4.1.) The Cubans have dedicated an entire key off the Cuban coast—known as the Isle of Youth—for the purpose of educating primary and secondary students. The schools on the Isle of Youth make a deliberate attempt to maintain the language and cultural identity of the students. Students from the same country are kept together by assigning entire schools to them, and they are taught by instructors from their home countries following work plans provided by their respective ministries of education.[56] Economic hardships in Cuba and political changes in the African countries, however, have led to an appreciable drop in the number of African students on the Isle of Youth. There were fewer than twelve thousand African students there as of June 1992, compared with sixteen thousand in 1988.[57]

In addition to primary and secondary education on the Isle of Youth, foreign students also have access to institutions of higher learning throughout the island where they can focus on engineering, agriculture,

Map 4.2   Cuban Civilian Assistance in Africa, 1992

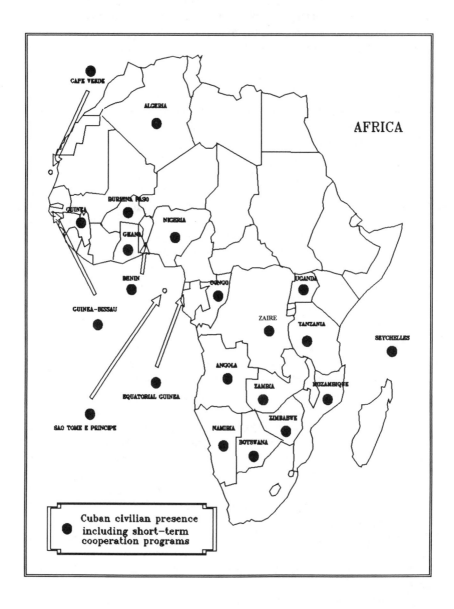

Source: Cuban Foreign Ministry (1992).

Table 4.1   African Students in Cuba, 1992

Country	Education[a]	University[b]	Technical[c]	Other[d]	Total
Algeria		1			1
Angola	4,778	323	316	76	5,493
Benin	34	31	10	17	92
Botswana		3			3
Burkina Faso	490	7	66	22	585
Burundi	4	35	9	13	61
Cape Verde	464	36	26	3	529
Congo	474	147	95	3	719
Ethiopia	154	477	150	18	799
Ghana	510	246	87	18	861
Guinea-Bissau	832	137	54	17	1,040
Equat. Guinea	7	16	6	2	31
Rep. Guinea	71	46	29	56	202
Kenya		2			2
Lesotho		9	7		16
Liberia		1			1
Madagascar	15	34	1		50
Malawi		3	1		4
Mali	36	33	18		87
Mozambique	1,987	145	196	31	2,359
Namibia	809	83	94	9	995
Niger		10	3		13
Nigeria		24	6		30
Rwanda		18	3		21
Sahara	1,592	131	84		1,807
São Tomé	61	16	22		99
Senegal	1	2			3
Seychelles	2	2	7	2	13
Sierra Leone	1	12	6	1	20
South Africa	21	14	1		38
Sudan	311	17	38	2	368
Swaziland			1		1
Tanzania		30	6		36
Uganda	1	24	3	2	30
Zambia		28	21	4	53
Zimbabwe	967	86	8	205	1,266
Total	13,622	2,229	1,374	501	17,728

Source: Cuban Foreign Ministry, June 1992.
Notes: a. Includes primary and secondary as well as "pre-university" students.
b. Does not include medical students.
c. Includes various technical vocation students as well as medical students.
d. Includes mostly sports and cultural education students.

medicine, economics, physical education, and mathematical disciplines. According to Cuban government sources, there is no tuition fee, and the students receive scholarships covering room and board, clothing, books, health care, and an allowance.[58]

The Cubans have been hard pressed to continue providing educational services in the current climate. In April 1992, Zimbabwean students complained to a monthly magazine in their home country that food shortages, lack of books, lack of response by their own ambassador to their problems, and the presence of sometimes hostile hosts had prompted them to request repatriation.[59] In addition, hundreds of Mozambican students rioted in December 1990, complaining that the clothing allotment and stipends were not sufficient.[60]

From 1978 until 1992, the Mozambicans have consistently sent about two thousand primary and secondary students to study at the Isle of Youth. Four schools were assigned to Mozambican students. In July 1992, however, the Mozambicans announced that Cuban and Mozambican economic difficulties would force the closure of the four schools within the next two years. Two of the schools will be turned over to the Cuban government by the end of 1992. Under an accord signed by the two countries, Cuba will receive only those Mozambican students attending higher-education courses. Commenting on the closure of the schools, Mozambique's deputy foreign education minister, Arnaldo Nhavoto, said that because of Cuba's economic difficulties students on the Isle of Youth were receiving a monthly allowance of only $5. Mozambique had not been able to augment that allowance because of its own economic difficulties, thus it was believed best for the students to return home.[61] Though there are still about eight hundred Ethiopian students studying in Cuba, their numbers are rapidly diminishing, as well. According to information received in June 1992 from the foreign ministry in Addis Ababa, "Cuba is in no position to provide Ethiopia with assistance. Students sent to Cuba by the Mengistu regime are there to complete their studies. No new arrangements are being made to take advantage of any Cuban scholarship opportunities."[62]

Medical Ties

Cubans proudly note that they have more physicians in Africa than the number fielded by the World Health Organization.[63] Cuban medical professionals have assisted in the establishment of several medical schools abroad, and Cuban physicians have served in the faculties of medical schools in Angola, Ethiopia, and Algeria.[64]

As of summer 1992, Cuba had medical cooperation agreements with the following African countries: Western Sahara, Angola, Zambia, Zimbabwe, Mozambique, Namibia, Nigeria, Botswana, Burundi, Uganda, Seychelles, Burkina Faso, the Republic of Guinea, Ghana, and Benin.

Technical Cooperation

Cuba has signed technical cooperation agreements with Uganda, Congo, Tanzania, and São Tomé and Príncipe.[65] The embassy of Sierra Leone in Washington also reports that there are several Cuban construction engineers in the country.[66] Several other agreements are being discussed with Zimbabwe and Nigeria.

DIPLOMATIC AND TRADE RELATIONS
AND COOPERATIVE AGREEMENTS

Information from the Cuban government indicates that Cuba maintains current diplomatic relations with forty-three of the fifty-three countries in sub-Saharan Africa.[67] Obviously, Cuba's ties are closest to those governments that espouse at least some socialist tendencies, such as Angola, Ghana, Mali, Mozambique, Congo, Guinea-Bissau, Tanzania, and Zimbabwe.[68]

A small amount of trade is conducted between Cuba and a few African countries. Trade is difficult because of the distance between Cuba and Africa, logistical difficulties, and lack of financing mechanisms. Also, many Cuban and African exports are similar. According to Cuban sources, the African countries that Cuba trades with include Egypt, Algeria, Libya, Congo, Cape Verde, Guinea-Bissau, Angola, Ghana, and Uganda.[69] There has been a declining trend in Cuban-African trade since 1980 when Cuba exported 237 million pesos' worth of goods to Africa—only 102 million pesos' worth were exported in 1985 and only 65 million pesos' worth in 1988. This represented only 1.2 percent of total Cuban exports in 1988. Trade has also been highly unbalanced toward Cuban exports, with only 24 million pesos in Cuban imports from Africa in 1985, dropping in 1988 to 12 million pesos, or 0.2 percent of Cuban imports.[70]

Cuba's main export to Africa is sugar, followed by semimanufactured goods and technical services. Those services include feasibility studies for industrial and agricultural projects; engineering projects; sugar industry consulting; training for hotel management personnel; and construction services.[71]

CONCLUSION

Broadly defined, Cuba's goals for its involvement in Africa for the last three decades have been to assist African countries in fighting colonial and neocolonial powers; increase its own standing as a leader in the developing world; and encourage as many African countries as possible to choose the socialist road to development.

Cuba successfully assisted several countries (Algeria, Angola, Rhodesia, and Namibia) in liberating them from colonial and neocolonial powers. Cuba can also claim credit for increasing world attention on the problem of apartheid in South Africa. Castro's close association with and support for the African National Congress has been unwavering over the years and is expected to continue.

For their willingness to shed blood for Africa's liberation, the Cubans were rewarded with the chairmanship of the Nonaligned Movement, thus allowing them to achieve their goal of increasing their status in the developing world. However, as the Cold War intensified and Cuba became clearly aligned with the Soviet camp (as exhibited by its support for the Soviet invasion of Afghanistan), Cuba's independence was questioned and its reputation in the Nonaligned Movement suffered.

Cuba has had the least success with regard to its goal of increasing the number of socialist states. Although the countries where Cuba has had the closest ties—Angola, Mozambique, and Ethiopia—implemented socialist policies in the 1970s and 1980s, they have since moved toward the West. The demise of the Soviet Union and Cuba's subsequent economic difficulties have led many to believe that the socialist model of development is not viable.

In addition, the change in Russian policy toward Africa and the declining support to Cuba from the former superpower has greatly reduced Cuba's ability to continue its internationalist foreign policy. Cuba's involvement in Africa has been so reduced that State Department officials in charge of Cuban and African policies have repeatedly stated that the numbers of Cubans in Africa are so insignificant that they do not keep track of them. They say that their main concern had been Cuba's involvement in Angola and Ethiopia, and as long as Cuban troops are out of those countries they do not consider the Cuban presence to be a threat.[72]

Cuba's priorities have changed as well. Castro has indicated that because of the severe economic difficulties Cuba is facing, internationalism should begin at home, and his first priority is to secure the survival of the Revolution. Although he has indicated that Cubans will continue to provide civilian humanitarian assistance, it is unclear as to how long they will be able to do so without Soviet aid. They will surely need to expand the "for pay" services to the maximum extent possible.

Cuba succeeded in achieving its goals in Africa when those goals coincided with the priorities of the African countries. When the African countries were fighting for independence and searching for economic models and leadership, Cuba was there. Now that their goal has changed from that of independence to that of survival, the Cuban model has failed to be exportable. Moreover, Cuba is in no position to assist Africa with its economic problems.

In the final analysis, neither side won the Cold War in Africa, and it was the African countries that suffered. As an African proverb says: "The grass suffers whether the elephants make love or war!" Years of civil wars destroyed what little infrastructure the colonial powers left, and desperately poor countries became poorer. Socialism in Africa has succumbed to poverty, and many former allies are adopting pragmatic approaches and changes in international ties. As one African diplomat succinctly said, "We are too busy trying to deal with the drought, famine and starvation to worry about relations with Cuba; maintaining good relations with the West means access to resources; maintaining good relations with Cuba means problems with the West."[73]

Cuba's future relations with the African countries will remain primarily on a pragmatic economic basis. Relations will be closest with those countries that share at least some socialist leanings—Ghana, Mozambique, and Angola (depending upon the outcome of the peace process and elections). The 1990s mark the end of an era for Cuba's involvement in Africa and its internationalist foreign policy in general, as economic and not political issues have become of paramount importance and each country must weigh whether close relations with Cuba will be to its benefit or its detriment.

NOTES

Special thanks are owed to Alastair Rodd for his substantive contributions to this chapter.

1. See books written or edited by William LeoGrande (1980); Carmelo Mesa-Lago and June S. Belkin (1982); Sergio Diáz Briquets (1989); and George Fauriol and Eva Loser (1990).

2. William M. LeoGrande, "Cuban-Soviet Relations and Cuban Policy in Africa," in Carmelo Mesa-Lago and June S. Belkin, eds., *Cuba in Africa*, Latin American Monograph and Document Series, no. 3 (Pittsburgh: University of Pittsburgh, 1982), p. 18.

3. Ibid.

4. Olga Nazario and Juan F. Benemelis, "Cuba's Relations with Africa: An Overview," in Sergio Díaz-Briquets, ed., *Cuban Internationalism in Sub-Saharan Africa* (Pittsburgh: Duquesne University Press, 1989), p. 16; and LeoGrande, "Cuban-Soviet Relations," p. 18. Cuban instructors were also provided for the Popular Movement for the Liberation of Angola (MPLA) and the African Party for the Liberation of Portuguese Guinea and the Cape Verde Islands (PAIGC).

5. Nazario and Benemelis, "Cuba's Relations with Africa," pp. 20–21.

6. Ibid.

7. Ibid., p. 17.

8. "Castro Ends Military Help for Revolution Abroad—U.S. Analysts," Reuters, January 13, 1992, AM cycle.

9. Nazario and Benemelis, "Cuba's Relations with Africa," p. 21; and Donna Rich, "Cuba's Role as Mediator in International Conflicts: Formal and Informal Initiatives," in H. Michael Erisman and John M. Kirk, eds., *Cuban Foreign Policy Confronts a New International Order* (Boulder and London: Lynne Rienner, 1991), p. 122.

10. See Pamela Falk, "Cuba in Africa," *Foreign Affairs* (Summer 1987), pp. 1084–1085.

11. Ibid., p. 1090.

12. *Granma Weekly Review,* December 17, 1989.

13. See Susan Eckstein, "Foreign Aid Cuban Style," *The Multinational Monitor* (April 1989), p. 16; and Falk, "Cuba in Africa," pp. 1093, 1095.

14. "Text of Pacts on Namibia Independence and a Pullout by Cuba," *New York Times,* February 23, 1988, p. A6.

15. Armando Entralgo González and Davíd López González, "Cuba and Africa: Thirty Years of Solidarity," in H. Michael Erisman and John M. Kirk, eds., *Cuban Foreign Policy Confronts a New International Order* (Boulder and London: Lynne Rienner, 1991), p. 102; and Armando Entralgo González and Davíd López González, "Cuban Policy for Africa," in Jorge I. Domínguez and Rafael Hernández, eds., *U.S.-Cuban Relations in the 1990s* (Boulder: Westview Press, 1989), p. 151.

16. Paul Taylor, "Angola Slips from Peace to War," *Washington Post,* January 18, 1993, p. A1.

17. Kenneth B. Noble, "As Angola Turns to West, Cubans Are Resentful," *New York Times,* April 9, 1991, p. A8.

18. Ibid.

19. "Southern Africa in Brief: Angola Cuban Envoy Says Future Relations Will Depend on Election Results," *British Broadcasting Corporation,* p. ME/1361/B1.

20. The Soviets and the Cubans often differed on approaches to Angola. The Soviets, for instance, supported a coup against Neto in 1977, while the Cubans helped Neto crush the attempt. LeoGrande, "Cuban-Soviet Relations," p. 36.

21. During his tour of Africa in March 1977, Castro made several attempts to mediate the conflict. Soviet president Nikolai Podgorny also attempted to mediate during a subsequent visit to Africa. For more discussion, see LeoGrande, "Cuban-Soviet Relations," p. 38; Nelson P. Valdés, "Cuba's Involvement in the Horn of Africa: The Ethiopian-Somali War and the Eritrean Conflict," in Carmelo Mesa-Lago and June S. Belkin, eds., *Cuba in Africa,* Latin American Monograph and Document Series, no. 3 (Pittsburgh: University of Pittsburgh, 1982), p. 68; and Rich, "Cuba's Role as Mediator," pp. 127–128.

22. The Cubans sent fifty military advisers after the WSLF guerrillas entered the Ogaden in May 1977 but did not send troops until January 1978, after Raúl Castro's visits to Addis Ababa and Moscow to coordinate the aid. See H. Michael Erisman, *Cuba's International Relations: The Anatomy of a Nationalistic Foreign Policy* (Boulder: Westview Press, 1985), p. 72.

23. Valdés, "Cuba's Involvement in the Horn," p. 73; and William Ratliff, "Cuban Military Policy in Sub-Saharan Africa," in Sergio Díaz-Briquets, ed., *Cuban Internationalism in Sub-Saharan Africa* (Pittsburgh: Duquesne University Press, 1989), p. 38. Ratliff estimates there were sixteen thousand to eighteen thousand Cuban troops in Ethiopia during 1977–1978 and three thousand to five thousand in 1988.

24. Cuba's Africa Role Said Growing," *Washington Post,* January 21, 1979, p. A21.

25. Zdenek Cervenka and Colin Legum, "Cuba and Africa in 1980," *Contemporary African Record,* 1980–81, p. A121.

26. Castro called for a federation in which Eritrea was granted regional autonomy but Ethiopia's territorial integrity remained intact. See Valdés, "Cuba's Involvement in Africa," pp. 80–81.

27. *CubaINFO* 1, no. 6 (September 17, 1989); *Diario de las Americas,* June 26, 1989, p. 13A.

28. Personal interview with Fisseha Adugna, counselor for political affairs, Ethiopian Embassy, Washington, D.C., May 15, 1992.

29. *Miami Herald*, May 14, 1992, p. 12A.

30. Personal interview with Adugna, Washington D.C., May 15, 1992.

31. Ibid.

32. Official response to questions submitted by this author to the Ethiopian government through the Ethiopian Embassy in Washington, D.C., May 1992.

33. LeoGrande, "Cuban-Soviet Relations," p. 45.

34. Valdés, "Cuba's Involvement in the Horn," p. 67.

35. LeoGrande, "Cuban-Soviet Relations," p. 42.

36. Gillian Gunn, "Cuba and Mozambique: A History of Cordial Disagreement," in Sergio Díaz-Briquets, ed., *Cuban Internationalism in Sub-Saharan Africa* (Pittsburgh: Duquesne University Press, 1989), p. 80.

37. Christopher Wren, "No U.S. Broker Role Here, Mozambique Says," *New York Times*, February 12, 1989, p. 14.

38. LeoGrande, "Cuban-Soviet Relations," p. 43.

39. In addition to the examples listed below, during the mid-1980s Mozambique applied for and was granted membership in the International Monetary Fund and the Lomé Convention. These moves did not endear them to the Cubans.

40. Ratliff, "Cuban Military Policy," p. 41.

41. Jill Smolowe, "Don't Call Us, Friend, We'll Call You," *Time*, March 5, 1990, p. 27.

42. Ratliff, "Cuban Military Policy," p. 41.

43. Gunn, "Cuba and Mozambique," p. 99.

44. Separate discussions with Shawn McCormick of the Center for Strategic and International Studies and Gillian Gunn of Georgetown University, May 1992.

45. Personal interview with anonymous Mozambican and Cuban officials, May 1992.

46. Smolowe, "Don't Call Us, Friend," p. 27.

47. "Mozambique: U.S. Offers to Take Formal Role in Peace Talks," *Inter Press Service*, May 18, 1992.

48. "U.S. to Join Mozambican Peace Talks," *Washington Post*, May 17, 1992, p. A27.

49. Gunn, "Cuba and Mozambique," p. 100.

50. Sergio Díaz-Briquets and Jorge Pérez-López, "Internationalist Civilian Assistance: The Cuban Presence in Sub-Saharan Africa," in Sergio Díaz-Briquets ed., *Cuban Internationalism in Sub-Saharan Africa* (Pittsburgh: Duquesne University Press, 1989), p. 48.

51. Ibid., pp. 50–51.

52. Entralgo González and López Gonzalez, "Cuba and Africa," p. 96. See also Eckstein, "Foreign Aid Cuban Style," p. 16. Eckstein says that countries began paying for services in 1977.

53. Díaz-Briquets and Pérez-López, "Internationalist Civilian Assistance," p. 53; and Entralgo González and López Gonzalez, "Cuba and Africa," p. 96.

54. "3,500 Students to Graduate from Cuba," *Xinhua*, June 15, 1992.

55. "Recession-Hit Cuba Forced to Limit Foreign Students," Reuters, April 24, 1992, AM cycle; and cable sent to Cuban Interests Section in Washington, D.C., from the Cuban Foreign Ministry, June 1992.

56. Díaz-Briquets and Pérez-López, "Internationalist Civilian Assistance," p. 67.

57. "3,500 Students to Graduate from Cuba," *Xinhua*, June 15, 1992; "Cuba's Isle of Youth Losing Its Foreign Students," *Agence France Presse*, February 23, 1992; and Díaz-Briquets and Pérez-López, "Internationalist Civilian Assistance," p. 71.

58. Díaz-Briquets and Pérez-López, "Internationalist Civilian Assistance," p. 71.

59. "Zimbabwe Students in Cuba Yearn for Home: Report," *Agence France Presse*, April 3, 1992.

60. Six hundred students were taken into police custody; one student died and twenty-one were injured. *CubaINFO* 2, no. 1, January 1990, p. 4.

61. "Mozambican Students in Cuba to Start Returning Home Next Week," *British Broadcasting Corporation*, July 10, 1992, p. ME/1429/B/1.

62. Official response to questions submitted by this author to the Ethiopian government through the Ethiopian Embassy in Washington, D.C., May 1992.

63. Personal interview with Cuban diplomat, Washington, D.C., May 18, 1992.

64. Díaz-Briquets and Pérez-López, "Internationalist Civilian Assistance," p. 57.

65. Cable sent to Cuban Interests Section from the Cuban Foreign Ministry, May 26, 1992.

66. Personal interview with diplomat from Sierra Leone who wished to remain anonymous, Washington, D.C., May 1992.

67. Cable sent to Cuban Interests Section from the Cuban Foreign Ministry, May 26, 1992.

68. Nazario and Benemelis, "Cuba's Relations with Africa," p. 21; and cable received from the Cuban Foreign Ministry, May 26, 1992.

69. Cable sent to Cuban Interests Section from the Cuban Foreign Ministry, May 26, 1992.

70. Nazario and Benemelis, "Cuba's Relations with Africa," pp. 23–24. Data from 1988 were obtained from "Cuba en Cifras, 1989," Comité Estatal de Estadísticas de Cuba, pp. 95–96.

71. Nazario and Benemelis, "Cuba's Relations with Africa," p. 22.

72. Off-the-record discussions with African and Cuban specialists at the State Department, April and May 1992.

73. Personal interview with African diplomat who wished to remain anonymous, May 1992.

5

Cuba and the Middle East:
The Gulf War and After

JOHN ATTFIELD

*We cannot be neutral in the struggle of the Arab peoples for the
return of the occupied territories and the recognition of the rights
of the Palestinian people; . . . between the rights of the Saharan
people and the occupiers of their territory; . . . between the
Yemeni revolution and Arab reaction; between the progressive
Arab countries and the reactionary Arab countries; . . . between
the progressive forces and the rightist forces in Lebanon. We
cannot be neutral in the face of imperialism,colonialism, neo-
colonialism, racism and fascism, and in any of the multitude of
political, economic and social struggles between the reactionary
and progressive forces in the world.*

—Fidel Castro

Cuba's relations with the Middle East are founded on the basic principles of Cuban foreign policy since 1959 and are thus anti-imperialistic,
anti–United States, pro–Third World, and prorevolutionary. In applying
these principles to the Middle East, Cuba has consistently been prepared to
put political commitment before considerations of economic gain or world
approval. Cuban troops backed Algeria in 1963 during its war with Morocco, even though at that time Cuba had more extensive trade with the
latter. Cuba condemned Egypt for the Camp David accords in 1978, despite good commercial relations with Egypt. And Cuba backed the Polisario guerrillas against Morocco in 1979 at the expense of its diplomatic
and trade ties with that country.[1] Most recently, Cuba's stand in the United
Nations in opposition to the U.S.-led Gulf War against Iraq served to further isolate Cuba at a time when it needed all the friends it could get.

Cuba's relations with the Middle East since 1959 have been marked by

- support for and political cooperation with friendly governments;
- support for revolutionary movements, especially the Palestine Liberation Organization (PLO);

69

- opposition to U.S. influence and to the main U.S. instrument in the Middle East, Israel; and
- opposition to "reactionary" Arab governments and to any moves seen as accommodating U.S. ambitions.

In general, Cuba has sought correct relations even with countries with which it has had political differences, such as Kuwait and North Yemen. Diplomatic relations have been broken, from Cuba's side, only in solidarity with progressive Arab opinion on matters of principle. For example, despite Cuba's hostility toward Israeli expansionism and oppression of the Palestinians, it did not break off relations with Israel until 1973, long after the Soviet Union did so. There have been recent moves to revive contacts.

Cuba's trade relations have been marked by a degree of pragmatism. It has often done its best business with countries with which it has had poor or nonexistent political relations. Exports to Egypt, for example, were unaffected by the political breach over Camp David. And Cuba has consistently done good business with Saudi Arabia despite the absence of diplomatic relations.

Central to Cuba's position in the Middle East since the 1970s has been support for the PLO. Cuba has consistently argued that withdrawal of Israeli troops and Israeli acceptance of the Palestinians' right of self-determination, including the right to establish their own state, are preconditions for a just and lasting peace in the Middle East.

Israel is portrayed by the Cuban leadership as the instrument of U.S. imperialism in the region. A 1980 Cuban Communist Party declaration stated:

> The USA is attempting, through the Zionist state of Israel, to achieve a privileged position in this key zone, threatening the southern flank of the Soviet Union, and at the same time to deny to the Arab countries the occupied territories and prevent the Palestinian people from establishing a national state on lands plundered by Israel.[2]

Elsewhere in the region, Cuba opposed "the imperialists' claims to control the energy resources of the countries in the area" (of the Gulf region) and the establishment of new military bases, which "created an explosive situation and seriously threatens international peace and security, with the concentration of a dangerous military force in the region."[3] The U.S.-led military action in the Gulf in 1991 was seen in this light.

Cuban support for progressive nationalist and socialist Arab states has stemmed from ideological affinity and a desire to assist Third World governments to resist imperialism. There has been extensive civilian collaboration with progressive Middle Eastern countries in fields such as construction, health care, and education. Some countries (e.g., South Yemen) have received cooperation in the form of aid. Others, such as Iraq and Libya, have paid for Cuban collaboration in hard currency. A two-hundred-person medical brigade was working in Iraq at the time of the Gulf War.

Cuban support has sometimes been given in military form, as in Algeria in 1963 and Syria in 1973. Cuba's political relations with most Arab countries improved significantly in 1973 when Cuba sent soldiers to Syria during the Yom Kippur War against Israel.

Cuba offers support to revolutionary movements that it believes represent oppressed peoples or an occupied country. Foremost among these movements in the Middle East have been the PLO and the Polisario Front, which were full members of the Nonaligned Movement (NAM) (the PLO is still, early in 1993; Polisario is not) and have received widespread international recognition. Cuba prefers to cooperate with what it views as mainstream movements rather than more extreme elements.[4]

Support for the so-called progressive camp is coupled with hostility to reactionary Arab states. Cuba identifies Saudi Arabia (and, prior to the overthrow of the shah in 1979, Iran) as the leader of the reactionary camp and a conduit for U.S. interests among Arab states.

Cuba has sought to influence Middle East affairs through international forums. Its support for and commitment to the United Nations is well known, and Cuba has regarded its acceptance within the UN as a key parameter of recognition of its place in world affairs. Cuba was elected to a nonpermanent seat on the Security Council some months before the outbreak of the Gulf War, giving it a significant role in political events during the Gulf crisis.

Cuba has been involved in NAM since the movement's formation. Arab countries have been among the greatest supporters of NAM, of which Egypt's Pres. Gamal Abdul Nasser was a founding father, and Cuba's active role has enhanced its prestige in the region. The Sixth Summit Conference of the movement was held in Havana in 1979. Cuba sees NAM as representing countries that, despite having differing social systems, share a common interest in opposing imperialism; as well, it sees it as an instrument for Third World economic independence. Within the movement, Cuba's acceptance of different social systems has not prevented it from lining up strongly against what it sees as reactionary forces among the nonaligned countries and those perceived as acting in the interests of U.S. imperialism (e.g., Egypt in regard to the Camp David accords). Cuba blamed "reactionary Arab states" for supporting Eritrean separatists against the Mengistu government in Ethiopia.[5]

In line with its support for a new world economic order, as chair of the Nonaligned Movement in 1979 Cuba argued in favor of the OPEC countries' efforts to raise the price of oil: "The petroleum exporting countries, which all belong to the developing world, almost without exception belong to the NAM, and at this moment find the support of the rest of our countries in their just demand for revaluation of their products and an end to unequal exchange and the squandering of energy resources."[6]

Cuba has also tried to play a mediating role in conflicts between members of NAM, as exemplified by its efforts to mediate at the time of the

Iran-Iraq war and its attempts to win acceptance within NAM for the revolutionary government of Afghanistan.[7]

ECONOMIC RELATIONS

To date, Cuba's economic relations with the Middle East have been characterized by a lack of synergy. The island's trade relations with the region have been almost entirely one-sided, with little more than sugar being exported to several Middle East countries and nearly nothing being imported. Because Cuba's oil supplies had been almost entirely sourced from the Soviet Union on preferential terms, there was previously no need to buy Middle East oil.

The Middle East has never been of major economic significance for Cuba, and the trend has actually been downward. The region represented less than 10 percent of Cuba's total nonsocialist exports in 1986–1988, compared with nearly 20 percent in 1983. The pattern of recent Cuban export trade with the Middle East is shown in Table 5.1.

Exports consist overwhelmingly of sugar. Sugar exports to Cuba's top three regional markets in 1988—Algeria, Iraq, and Egypt—totaled 48.8 million pesos (roughly equivalent to dollars) and represented 99 percent of the value of Cuba's exports to these three countries. Values have fluctuated according to the world value of sugar. In volume terms, sugar exports to these three markets fell from 488,000 tons in 1983 to 255,000 tons in 1988 and 264,000 tons in 1989; exports rose again to 499,000 tons in 1990. In 1990, the Middle East accounted for 10 percent of total Cuban sugar exports by volume, or 20 percent of non-Soviet exports. Thus the Middle East is far more significant for Cuba's sugar economy than for Cuban exports as a whole. The figures in 1990 were significantly higher than those in 1989, as shown in Table 5.2.

Apart from sugar, another major Cuban export to the region has been canned mango juice. Although this product may be too sweet for Western European palates, it is ideal for Middle Eastern tastes, and the Cuban product (sold under the Taoro brand name) has had a high reputation in the region. Cuban mango juice has been sold in Kuwait, Jordan, Saudi Arabia, and elsewhere in the region. During the 1970s and early 1980s, Taoro was the brand leader in Saudi Arabia.

Saudi mango juice imports from Cuba were valued at $573,000 in 1987, the last year during which significant quantities were imported. Quantities were at a peak in the early 1980s, with nearly 8,000 tons imported in 1983 at a value of some $4 million. However, imports fell to about 1,300 tons in 1987 and to negligible quantities in 1988 and 1989.[8] Trade resumed in 1990 but was disrupted by Cuban production and shipping

Table 5.1 Cuban Exports to the Middle East (in millions of pesos)

	1983	1986	1987	1988	Avg. 1986–1988
Algeria	44.1	13.6	7.4	28.6	16.5
Egypt	51.0	24.0	11.9	5.1	13.7
Iraq	25.6	8.1	4.5	15.8	9.5
Syria	18.5	6.1	10.5	5.2	7.3
Libya	19.1	9.1	9.0	2.0	6.7
Tunisia	2.4	4.8	4.0	1.6	3.5
S. Yemen	0.1	2.3	1.5	0.6	1.5
Lebanon	4.6	0.4	3.2	0.1	1.2
Saudi Arabia	7.4	—	0.9	0.5	0.5
Iran	10.8	—	—	—	—
Total	183.6	68.4	52.9	59.5	60.4
% of Cuban Exports to:					
World	3.3	1.3	0.9	1.1	1.1
Nonsocialist countries	18.7	10.9	8.0	7.8	8.8

Source: Anuario Estadistico de Cuba, 1988.

Table 5.2 Cuban Sugar Exports to the Middle East (in thousands of tons)

	1989	1990
Algeria	188.1	195.3
Egypt	38.5	277.8
Iraq	37.0	26.0
Libya	40.8	79.7
Syria	64.0	84.8
Tunisia	72.4	51.4
Total	440.8	715.0
% of Total Exports	6.2	10.1
% of Non-USSR Exports	12.2	20.0

Source: International Sugar Journal 93, no. 1111 (1991).

problems. The decline in this business of late has had less to do with the state of political relations between Saudi Arabia and Cuba than with practical considerations, including the end of the Saudi economic boom in the mid-1980s, the difficulty of maintaining market shares in this highly competitive and anarchic market, and Cuba's own production problems.

More recently, Cuban exporters have made serious attempts to find new markets in the Middle East for both mango juice and other fruit products, such as citrus juices and fresh citrus fruits, to replace lost markets in Eastern Europe and the Soviet Union.[9]

Another Cuban export with wide currency throughout the Middle East is cigars, exported by the Cuban enterprise Cubatabaco through an agent in Switzerland. Statistics are not available, but Cuban brands such as Montecristo, Romeo y Julieta, and Partagas can be seen for sale in Middle Eastern supermarkets and hotels.

As previously mentioned, Cuban imports from the region are minor. Cuba's trade statistics showed imports valued at 9.0 million pesos from Tunisia and Algeria in 1983, and 10.0 million pesos from Tunisia in 1987 falling to 0.8 million pesos in 1988.

There are significant commercial relations between Cuba and the Middle East in the area of construction. An important role has been played by the Cuban construction enterprise UNECA, which has regional subsidiaries in Tripoli (Libya), Algiers (Algeria), and Baghdad (Iraq). UNECA construction projects in the Middle East, paid for by the recipient countries in hard currency, have included a 183-km Sahara desert highway, three apartment buildings, and five schools in Libya; and a 146-km highway and four thousand dwellings in Iraq.[10]

UNECA works mainly in politically friendly countries and has therefore missed out on most of the lucrative construction projects connected with the oil-rich Middle East countries in recent years. However, Cuban construction enterprises have carried out at least one commercial project in Kuwait, in 1984.[11] (Currently, most of UNECA's activities take place in Cuba, especially connected with the expansion of Cuba's tourism program. It is not clear how long UNECA's activities in the Middle East will be maintained.)[12]

CUBA'S FRIENDS IN THE MIDDLE EAST

Cuba's longest-standing diplomatic relations in the Middle East have been with Algeria, Lebanon, Iraq, and Syria since the 1960s; Libya, South Yemen, Kuwait, Jordan, and Iran since the 1970s; and North Yemen since 1982.[13] Relations with Israel survived the Six Day War but were broken off during the Yom Kippur War in 1973. Relations with Egypt were breached after the Camp David accords in 1978 but have since resumed.

Relations with Morocco were broken in 1979 over Cuba's support for the Polisario guerrillas and its recognition of the Saharawi Arab Democratic Republic.[14]

Cuba regards as its closest friends countries that have adopted a socialist or progressive stance internally and in foreign affairs. Within the Nonaligned Movement, according to President Castro in 1980, Cuba's "most permanent and extensive relations, our shared view of the main problems of international life, has been achieved with those countries which have proclaimed socialism or have assumed a socialist orientation"; Castro named such countries in the Middle East as Algeria, Iraq, Syria, Libya, and Democratic (South) Yemen.[15] These, together with the PLO, have remained Cuba's most consistent political friends in the region; along with Egypt, they are also Cuba's most important regional trading partners. Recently, Iran has also assumed greater importance.

In line with majority Arab opinion, Cuba recognizes the PLO as the government of a state and the legitimate representative of the Palestinian people. It regards Israel as an illegal occupying power. The resolution made on international policy at the Second Congress of the Cuban Communist Party, in December 1980, provides an accurate expression of Cuba's position:

> US policy toward the Middle East has been aimed at completely submitting this region to its domination, and to eliminating the Palestinian Resistance. . . . Through the Camp David accords, which have received wide international condemnation, U.S. imperialism seeks to establish an aggressive and reactionary alliance with Israel and the Egyptian regime. We condemn Zionism and its expansionary practices, which are causing enormous suffering to the Palestinian people and constitute a permanent threat to all the Arab peoples in the region. Cuban Communists reaffirm solidarity with the just cause of the Arab people, and especially with the Palestinians, and reaffirm the conviction that only through a recognition of their legitimate rights, including the existence of a sovereign state based on the leadership of the Palestine Liberation Organization, and the withdrawal of Israel from the occupied territories, can a just and lasting peace in the Middle East be achieved.[16]

The PLO has an embassy in Havana and was a member of the Coordinating Bureau of NAM during Castro's chairmanship. Cuba sees its relationship with the PLO and its leader, Yasser Arafat, as a focal point for its diplomacy in the Middle East and within NAM.

Relations with the PLO were nevertheless slow to develop. Agreement was first reached to open a PLO office in Cuba after Arafat's visit to the island in November 1974. The office—the first PLO headquarters in Latin America—was later raised to embassy status. Since then, relations have always been close. PLO officials and cadres have been trained at Cuba's top party training school.[17]

Cuba continues to be one of the PLO's strongest supporters in the UN and NAM. The coincident views of Cuba and the PLO over the Kuwait crisis and the Gulf War in 1990–1991, despite severe international criticism, further helped to cement relations, and the two leaders continue to consult on Third World policy. Since the start of the Palestinian uprising (intifada), Cuba's support for Yasser Arafat has helped dampen criticism of Cuba's role by presenting Cuban support for the PLO as a brake on extremist tendencies, helping to open the way for diplomatic initiatives.[18]

ISRAEL—TOOL OF IMPERIALISM

From the early days of the Revolution, Cuba regarded Israel essentially as a dependency of the United States. Maintaining diplomatic links with Israel, when other Soviet allies broke relations in 1967, could be seen as a way for Cuba to keep a line open to Washington. Israeli technicians had played an important role in establishing the citrus plantations on the Isle of Youth, and Cuba maintained trade with Israel until relations were broken off in September 1973. After that, the relationship descended to a level of mutual antagonism, although there is evidence that unofficial contacts took place. The break in relations in 1973 has been interpreted by some commentators as designed to placate NAM countries, such as Libya, that were casting doubt on Cuba's credentials of nonalignment.[19] Nevertheless, Cuba's position boosted its standing among Arab opinion.

Cuba subsequently supported the UN resolution equating Zionism with racism.[20] While arguing that Cuba was not opposed to the Jewish people as such, the country made clear its opposition to Zionism and the Israeli government, with Castro comparing the actions of Israel with those of the Nazis: "Robbed of their lands, expelled from their own country, dispersed throughout the world, pursued and assassinated, the heroic Palestinians constitute an impressive example of self-denial and patriotism, and are a living symbol of the greatest crime of our age."[21]

A slight thaw occurred in 1989–1990, although prospects for a complete warming remain remote. In 1989 a representative of the Israeli opposition Mapam Party became the first representative of an Israeli Zionist party to visit Cuba since 1973. In February 1990, plans were announced for an Israeli scientific and trade delegation to visit Cuba. Another Mapam official visited in July 1990 and reported that Cuban officials had accepted an invitation to visit Israel later in the year. There was speculation that the two countries were preparing to reestablish diplomatic relations.[22]

According to press reports, the head of Israeli intelligence activities in Central America, Mike Harari, visited Cuba several times during the 1980s to discuss diplomatic and commercial relations. According to senior Panamanian army officers debriefed after the U.S. invasion of Panama, Harari, who also acted as adviser to General Noriega, visited Castro on several occasions using Noriega's close connections with Cuba to arrange access. Harari told his Panamanian contacts that he had been instructed by the Israeli government to open unofficial talks with Cuba toward establishing diplomatic relations because "Castro is a leader among the nonaligned states, many of them Arab."[23]

As a founding member of NAM, Cuba could not ignore possible changes in attitude toward Israel on the part of other nonaligned countries. Moreover, any improvement in Cuban-Israeli relations could be a factor in improving Cuba's relations with Washington. But a reestablishment of formal ties depends on Israel taking a significant step toward solving the Palestinian problem. In making gestures toward improving relations with Israel, Cuba was careful not to compromise its contacts with the Palestinians.[24] Cuba has always argued in international forums in favor of a resumption of the Geneva talks toward a general settlement in the Middle East in accordance with UN Resolution 3236, with the participation of all parties, including the PLO. The ongoing direct negotiations between Israeli and Palestinian negotiators with tacit PLO agreement signal the elimination of a major hurdle to better Cuban-Israeli relations.

IRAN—CUBA'S NEWEST ALLY

Cuba welcomed the overthrow of the shah of Iran (described as "the favorite gendarme of US imperialism")[25] in 1979 and the subsequent emergence of what it described as a "popular process with an evidently anti-imperialist orientation."[26] Diplomatic relations with Iran were established in that year but were later suspended during the fundamentalist rule of Ayatollah Khomeini and the war with Iraq, during which Cuba sought to mediate through NAM. The war between "two progressive and nonaligned countries," in Cuba's view, "debilitates the common front of struggle against imperialism and Zionism, [and] threatens to contribute once more to aggravating the already difficult economic situation of the non-oil countries of the Third World."[27]

Since the death of Khomeini and the emergence of Pres. Ali Akbar Rafsanjani in 1989, relations between Cuba and Iran have become extensive. The first joint commission on Cuban-Iranian economic cooperation was held in Teheran in that year.[28] Considered in 1992, Cuba's relations with Iran are among the warmest and most active in the region, marked by substantially similar views about the Gulf War and joint mediation attempts by the two countries through the Nonaligned Movement.

In January 1991, Cuba and Iran signed a far-reaching agreement on cooperation in the sugar industry, including plans for a research center for agriculture and industry, as well as exchange of information on sugar derivatives. Cuba agreed to share technical skills and set up mills and by-product plants in association with other international investors. Cuba also hopes to sell its KTP-2 sugarcane harvester in Iran.[29]

Iran's minister of public health, Iraj Fazel, visited Havana in December 1990 and signed an agreement that involved trade in medical products and an exchange of medical students; it was also agreed that Cuban doctors would work in Iranian community hospitals and teach in Teheran's medical school. Iran's agriculture minister, Dr. Issa Kalantari, visited Cuba the following month to sign a further cooperation agreement. There has also been discussions on cooperation in education, science, sports, and the petroleum and paper industries.[30] Later in 1991, Cuba and Iran signed a two-year scientific cooperation program in the field of nuclear energy.[31]

The third Cuba-Iran joint commission was held in Teheran early in 1992.[32] In February 1992, Cuba's vice president, José Ramón Fernández, signed an agreement with Iran to expand cooperation in agriculture, sports, health care, and industry. Iran's official radio later reported that Cuba was seeking an oil agreement with Iran. Cuba will also sell sugar to Iran for the first time in ten years. The oil-for-sugar barter deal involves the exchange of 200,000 tons of sugar for an unspecified quantity of Iranian oil. According to Western reports, Iran was also offering to buy all or part of Cuba's recently built oil refinery in Cienfuegos.[33]

IRAQ AND THE GULF WAR

Cuba and Iraq have maintained diplomatic relations since 1960; and since the ascendancy of the nationalist Ba'th Party, Cuba has regarded Iraq as one of its closest Middle Eastern friends. There has been substantial cooperation in civilian projects since 1979, but Cuba has criticized Iraq in the past for its equivocal political role in the region.[34]

When the Middle East crisis broke in August 1990, Cuba had been serving for some months, for the first time ever, as one of the nine non-permanent members of the UN Security Council. This was the very body the United States used for its diplomatic efforts against Iraq following the invasion of Kuwait on August 2. Since the first vote on Resolution 660 of the Security Council (August 2), Cuba supported the demand that Iraq unconditionally withdraw its troops from Kuwait. Cuba supported Resolution 662 (August 9), which declared the annexation of Kuwait to be illegal, and Resolution 664 (August 18), instructing Iraq to allow foreign nationals to leave the area.

On the other hand, Cuba opposed from the beginning the buildup to the use of force against Iraq. At the start of the crisis, the Cuban Foreign Ministry issued a statement that Iraq's entry into Kuwait should not serve as a pretext for the U.S. government or its allies to increase their military presence in the region.[35] Castro sent a message to the leaders of the Arab countries on August 7, warning of the consequences of the Gulf crisis and the U.S. military buildup: "Castigating Iraq for its lamentable and unacceptable action in Kuwait is only a pretext for the United States . . . to legitimize its armed intervention put in place in the name of the international community."[36]

Cuba abstained, together with Yemen, on Resolution 661 (August 6), calling for a trade, finance, and military embargo against Iraq, and Resolution 665 (August 25), authorizing the use of force. It voted against Resolution 666 (September 13), which imposed a food embargo on Iraq, and Resolution 670 (September 25), which extended the air and naval blockade. Cuba also voted, again together with Yemen, against the fateful Resolution 678 (November 29), which contained the ultimatum on Iraq to leave Kuwait by January 15, 1991. In a speech to the UN on September 27, Foreign Minister Isidoro Malmierca of Cuba criticized the haste with which the UN was raising the stakes in the Gulf crisis. Cuba also argued for the UN to take action against Israel's treatment of the Palestinians, especially following the Temple Mount killings on October 8, 1990.[37]

Despite having opposed the UN economic embargo in the Security Council, Cuba made gestures to comply with it. It canceled exports of sisal, textiles, rum, and other items and withdrew some civilians working in Iraq in nonmedical fields. Cuba denied U.S. allegations that it received a shipment of petroleum from Iraq after the imposition of sanctions. On the other hand, Cuba continued its sugar agreement, which it declared a "humanitarian program," and its program of medical assistance to Iraq.[38] Approximately two hundred Cuban doctors and nurses continued to work in Iraq during the crisis. After the outbreak of fighting, Cuba placed the services of its medical personnel at the disposal of the International Red Cross.[39]

Cuba took a position of blaming all sides, especially "the hegemonic policies of the United States," for the conflict.[40] Castro said that the United States and its Western allies were able to "capitalize on the logical indignation in the world community provoked by Iraq's actions against Kuwait."[41] In an interview with *Prensa Latina*, Cuba's ambassador to the UN, Ricardo Alarcón, said that the military attack was "carefully planned by the United States from the start of the Gulf conflict with the objective of gaining control over the oil resources of the region." The U.S. objective, said Alarcón, was "not the liberation of Kuwait or to prevent a supposed attack against Saudi Arabia, but the barbarous destruction of an Arab nation which with its independent positions was frustrating the hegemonic ambitions of the US administration in the richest oil producing zone in the world."[42]

Economic sanctions had not been given enough time, nor had diplomatic overtures been exhausted, declared President Castro. War resulted because of the "failure of the UN and the politicians of our times to solve problems by peaceful means." Blaming the United States for "firing the first shots," Castro said, "I think the mind-set of Arab countries was not taken into account." He said he felt "a very deep bitterness in terms of the loss of life and the great material losses that will result in a war that never should have happened. . . . We'll send doctors, even to the Americans if they need them."[43]

Castro charged the international community with double standards in failing to condemn the U.S. invasion of Panama, the U.S. attack on Libya, and the Israeli occupation of the West Bank and Gaza Strip.[44] Cuba argued that the use of force by the UN was unprecedented and had never been adopted against other aggressor countries. The UN, Cuba argued, was pushed into hasty actions by U.S. interests, without waiting for the chance for a peaceful solution.[45]

Cuba's position expressed the interests of the Third World in the conflict. It emphasized the destructive potential of the conflict on the economies of non-oil-developing countries. Cuba itself could not remain immune from the negative economic consequences of war in the Gulf. It feared the impact of the war on the Soviet Union's ability to supply oil, which was then being sold at world market prices. Castro was afraid that the price for such oil would rise, saying, "If oil prices shoot up dramatically, that will be prohibitive for Cuba and will force us to greater sacrifices because of our inability to go elsewhere."[46]

Cuba backed initiatives within the UN, NAM, and the Arab League to broker a peace settlement that would cut out the United States. Cuba, with Yemen, Malaysia, and Colombia, sought to sponsor proposals that would allow Iraq room to maneuver its way out of confrontation with the UN. Ambassador Alarcón gave support to Soviet efforts to broker a proposal for Iraq's withdrawal. Together with Sudan, Yemen, and the Magreb countries, Cuba pressed for a formal recall of the Security Council before the start of the allied ground offensive. The United States and Britain used their veto to block the move.[47]

Cuba pursued intense diplomacy within the Nonaligned Movement. On the first day of the crisis, August 2, 1990, Cuba sent a message to the Yugoslav president of the movement, Janez Drnovšek, urging that NAM's influence be used to seek a peaceful solution.[48] On February 12, 1991, Cuba participated in a specially convened meeting of sixteen foreign ministers of NAM in Belgrade to promote a new peace initiative.[49] The group agreed to send the foreign ministers of Cuba, Yugoslavia, Iran, and India to visit Saddam Hussein in Baghdad.[50]

During the war, the Cuban press and radio reported the course of hostilities in minute detail. The Cubans were fascinated as well as shocked by the war and sought information from whatever sources they could find.[51] After the first red-ink headline in *Granma* on January 17, "CRIMINAL YANKEE BOMBARDMENT OF BAGHDAD," most day-to-day battle reports were taken from Western press agencies (such as CNN, EFE, and AFP) and were factual and nonrhetorical, although they took pains to emphasize the human and material costs of the war. Special placement was given to reports of U.S. bombings of Iraqi homes, hospitals, and health centers and to antiwar actions, demonstrations, and statements by politicians and intellectuals around the world. Prominence was given to expressions of anti-Western and anti-U.S. sentiment in the Arab world and Latin America.

After Iraq's expulsion from Kuwait at the end of February 1991, Cuba was the only member of the Security Council to vote against the resolution (April 3) approving the strict cease-fire terms to end the war. Cuba criticized the resolution for providing for the military occupation and dismemberment of Iraq. Yemen, hitherto Iraq's most consistent supporter in the Security Council, abstained in this vote, reportedly under pressure from U.S. threats to withdraw economic aid.[52] Cuba subsequently voted against the Security Council resolution on April 5 condemning Iraqi persecution of its Kurdish population.[53] This made Cuba the target of Kurdish demonstrations in various cities in Europe. In Germany two diplomats were expelled after firing guns inside the Cuban embassy in Bonn when Kurdish demonstrators broke in to protest Cuba's position.[54]

CUBA'S MIDDLE EAST RELATIONS AFTER THE GULF WAR

It is not true, as is sometimes suggested, that Cuba supported Iraq's invasion of Kuwait or recognized Kuwait's incorporation into Iraq. Nor was Cuba's stance as isolated as some commentators have implied. Cuba, fearing that war would result in increased U.S. hegemony and would damage Third World interests, opposed by all means the use of force and promoted a negotiated settlement among Arabs that would not enhance U.S. influence. Castro argued that, from a political viewpoint, whatever justifications Iraq saw for its actions it played into the hands of the United States, enabling the superpower to line up a powerful coalition, including many Arab states, against the invader.[55] It was a view that found support in many Middle East quarters of anti-U.S. opinion, including in Iran, which is increasingly emerging as a major regional player.

Regarding the twelve Security Council resolutions leading up to the war, Cuba voted consistently in favor of those that condemned Iraq's annexation of Kuwait and declared it illegal; it also voted in favor of the resolutions that condemned hostage-taking and Iraq's actions against foreign embassies. It abstained or voted against resolutions that imposed sanctions or authorized the use of force. Its seat on the Security Council placed Cuba in the spotlight of international diplomacy. It led the United States, for the first time in three decades, to make serious efforts to gain

Cuba's acquiescence for its policy. A meeting between U.S. secretary of state James Baker and Cuban foreign minister Malmierca in November 1990 to discuss Cuba's position on the Security Council was the highest-level meeting between the two countries since 1959 and was seen by some commentators as a sign of the times in the post–Cold War world.[56]

Nevertheless, Cuba's line was extremely risky from both pragmatic and principled viewpoints. Cuba (along with Arafat and the PLO) risked isolation by adopting a policy at odds with the majority of UN members, including some with hitherto excellent relations with Cuba, and some of Cuba's most important trading partners. It was the first major world crisis in decades toward which Cuba's view differed seriously from that of the Soviet Union.

In terms of principle, Cuba's argument that the crisis should be solved in the context of a general Middle East settlement risked implying that Cuba accepted Saddam Hussein's crude "linkage" of Iraq's occupation of Kuwait with Israel's occupation of Palestine—a stance that had seriously harmed the Palestinian cause. Diplomacy alone (i.e., calling for a peaceful solution) may have failed to remove Hussein from Kuwait. Although true, the argument that previous cases of aggression by the United States and Israel had gone unpunished was no argument for not punishing this aggression.

Cuba faced a dilemma of principle: to uphold Kuwait's independence and the supremacy of the UN while supporting Palestinian claims, resisting U.S. hegemony, and insisting on the peaceful settlement of disputes. Cuba claimed that it emerged from the crisis with its anti-imperialist principles intact.

During and after the Gulf War, the United States tried to capitalize on Cuba's isolation. Even before the war ended, U.S. diplomats started extensive worldwide lobbying in favor of the most critical resolution ever adopted against Cuba at the Human Rights Commission in Geneva. The commission agreed to send an observer to investigate conditions in Cuba and monitor the situation over the following twelve months.[57] Presumably, as a reward for Cuba's stand, Iraq voted against the resolution, along with China and the Soviet Union.

It was argued in U.S. circles that Cuba's status as a champion of the Third World was incongruous with the perception that it was out of step with world views and was squandering political capital on lost causes. According to Alarcón, however, Cuba's influence was not dented by the Gulf War, although U.S. influence rose. He pointed to the systematic pressure that the United States exerts over members of the UN; only Cuba is impervious. "We don't see it as a failure," commented Alarcón on Cuba's lonely no vote. "We view it with pride; to be one of the few countries in a position to vote according to their ideals."[58]

The Gulf War led Cuba to question the UN's ability to preserve peace. Cuba had always revered the UN as a focus for its policy of anticolonialism and nonalignment. Now, while Western commentators praised the UN's newfound ability to deal effectively with international conflicts, Cuba condemned its loss of moral authority. The war, declared Alarcón, dealt the UN "a severe legal and moral blow, when the Security Council approved the use of force against a member state without exhausting the diplomatic possibilities or awaiting the results of economic sanctions and the blockade."[59] He said that the Security Council resolutions were worded "in language that can be used for any purpose the generals decide upon."[60]

Once armed force was decided upon, the UN itself should have assembled the forces, taken command, and controlled the operations. Instead the operation was planned and controlled by the United States, and "the Security Council, which supposedly authorized and initiated the attack, was informed of the opening of hostilities through the medium of American television."[61] The approval of Resolution 678 was "a flagrant violation of the UN Charter,"[62] which would "remain in the annals of this organization as a moment of shame when the Security Council abdicated its fundamental obligation . . . to preserve international peace and security."[63]

Cuba's post–Gulf War situation is related to its post–Cold War dilemma. At the time of the war the Warsaw Pact and the COMECON system had already disintegrated, and a process of estrangement between Cuba and the Soviet Union was under way. Following the war, when the Soviet Union finally broke apart, Cuba lost its main source of economic support and was set adrift in a world with only one remaining superpower, a hostile one.

To survive the Soviet collapse, Castro's Cuba must address the need for new sources of political and economic sustenance. New areas for trade and cooperation are needed, and political considerations dictate that these be found first in the Third World. Cuba has not been slow in identifying the Middle East, where it already has a number of allies, as a potential source of new trading partners and political friends.

In February 1992, Vice President Fernández made an important two-week tour of Syria, Iran, Libya, and Tunisia (including a meeting in Tunis with Yasser Arafat) to strengthen diplomatic and economic relations with the region. Cuban officials said they were highly satisfied with the results. According to reports, the governments of all the countries—including those that had supported the anti-Iraq alliance—expressed understanding of Cuba's position on world questions and, above all, the view that Third World countries should seek a coordinated policy.[64] The implication is that Cuba's diplomatic isolation following the war has not permanently damaged its standing among Arab countries. However, the region's long-standing problems, especially the Palestinian question, remain unsolved. Not all countries, and certainly not in the Middle East, welcome the United States as the world's unchallenged police guard, and the concept of anti-imperialist nonalignment that Cuba advocates still finds a powerful echo.

On the economic front, can the Middle East help Cuba? Despite the global trend toward market economy, business can still be done in many Middle East countries—such as Iraq, Libya, and Iran—through old-style, government-to-government and barter trade agreements of the kind to which Cuban enterprises are accustomed. Cuba sees the Middle East as an important source of support to replace lost Soviet aid.[65] Recent Cuba-Iran developments show the potential for synergy between Cuban sugar and Middle Eastern oil—Cuba badly needs oil and the Middle East needs sugar. The new relationship with Iran, including the oil-for-sugar deal, must count as one of Cuba's most important diplomatic and commercial successes of recent times.

Links with the Middle East alone are not enough for Cuba's survival, however. Cuba cannot expect to find Middle East sources of economic subsidy to replace its special relationship with the Soviet Union. The Middle East cannot absorb enough sugar to pay for Cuba's present oil needs at world market prices, so Cuba will have to both find additional outlets for sugar and continue to reduce its oil consumption. Nevertheless, in the new post-Soviet global context, Cuba's relations with the Middle East are bound to acquire new significance.

NOTES

The epigraph that opens this chapter is from a speech given by Castro in Santiago de Cuba on July 26, 1978, and is quoted from *Granma*, July 27, 1978; La Política Exterior de la Cuba Socialista, Editorial Progreso, Moscow, 1982, pp. 383–384.

1. Jorge I. Domínguez, *To Make a World Safe for Revolution: Cuba's Foreign Policy* (Cambridge: Harvard University Press, 1989), p. 7.

2. Castro's speech at the First Congress of Cuban Communist Party, December 1975, La Política Exterior, p. 46.

3. Resolution of the Second Congress of Cuban Communist Party, December 1980, La Política Exterior, pp. 106–107.

4. Domínguez, *To Make a World Safe*, p. 128.

5. Speech by Guillermo García Frías at the Eleventh Congress of League of Communists of Yugoslavia; *Granma*, June 24, 1978; La Política Exterior, p. 206.

6. Castro's speech at the Sixth Nonaligned Summit in Havana, September 1979; *Granma*, September 4, 1979; La Política Exterior, p. 276.

7. La Política Exterior, Preface, p. 28.

8. Saudi Arabian trade statistics.

9. Author's interviews with Cuban trade officials.

10. *Cuba Business* 3, no. 4 (August 1989).

11. Domínguez, *To Make a World Safe*, p. 210.

12. *Cuba Business* 3, no. 4 (August 1989).

13. Pamela S. Falk, *Cuban Foreign Policy: Caribbean Tempest* (Lexington: Lexington Books, 1985), pp. 116–117.

14. Ibid., p. 116; *Granma*, December 20, 1980; La Política Exterior, p. 79.

15. *Granma*, December 20, 1980; La Política Exterior, p. 79.

16. La Política Exterior, pp. 106–107.

17. Domínguez, *To Make a World Safe,* pp. 129–130.

18. Informe Latinoamericano, July 20, 1989.

19. Ibid.

20. Ibid.

21. Castro's speech to UN General Assembly, New York, October 12, 1979; La Política Exterior, p. 293.

22. *Cuba Business* 3, no. 4 (August 1989); 4, no. 1 (February 1990); and 4, no. 4 (August 1990).

23. *Guardian,* July 28, 1990.

24. Informe Latinoamericano, July 20, 1989.

25. Resolution of the Second PCC Congress, December 1980; La Política Exterior, p. 102.

26. Castro's speech at the Second PCC Congress, 1980; *Granma,* December 20, 1980; La Política Exterior, p. 64.

27. Resolution of the Second PCC Congress, December 1980; La Política Exterior, pp. 106–107.

28. *Cuba Business* 3, no. 4 (August 1989).

29. *Cuba Business* 5, no. 1 (February 1991); *Public Ledger,* January 29, 1991.

30. *Cuba Business* 5, no. 1 (February 1991).

31. *Cuba Business* 5, no. 5 (October 1991).

32. *Miami Herald,* February 25, 1992.

33. *CubaINFO* 4, no. 3, p. 2; and 4, no. 4, p. 4, 1992.

34. Castro's speech at the First PCC Congress, 1975; La Política Exterior, p. 46.

35. *Granma,* January 18, 1991; Wolfgang G. Lerch, *Kein Frieden für Allahs Völker* (Fischer Frankfurt/Main: 1992), Taschenbuch Verlag, pp. 117, 132, for Cuba's voting behavior in the UN Security Council.

36. *Granma,* January 25, 1991.

37. *Granma,* February 11, 1991.

38. *Cuba Business* 4, no. 5 (October 1990).

39. *Granma,* January 25, 1991.

40. Castro press conference in Havana; *Granma,* January 17, 1991.

41. Castro's letter to Arab leaders on August 7, 1990; *Granma,* January 25, 1991.

42. *Granma,* January 18, 1991.

43. *Miami Herald,* January 17, 1991.

44. *Cuba Business* 4, no. 5 (October 1990).

45. *Granma,* January 18, 1991.

46. *Miami Herald,* January 24, 1991.

47. *Cuba Business* 5, no. 1 (February 1991); *Granma,* January 24 and February 1, 1991.

48. *Granma,* January 18, 1991.

49. *Granma,* February 13, 1991.

50. *Newsday,* February 25, 1991.

51. *Miami Herald,* January 24, 1991.

52. *Cuba Business* 5, no. 2 (April 1991); *Miami Herald,* April 7, 1991.

53. *Miami Herald,* April 7, 1991.

54. *Cuba Business* 5, no. 2 (April 1991).

55. *Granma,* January 17, 1991.

56. *Cuba Business* 4, no. 6 (December 1990).

57. *Miami Herald,* March 7 and April 7, 1991.

58. *Miami Herald,* April 7, 1991.
59. Interview in *Granma,* January 18, 1991.
60. Speech by Ricardo Alarcón at UN on cease-fire debate, April 3, 1991.
61. *Granma,* January 18, 1991.
62. Ibid.
63. Alarcón speech, April 3, 1991.
64. *El Nuevo Herald,* February 23, 1992.
65. *CubaINFO* 4, no. 3, p. 2, 1992.

PART 2

CUBA'S RELATIONS
WITH EUROPE

6

The Relationship Between the European Community and Cuba

WOLF GRABENDORFF

For the second time since its socialist revolution in 1959, Cuba has become an important issue in world politics.[1] Whereas its international participation during the East-West conflict assured its top ranking in global politics, the reasons for current international attention on the small Caribbean island are quite different. Events to date in the 1990s indicate that the Cuban model of socialism is doomed to failure. Moreover, Cuba has been abandoned by its allies in Europe and Latin America, and the collapse of the Castro regime, or at least its transformation, appears to be only a question of time.

Cuba is one of the few countries with a dual identity: it is a Third World country on the one hand and part of the group of "Second World" countries on the other. Because of this unique position, Cuba is the point of intersection between North-South and East-West conflicts. Because of its size and geographic location, Cuba developed a foreign policy conditioned by a strong economic dependence on one central ally at a time—namely, the United States during Cuba's prerevolutionary era, and later the Soviet Union. Furthermore, Cuba's foreign-policy profile represents a blend of its Latin American, North American, and African cultural and political influences. The island's thirty-three-year relationship with the Soviet Union and Eastern Europe has also influenced its policies.

The European Community (EC) has never been a priority on Cuba's foreign-policy agenda, nor has Cuba been a priority on the agenda of the EC. Consequently, neither has ever defined a clear political strategy toward the other. EC-Cuban relations have traditionally been highly dependent on the international and respective regional climate and each one's commitments therein. The bipolar international system involving relations of the Atlantic Triangle—the United States, the EC, and Latin America—and events surrounding East-West and North-South conflicts have served as the backdrop for Cuban-European relations. Moreover, direct supranational and bilateral links between Europe and Cuba have involved overlapping interests in three regions—the Caribbean Basin, Africa, and Central America

—mostly relics from the European colonial past. Although the following analysis will focus on the different levels (namely, international, supranational, and bilateral) of past and future political and economic relations between Cuba and Western Europe, these three conflictive regions also have to be viewed as representing unique historical conditions contributing a specific weight to the bilateral pattern of EC-Cuban relations.

EUROPE AND CUBA IN THE INTERNATIONAL ARENA

In the global context, from the Cuban Revolution in 1959 to the collapse of socialism in the 1990s, EC and Cuban perceptions were determined by their ideological commitments in the Cold War. Cuba, as part of the socialist bloc and member of the Council for Mutual Economic Assistance (CMEA), was treated by the Europeans as a communist country rather than a Latin American country. Europe, from the Cuban perspective, was seen as a U.S. ally but also as a buffer zone between the two superpowers.

The positions of Europe and Cuba in the international system were radically altered following the collapse of the Eastern bloc and the dissolution of the Soviet Union. Cuba became one of the few remaining isolated socialist countries, abandoned by all its traditional political and economic allies in Eastern Europe, a group that accounted for 85 percent of Cuban trade. At the same time, a unified Europe developed its own independent position in international politics and, together with Japan and the United States, is now competing for the world domain. With the dissolution of the CMEA on June 28, 1991, relations between Europe and Cuba represent no longer a dialogue between different ideological blocs but rather one between an isolated socialist country in the Caribbean and a bloc of twelve integrated European countries.

Cuba's international isolation was aggravated by a number of events: the end of the Sandinista regime in Nicaragua, the unification of the two Germanys, the return of democracy in Latin America, and, last but not least, Cuba's withdrawal from Africa. Moreover, the new international environment was dominated by two general trends: (1) the worldwide shift from one-party systems toward Western multiparty systems and free elections and (2) the formation of regional trading spheres. Consequently, without political and economic reforms, Cuba will confront serious difficulties in reinserting itself into patterns of international relations.

Because of dramatic cuts in foreign aid, a weakening demand for its imports, and the end of Soviet subsidization, Cuba is suffering the worst economic and social crisis of its history and has been forced to search for alternatives. In fact, Cuba's new economic strategy, designed in 1990, concentrates on integrating parts of the Cuban economy into the world market by establishing stronger trade links with capitalist countries without abandoning its socialist principles. Thus, Cuba's foreign policy in the 1990s envisages three principle aims: (1) to reintegrate Cuba into the community of Latin American countries; (2) to create closer links with Asian countries, mainly China and Japan; and (3) to reactivate diplomatic and trade links with Western countries—namely, Canada and the countries of the EC.

However, improving relations with Western Europe is hindered by several major obstacles. Cuba's human rights situation, harshly criticized by the EC and its member states, represents the major stumbling block for strengthening mutual ties. The path to the West is blocked also by Cuba's outstanding debt obligations with EC countries. Finally, ideological differences remain.

Although Western Europe counterbalanced the negative effects imposed by the U.S. trade embargo (albeit in part because the situation was viewed as an opportunity for Europe to demonstrate it had a foreign policy independent of the United States), this position was modified at the beginning of the 1990s in favor of closer political ties toward U.S. policy on Cuba. In the new international order of the 1990s, the EC and most European countries are beginning to openly criticize the Cuban regime and are pressuring for internal political changes. In its February 13, 1992, resolution on Cuba, the European Parliament condemned the government's human rights violations and its application of the death penalty. The European Parliament has appealed to the "'totalitarian' Cuban regime to create the necessary conditions for the introduction of a democratic process in Cuba."[2]

Conflicts of Interest in the Central American Crisis

Within the European–Latin American framework, Cuba and the EC are directly involved in interregional, subregional, and bilateral conflicts. The Central American conflict best illustrated that Latin America offered a stage for open conflicts or sharp contrasting ideological differences between the European Community and Cuba.

Since the 1959 revolution, Cuba has played an active role in Third World policies and has been directly involved in political conflicts in Latin America and Africa. Cuban actions have not been mere reflections of Soviet strategies. On the contrary, Cuban involvement in the Third World is best characterized as an independent initiative representative of Cuba's own revolutionary vanguard model. Through the implementation of South-South normalization initiatives and the exportation of its revolutionary posture, Cuba had hoped to gain new partners in the South.

In the 1980s, Central America provided one of the main stages for the activities of foreign-policy makers with different ideological standpoints— namely, Mexico, Venezuela, Panama, the EC, and Cuba. From 1984 on, when the Central American countries established a formal dialogue with the

EC in the so-called San José process, the EC developed its own Central American policy profile in close collaboration with the Contadora peace initiative initiated by Mexico, Venezuela, and Panama to promote a peaceful democratic solution in the region.[3] In contrast, the Cuban stance in the Central American crisis was somewhat ambivalent: while Cuba aided guerrilla groups in El Salvador and Guatemala and was one of the main allies of the Sandinistas in Nicaragua, it also supported the peace initiatives of the Contadora group as a regional solution to the crisis.

Cuban assistance to guerrilla groups in El Salvador and Guatemala, as well as Cuban military and political assistance to the Sandinista government, was perceived by the Europeans as a dangerous and counterproductive force against reaching a peaceful solution to the regional conflict. And although both Cuba and the EC supported the Contadora peace initiative, their motives varied: while the EC promoted peace negotiations in Central America to contribute to the democratization process and to advocate respect for human rights, Cuba hoped for the consolidation of a Sandinista government that would contribute to the strengthening of its own revolutionary regime in the region.

However, Cuban hopes set on the Sandinista consolidation were short lived. The defeat of the Sandinistas in the democratic elections of February 1990 signified not only a peaceful end to the long-standing Central American crisis but also the end of friendly relations between Nicaragua and Cuba. Cuba's influence in Central America was further reduced by the end of the Noriega regime in Panama in December 1989 and the peace agreement signed between the Salvadoran government and the Farabundo Martí Front for National Liberation (FMLN) in December 1991.

These events and the general trend toward liberal democracies in Latin America in the 1980s isolated Cuba and displaced it from its relatively protagonistic role in the region. Cuba became a minor issue for the Europeans, and they began to see the crumbling of the Castro regime as just a question of time and hoped for a nonviolent change of regime.

THE EUROPEAN COMMUNITY AND CUBA:
BETWEEN COMMON APPROACHES AND CONFLICTS

There are two main European political actors involved in EC-Cuban relations: the European Commission (the Commission) and the European Parliament (EP) along with its different political groups. While the Commission is involved mainly in trade and aid relations, the EP, and especially the Socialist Group,[4] have been the most interested parties in establishing stronger political links with Cuba.[5]

Economic ties are the main anchor for EC-Cuban relations, while political relations have been highly dependent on international political cycles. Cuba's cultural ties with Western Europe have been traditionally limited to bilateral relations with Spain and to some extent with France and Italy, but Cuba's strong links with the Eastern and central European countries can be expected to have a certain impact on the future patterns of cultural ties with the countries of the European Community.

Because of Cuba's double identity as both a socialist and a Latin American country, contacts between Cuba and the EC in the framework of European–Latin American relations are not based on an extensive institutional framework. The only institutionalized forums in which both actors participate are the regular meetings of Latin American ambassadors to the EC in Brussels (GRULA), a group to which Cuba has belonged since October 1979. Nevertheless, Cuba's participation in the biregional meetings has always been conflictive because of Cuba's differing ideological approach. As a member of the Latin American Parliament since 1985, Cuba also participates in the biannual interparliamentarian meetings between representatives of the European Parliament and the Latin American Parliament.

POLITICAL CONTACTS
DURING AND AFTER THE COLD WAR

The EC has never defined a clear political strategy on Cuba. Its attitude toward the island has been highly dependent on its relationship with the United States and the nine members of the CMEA. Nevertheless, despite Cuban ties to the socialist bloc, EC countries have maintained their economic and diplomatic relations with Cuba, for several reasons. Because European interests in the Caribbean were quite limited, most Europeans did not perceive the small Caribbean country as a real security threat and, consequently, were not disposed to back U.S. confrontational policies toward Cuba.[6] In fact, as previously stated, some European countries saw Cuba as presenting an opportunity to demonstrate a foreign policy independent of the United States. Thus, European policy toward Cuba can be best characterized as a European intent to create a third pole of influence as a counterpart to that of the United States and the Soviet bloc.[7]

However, the major obstacle for the normalization of EC-Cuban relations was less U.S. policy in Cuba than Cuba's close relationship with Eastern Europe. Cuba's participation in the CMEA transformed EC-Cuban relations—for nearly thirty years—into a supranational dialogue between two ideological blocs: the EC and the CMEA. As the evolution of mutual relations shows, the intensity of EC-Cuban relations was highly dependent on the EC's ties with CMEA. However, the formal dissolution of the economic organization of socialist countries in June 1991 put relations in a new light: Cuba was finally seen by the EC as an individual Latin American country, albeit a socialist one.

During the first decade of Castroism in the 1960s, when Cuba defended its own independent, homemade revolution, both the EC and Cuba maintained diplomatic and economic relations in opposition to U.S. policy and the U.S. trade embargo of 1962. In the 1970s, relations were determined by Cuban closeness to the Soviet Union and overshadowed by the Cuban endorsement of the 1968 Soviet invasion in Czechoslovakia. Cuba's deepening ties to Eastern Europe culminated in July 1972, when Cuba became the first full non-European member state of the CMEA. Cuba's integration into the socialist community and its strong links with the eastern part of the Iron Curtain provoked a serious deterioration of EC-Cuban relations. Moreover, Cuba's direct political and military involvement in Africa—seen by some as a traditional European sphere of influence—provided a further reason for Europe to distance itself from the Cuban government. More so than in Latin America, Europeans perceived Cuba as a security threat in Africa, since Cuban activities endangered an important European export market, given that Africa is a member of the African, Caribbean, and Pacific (ACP) country group strongly linked to the EC.

Improved EC-Cuban relations in the 1980s were a result of mutual recognition between the EC and the CMEA on September 25, 1988. Four days later, the EC and Cuba restored formal diplomatic relations. This marked the beginning of the short-lived "honeymoon" between the EC and Cuba from 1988 to 1990. In May 1989, the EC and Cuba began to exchange ambassadors, and on April 22–24, 1990, the president of the EP delegation for Central America and Mexico, Fernando Suárez, made an official visit to Cuba. This new political dialogue triggered a series of common programs and activities in specific economic sectors, and for the first time there was discussion of a possible general agreement between Cuba and the EC. In order to intensify relations with the European Community, in December 1989 the Cubans created the National Group of Attention to the EC for the preparation of cooperation projects. Good relations were short lived, however: one year later, all current projects were stopped in response to a refugee conflict in Havana that occurred in July 1990.

Relations between Cuba and the EC in the 1990s were complicated not only by human rights conflicts but also by the new international order, when Eastern and Central European countries announced the dissolution of the socialist bloc. As one of the few countries belonging to the former economic bloc of socialist countries that was unwilling to undergo reform, Cuba could not benefit from the new ties established by the EC with other CMEA members.

As has been the case with Eastern European countries, the normalization of EC-Cuban relations is highly dependent on the island's implementation of democratic reforms, including the improvement of human rights and the formalization of free elections. This reflects a general trend in the EC's Latin American policy. In order to promote liberal democracies in the region, the EC has explicitly made development cooperation conditional on respect for human rights and formal moves toward democratization. These guidelines were also adopted in the Cuban case. From 1990 to 1992 the European Parliament approved a number of resolutions against human rights violations and in support of democratic reforms in Cuba. The human rights situation in Cuba has been responsible for two problematic events in EC-Cuban relations in the 1990s: the embassy crisis in July 1990 and the increasing repression of internal opponents that culminated in the execution of a regime opponent in 1992.

The first diplomatic conflict related to human rights took place in July 1990, when Cuban refugees occupied several European embassies in Havana (the embassies of Czechoslovakia, Spain, Belgium, and Italy) demanding political asylum in the respective countries. The events escalated to shootings in the embassies and were followed by a dramatic exchange of political statements between both sides. Cuban authorities interpreted the incidents as an "international conspiracy" against Cuba. At Spain's request, on July 20 the EC responded with the suspension of recently established cooperation programs with Cuba and the suspension of diplomatic relations.[8]

The continuing repression of regime opponents in Cuba[9] led to the second problematic event: the execution of the leader of a sabotage mission on January 20, 1992. Commissioner Abel Matutes of the EC qualified the execution as a "serious obstacle to the normalization of relations between the Community and Cuba."[10] On the same day, the European Commission canceled all running cooperation programs with Cuba, and later it refused an official Cuban invitation to study future cooperation projects in Havana. Individual European governments, including those of France, Spain, and Germany, expressed their "profound consternation."

Although these two conflicts have demonstrated that the EC is shifting closer to the U.S. stance on Cuba, the EC, especially the European Parliament, has continued to be an intermediary link between the United States and Cuba, appealing to both governments to initiate a bilateral dialogue and promoting Cuba's reintegration into the Organization of American States (OAS).[11]

At present, the EC pursues a more ambivalent strategy toward Cuba than does the United States. On the one hand, the EC has tightened pressure on Cuba for democratic reforms; but on the other, it has expressed doubts on the efficiency of the U.S. strategy. Recent debates in the EC have shown that the U.S. trade blockade against Cuba is still a controversial subject. In contrast to a U.S. confrontational policy, most Europeans see the insertion of Cuba into the international community and the lifting of the U.S. blockade as a way of opening Cuba's ideological system, thus providing room for a gradual peaceful democratization process. Most Europeans agree that the U.S. strategy to isolate Cuba may be counterproductive, since it could strengthen Cuban loyalty to Castro in his "fight between David and Goliath."

Development Cooperation and Economic Ties

As has already been pointed out, EC cooperation programs with Cuba have been conditioned by political factors. Since its inception in 1984, EC development assistance targeted for Cuba has been negligible. Moreover, Cuba is the only Latin American country that has not yet signed a general agreement with the European Community. Within the framework of EC development cooperation, Cuba has actually only benefited from the General System of Preferences (GSP), by which EC concessions for special products—including Cuban tobacco, nickel, fish, honey, and cocoa—expanded from 31 percent in 1976 to 64 percent in 1985. From 1990 onward, the EC system of trade preferences has also included Cuban textiles.

Although development cooperation was subordinated to politics, political differences had nearly no impact on trade relations between Cuba and the EC. Given that the international system is less hierarchical and more polycentric in economic relations than in political ones,[12] Cuba and the EC have maintained relatively stable economic ties linked to their respective economic interests and to price fluctuations in the world market.

For Cuba, trade relations with Western European countries have been of great importance, since these countries, along with Canada, represent the main access to the world market of freely convertible currency.[13] Moreover, economic links with Europe and other capitalist countries have undermined the efficacy of the U.S. trade embargo and, consequently, have protected Cuba from world market isolation.

The EC is one of the most important noncommunist trade partners for Cuba; it accounted for 45–50 percent of total Cuban trade with the noncommunist world in 1987 (see Tables 6.2 and 6.3). However, the share of Cuban trade with noncommunist countries accounted for only approximately 11 percent of total Cuban trade, given that CMEA countries have traditionally accounted for over 80 percent (approximately 70 percent with the Soviet Union and 10 percent with Eastern Europe).

Cuba is one of the world's largest sugar exporters. More than 70 percent of Cuba's exports are based on sugar, followed by petroleum, base metals, fish, tobacco, and nickel (see Table 6.4). Of these, tobacco and seafood are exported to the EC (Cuban honey is also exported there). However, because the EC is a major net exporter of sugar, Cuba's sugar exports to the EC and its member states are insignificant (see Table 6.5). Cuba, on the other hand, receives mainly industrial goods and technology from the EC.

Among the twelve EC member states, Spain, Germany, the United Kingdom, and France are Cuba's most important Western European trade partners (see Table 6.6). In 1989, the United Kingdom accounted for 26

RELATIONS WITH THE EUROPEAN COMMUNITY   97

Table 6.1 Official Development Aid Received by Cuba, 1980–1990 (in millions of US $)

	1980–1984	% of Total DAC	1985–1989	% of Total DAC	1990	% of Total DAC	1980–1990
Belgium	1.4	5.2	0.0	0.0	0.0	0.0	1.4
Denmark	0.3	1.1	0.0	0.0	0.0	0.0	0.3
France	1.8	6.7	4.7	8.1	0.8	2.4	7.3
Germany	0.2	0.7	0.7	1.2	1.1	3.3	2.0
Italy	1.1	4.1	5.8	10.0	10.5	31.2	17.4
Netherlands	4.8	18.0	0.6	1.0	0.0	0.0	5.4
Spain	n.a.	n.a.	n.a.	n.a.	17.5	51.9	17.5
United Kingdom	0.0	0.0	0.0	0.0	0.0	0.0	0.0
Total EC countries	9.6	35.8	11.8	20.3	29.9	88.8	51.3
EC commission	3.2	12.0	31.5	54.4	0.1	0.3	34.8
Japan	0.6	2.2	1.4	2.4	0.6	1.8	2.6
Total DAC[a]	26.7	100.0	57.9	100.0	33.7	100.0	83.5

Sources: OECD, Database on Financial Flows to Developing Countries, Paris; State Secretariat for International Cooperation and Latin America, various publications; EC Commission, Database; and IRELA.
Notes: n.a. = not available
a. Development Assistance Committee of the OECD

Table 6.2   Main Destinations of Cuban Exports (as % of total exports)

	1980	1985	1987	1988
Socialist countries				
in Eastern Europe	59.6	86.1	86.8	n.a.
in Asia	3.0	2.9	2.0	n.a.
	62.6	89.0	88.8	86.4
Nonsocialist countries				
European Community	4.3	3.1	5.2	n.a.
United States/Canada	2.9	0.5	0.7	n.a.
Japan	2.8	1.3	1.4	2.0
Developing countries	8.3	2.8	2.5	n.a.
Other countries	19.1	3.3	1.4	n.a.
	37.4	11.0	11.2	2.0

Sources: United Nations Conference on Trade and Development, *Handbook of International Trade and Development Statistics*, Geneva 1991; Economist Intelligence Unit (EIU), *Country Profile*, no. 4, 1991; and IRELA calculations.
Note: n.a. = not available

percent of Cuban EC exports; Spain for 19.7 percent; Germany, 16.3 percent; and France, 12.4 percent. Spain is Cuba's main supplier of EC imports (38.5 percent), followed by the United Kingdom (17 percent) and Germany (16 percent) (see Table 6.7). Regarding total trade turnover between Cuba and Western Europe in 1989, Spain, with 29.1 percent, was Cuba's main trade partner, followed by the United Kingdom, with 21 percent, and Germany, with 16.1 percent. The importance of Italy and France in Cuban trade fell back considerably at the end of the 1980s, reaching only 10.7 and 9.7 percent, respectively.

In the 1980s, mutual trade relations suffered a serious setback and Cuba began to maintain a chronic trade deficit. This crisis was directly related to the rise of oil prices in the world market. Consequently, Western Europe's share of Cuban imports fell from 13.4 percent in 1981 to 6.3 percent in 1988. Today, the EC's participation in total Cuban trade is estimated at 6 percent.[14]

In the beginning of the 1990s, following the disintegration of the socialist bloc, noncommunist countries increased trade with Cuba. Nevertheless, Cuba's capacity to strengthen trade relations with such countries is strongly limited. Given that more than 85 percent of Cuban trade, much of it subsidized, was directed toward the Eastern bloc, the end of subsidized

Table 6.3   Main Origins of Cuban Imports
             (as % of total imports)

	1970	1975	1985	1988
Socialist countries				
in Eastern Europe	62.2	48.3	80.4	n.a.
in Asia	n.a.	n.a.	3.3	n.a.
	62.2	48.3	83.7	87.4
Nonsocialist countries				
European Community	20.4	22.3	6.8	n.a.
United States/Canada	2.1	3.2	0.7	n.a.
Japan	2.5	11.6	2.8	n.a.
Developing countries	1.6	n.a.	4.9	n.a.
Other countries	11.2	14.6	1.1	n.a.
	37.8	51.7	16.3	13.0

Sources: United Nations Conference on Trade and Development, *Handbook of International Trade and Development Statistics,* Geneva 1991; Economist Intelligence Unit, *Country Profile,* no. 4, 1991; and IRELA calculations.
Note: n.a. = not available
In 1989, the Cuban authorities ceased publication of statistics.

relations means that Cuba must pay for its imports (mainly grains and oil) at market prices. Since hard currency reserves have consequently been severely reduced, the Cuban government has been obligated to cut imports by more than half.[15]

Foreign direct investment. Fostering direct investments from abroad has provided a good strategy to guarantee the survival of the Cuban economy without Soviet help. In 1990, there were important internal modifications of the Cuban economic structure: opening to noncommunist countries, attraction of foreign capital, and promotion of tourism were the main elements of a new long-term strategy. The promotion of an economic opening via the creation of a few economic capitalist enclaves was initially tested in tourism and biotechnology and later expanded to nearly all economic sectors. On the other hand, as a short-term measure to counterbalance the dramatic loss of Soviet and Eastern European supplies, in 1989 the regime implemented a radical economic emergency program, the Special Period in Time of Peace, modified one year later into the "zero option." In some aspects, the Cuban concept at the beginning of the 1990s can be compared

Table 6.4   Main Cuban Exported Commodities
(based on 1987–1988 averages)

	% of Total	% of Exports of Developing Countries	% of World Exports
Sugar and honey	74.43	60.21	38.78
Petroleum products	4.87	0.95	0.40
Base metals	3.68	3.78	1.81
Shellfish, fresh frozen fish	2.35	2.23	1.36
Tobacco, manufactured	0.94	9.69	0.70
Coffee and substitutes	0.76	0.42	0.36
Fruit, fresh and dried nuts	0.69	0.62	0.25
Crude petroleum	0.64	0.04	0.02
Tobacco, unmanufactured	0.60	1.94	0.84
Iron and steel scrap	0.55	9.97	0.82
Medicinal, pharmaceutical products	0.54	2.06	0.11
Iron, steel shapes, etc.	0.47	1.20	0.18
Cocoa	0.43	0.69	0.52
Fruit, preserved and prepared	0.40	0.80	0.32
Alcoholic beverages	0.32	2.47	0.13
Alcohols, phenols, etc.	0.29	1.55	0.26
Others	8.03	n.a.	n.a.
All commodities	100.00	1.07	0.21

Sources: United Nations Conference on Trade and Development, *Handbook of International Trade and Development Statistics*, Geneva 1991; and IRELA calculations.
Note: n.a. = not available

with the strategy pursued by its increasingly important partner, China. In both countries, strengthened political indoctrination to protect the regime has been complemented by a more pragmatic economic concept, based on the partial introduction of capitalist elements. (See Chapter 2.)

Joint ventures. The campaign to attract joint ventures began in 1988, and in the following years Cuba strengthened its joint venture diplomacy by approving legislative modifications to Law 50, established on February 15, 1982, by conceding up to 50 percent of foreign participation in Cuban firms (see Chapter 14). Cuba's new joint venture diplomacy is employed principally in the tourist sector but also in the pharmaceutical, oil drilling, metallurgy, and transport industries. In October 1991, the state-owned investment company Cubanacán agreed to joint ventures with companies from Spain, Italy, the Netherlands, and Germany. Because of the end of subsidized Soviet oil supplies, the Cubans have invited European enterprises to

Table 6.5   Main Cuban Exports by Product to the EC (in thousands of pesos)

	1980	EC Market Share of Total Cuban Exports (%)	As % of Total Exports to EC	1987	EC Market Share of Total Cuban Exports (%)	As % of Total Exports to EC
Tobacco	10,406	29.8	9.6	60,990	73.5	22.6
Nickel and copper	30,342	32.5	26.0	18,893	n.a.	7.0
Seafood	18,242	22.7	15.9	64,833	46.5	24.0
Sugar and honey	27,982	n.a.	24.3	5,689	n.a.	2.1
Others	27,858	n.a.	24.2	119,192	n.a.	44.2
Total	114,830	n.a.	100.0	269,597	n.a.	100.0

Sources: Anuario Estadístico de Cuba, 1973–1989; and IRELA calculations.

Table 6.6   Cuban Exports by Country to the EC (in thousands of pesos)

	1980–1984	% of Total EC	1985–1988	% of Total EC	1989	% of Total EC
Belgium	44,048	5.7	47,733	4.4	28,930	6.6
Denmark	4,841	0.6	3,617	0.3	135	0.0
France	211,413	27.5	235,351	21.5	54,429	12.4
Germany	157,251	20.4	128,998	11.8	71,395	16.3
Greece	231	0.0	3,136	0.3	9	0.0
Ireland	2,360	0.3	1,049	0.1	67	0.0
Italy	127,391	16.5	135,461	12.4	36,163	8.3
Netherlands	121,484	15.8	178,571	16.3	34,005	7.8
Portugal	0	0.0	4,065	0.4	12,774	2.9
Spain	0	0.0	254,622	23.3	86,031	19.7
United Kingdom	100,765	13.1	100,213	9.2	113,782	26.0
Total EC	769,784	100.0	1,092,816	100.0	437,720	100.0

Sources: Anuario Estadístico de Cuba, 1973–1989; and IRELA calculations.

Table 6.7 Cuban Imports from the EC (in thousands of pesos)

	1980–1984	% of Total EC	1985–1988	% of Total EC	1989	% of Total EC
Belgium	82,219	4.8	46,408	2.8	9,880	2.1
Denmark	27,871	1.6	22,291	1.4	5,906	1.2
France	456,333	26.7	223,660	13.6	34,650	7.2
Germany	392,167	22.9	276,971	16.8	76,612	16.0
Greece	0	0.0	0	0.0	0	0.0
Ireland	6,453	0.4	0	0.0	2	0.0
Italy	174,671	10.2	219,736	13.3	62,577	13.0
Netherlands	194,519	11.4	79,680	4.8	22,875	4.8
Portugal	0	0.0	7,179	0.4	924	0.2
Spain	0	0.0	458,981	27.8	184,865	38.5
United Kingdom	374,593	21.9	313,907	19.0	81,769	17.0
Total EC	1,708,826	100.0	1,648,813	100.0	480,060	100.0

Sources: Anuario Estadístico de Cuba, 1973–1989; and IRELA calculations.

explore for oil in Cuba. The Cuban Petrol Union signed its first agreement with the French petrol consortium composed of Total Petroleum and Compagnie Européene des Pétroles in December 1990.

Tourism. The development of the tourist sector to gain hard currency has become a principal target of Cuba's new economic agenda. First successes were reported at the end of 1991, when official sources counted nearly five hundred thousand tourists.[16] In 1988, nearly half of the tourists to Cuba came from Europe, and of the 340,000 tourists in Cuba in 1990—a group that spent nearly $250 million there—the largest number came from Canada, Germany, Spain, and Italy. According to predictions made by the Cuban Institute for Tourism (INTUR), Western European tourism to Cuba will increase by approximately 50 percent in the period 1991–1995.[17] Many of the new hotels on Cuba's beaches have been built and are managed by European partners, with a 50 percent foreign capital stake. Spanish enterprises are the most interested partners for investments in Cuba's tourist sector, and at the beginning of 1992, Spanish banks and enterprises announced their willingness to invest about $250 million in a gigantic tourist project on the Isle of Youth in Cuba.

Future prospects. Apart from the uncertainty of Cuba's future economic scenarios, current efforts to intensify economic relations with the EC confront three main obstacles: the external debt, the Single European Market, and stronger opposition from European countries to the Cuban regime. Because of its severe solvency problems, in April 1986 Cuba announced the unilateral suspension of its debt payments; Cuba's external debt owed to Western countries is estimated at $8 billion. The EC reply to Cuba's announcement was prompt: the cancellation of all credits and financial cooperation projects with Cuba. Cuba's external debt problem is still unresolved, and, coupled with an aggravated economic situation, the debt burden is still one of the main obstacles to improved trade with Europe.

Although Cuban trade relations with the EC traditionally have been difficult because of mutual competition in the international sugar market, a further deterioration of EC-Cuban relations can also be expected because the integration of EC member states after 1992 will also include the gradual unification of their respective foreign policies. Because bilateral relations with European countries have been much more significant for Cuba than links with the EC, European integration and the consequent loss of bilateral contacts may seriously affect political and economic relations between Europe and Cuba. Moreover, the current tendency toward the formation of regional economic blocs in Europe and Latin America could further accentuate Cuba's growing isolation.

Cuba thus remains a special case for the EC, and the path leading to normalization of trade relations is still long and arduous. From the European

Table 6.8   Tourism to Cuba (number of visitants received by INTUR)

	1988	% of Total	1992	% of Total	1995	% of Total
North America	43,009	22.57	124,753	23.50	179,490	22.00
Latin America/Caribbean	45,382	23.81	134,308	25.30	169,699	20.80
Western Europe	100,950	52.97	262,246	49.40	453,048	55.53
Austria	6,681	3.51	—	—	—	—
France	7,117	3.73	—	—	—	—
Germany	37,186	19.51	—	—	—	—
Italy	17,125	8.99	—	—	—	—
Spain	26,219	13.76	—	—	—	—
United Kingdom	491	0.26	—	—	—	—
Other Europe	6,131	3.22	—	—	—	—
Others	1,237	0.65	8,494	1.60	13,625	1.67
Total	190,578	100.00	529,801	99.8	815,862	100.00

Source: INTUR, Estadísticas, 1991.
Note: Figures for 1992 and 1995 are projections.

perspective, the main obstacle to intensifying mutual relations is the incompatibility of Cuba's economy with the norms established in the international system and the uncertain outcome of Cuba's current social and economic crisis.

It can be expected that the contradiction between economic opening and political intimidation of internal opposition and criticism will serve to further complicate relations with the EC. The internal contradictions of the Castro regime, combined with the economic crisis and the negative impact of repressive political strategies in Cuba for some Western European and Latin American countries, even give rise to interpretations of an imminent collapse of Cuban socialism.[18]

BILATERAL PATTERN OF EC-CUBAN RELATIONS

In general, bilateral relations between individual European countries and Cuba have been more important than EC contacts.[19] Nearly all EC member states have signed cooperation agreements with Cuba and some hold friendly political contacts with the Castro government. Although countries such as Italy and the Netherlands have also been of certain importance for Cuba, its main bilateral EC partners have traditionally been Spain and France and, more recently, Germany and the United Kingdom. (See Chapter 7 for a discussion of Cuban-British relations.)

The nature of bilateral contacts between European countries and Cuba have been determined basically by European historical ties with Cuba and respective relations with the United States. For example, links between Cuba and Spain have their roots in a common cultural and historical heritage, given that Cuba was the last of many Spanish colonies. Cuba's relations with France have also been dominated by cultural ties, although political relations have been complicated by competing Cuban-French activities in Africa. By contrast, Cuba's cultural ties with the former West Germany and the United Kingdom are almost nonexistent, and political links have been strongly limited by different commitments in the Cold War. Moreover, German unification on October 3, 1990, hit Cuba hard because it meant losing a very important partnership with East Germany. Nevertheless, trade and investment relations have been the focus of Cuban relations with both these countries.

Spain: Historical Links and Political Differences

Spain has been of strategic importance in Cuba's relations with the EC for three main reasons: (1) strong historical and cultural ties have allowed Spain to act as a bridge in European–Latin American affairs; (2) Spanish mistrust of U.S. involvement in Latin America, traditionally a Spanish zone of influence, prompted Spain to act as a guardian of the region; and (3) the loss of Cuba, the last Spanish colony, marked the end of the Spanish colonial era and thus took on special significance for Spain.

This special relationship has translated into intense political and commercial links. Spain is Cuba's most important Western European trade partner, and Cuba has become Spain's most important partner in the Caribbean Basin.[20] Spanish contribution to Cuban development is the most significant among EC countries, Cuba being the largest single recipient of Spain's development assistance in the Caribbean Basin. Donations from Spain are estimated to be $2.5 million annually. In 1990, Cuba received 10 percent of the total development assistance targeted for the Caribbean Basin, compared with 0.4 percent received by Haiti and 0.7 percent received by the Dominican Republic.[21]

Spain's share of total Cuban trade is estimated at 3 percent; its participation in Cuban trade among capitalist countries is 12 percent. Hence, Spain is among the top ten most important trade partners for Cuba.[22] In contrast, Cuba's participation in Spanish trade is much lower. With a contribution of only 0.3 percent in the 1980s, Cuba ranked forty-fourth in total trade with Spain. In general, Cuban imports from Spain have been much more significant than Cuban exports to Spain.

From Cuba, Spain imports mainly tobacco, in addition to coffee and seafood; in turn, Spain is an important supplier of machinery, technology, and industrial goods and plants to Cuba. Apart from commercial exchanges, Spanish firms have recently become prevalent signatories of joint venture agreements in Cuba, as well as constituting the largest group of Western European investors in Cuban tourist projects.

Despite policy differences during the two main periods of modern Spanish politics—the Franco term and that of the current socialist president, Felipe González—Spain maintained consistent trade and diplomatic ties with Cuba. Paradoxically, bilateral economic links were cemented during the Franco regime, in spite of obvious ideological differences and in defiance of U.S. policy in Cuba. By the 1960s Spain had already become Cuba's largest Western European and noncommunist trading partner, accounting for 6.5 percent of total Cuban trade. During the Spanish transition period following the death of Franco in 1975, Castro's political relationship with Spain's first democratically elected president, Adolfo Suárez, also acquired special importance.

One reason for strong links between the unequal partners was their shared regional isolation: Cuba as a socialist country in Latin America, Spain as a dictatorial regime in Europe. Moreover, Spain was not disposed to joining the U.S. embargo policy and, in fact, with the November 1963 signing of a three-year bilateral trade agreement with Cuba, initiated the first formal break by a Western European country from the embargo. This action was strongly influenced by Spain's own experience with the embargo imposed by European states in protest of the dictatorial Franco regime.

Cuban relations with the socialist government of President González can be divided into three periods: 1982–1986; 1986–1990; and 1990–present. The period from 1982 to 1986 can generally be characterized by strong diplomatic contacts, support for Cuba's Third World policy orientation, and a limited solidarity with the Cuban Revolution. However, Spain's accession to the EC in 1986 marked a deterioration of Spanish-Cuban relations, and from the mid-1980s onward, Spanish policy toward Cuba was more in line with the EC position. Because of conflict over Cuba's human rights abuses, there has been a gradual erosion of political contact between Spain and Cuba in the 1990s.

When González came to power in 1982, the government's political agenda more closely resembled the Cuban position, although there were ideological differences on Latin American policy issues, as exemplified by each country's handling of the Central American crisis. In this particular case, Cuba and Spain became key external actors in the region's peace process: Cuba as an interlocutor for Nicaragua, and Spain as a more moderate mediator in the conflict. This division gave rise to a kind of Spanish-Cuban rivalry.

The 1986 entry of Spain into the EC marked the first rupture of relations with Cuba. Spanish policy toward Cuba was determined, more than ever, by its international commitments in line with the global trend toward democratic transition. Spain's entry into the EC also seriously affected trade relations with Cuba. Cuba's sugar exports to Spain and Portugal slumped to zero because of an increase of imports from the ACP countries and the EC.[23] In addition, Spanish EC membership meant the loss of preferential treatment given to Cuban tobacco exports to Spain. The further gradual dismantling of Spain's trade links with Cuba was also in part determined by Spain's high internal costs of European integration.

The Spanish involvement in the 1990 asylum crisis provoked the second serious setback of mutual relations. Fearing international destabilization from outside, the Cuban authorities overreacted by accusing the Spanish government of having manipulated the refugees. Luis Yañez Barnuevo, former Spanish secretary of state for international cooperation, commented on the conflict as follows: "Spain has been Cuba's umbilical cord with the EC and Cuba is cutting off links with its sole friend in Europe."[24] In protest of the accusations from the Cuban government against Foreign Minister Francisco Fernández Ordóñez of Spain, Spain suspended its aid program to Cuba, forecasted at $2.5 million. The cooperation program was not restored until November 1991.

More recent Spanish policy toward Cuba has been ambivalent. On the one hand, Spain has established an official dialogue with exiled Cuban human rights activists and regime opponents.[25] On the other hand, the

Spanish government has maintained a dialogue with Castro and has continued to be the European mediator for the liberation of political prisoners. In any case, the arising conflicts on human rights abuses did not exclude Cuba from the annual summits of Ibero-American states, first celebrated in summer 1991 in Mexico. Spain's 1993 full integration into the Single European Market will undoubtedly only further reinforce a relationship in decline, although it is one with a strong emotional impact.

Germany: The Burden of Cuban–East German Relations

While relations between Cuba and the Federal Republic of Germany have been almost nonexistent since the Cuban Revolution, the former German Democratic Republic (GDR) had been Cuba's second largest trade partner and political ally next to the Soviet Union. Moreover, the GDR had also been Cuba's main partner in technical and scientific cooperation; in fact, it was responsible for the technical and academic training of thirty thousand Cubans in East Germany. In addition, the East Germans, as well as the Soviets, granted Cuba special trade preferences and credits with low interest rates.

For a unified Germany, the special Cuban–East German relation, including the outstanding $500 million burden, became a much-debated issue in the German foreign-policy agenda. The key question was whether to maintain or dissolve the long-standing trade and cooperation agreements.

The Federal Republic chose the latter option, and one of the first decisions taken by Chancellor Helmut Kohl immediately after reunification, was to cancel the seven financial cooperation agreements established by the former GDR government. However, the German authorities have not yet restructured their economic cooperation policy with Cuba, and the political stance on Cuba is still an open question. It is expected that, from 1991 onward, cooperation will be based on credits in free convertible currency. Considering the state of human rights violations in Cuba under the current regime, there is little expectation that German policy toward Cuba will be reformulated.

The dramatic effects of German unification were severely felt by Cuba's economy, and on September 17, 1990, Cuba appealed to the EC to consider the economic repercussions of German unification on Cuba by granting it provisional trade preference measures. In response, the EP started a campaign in favor of a resolution on the impact of German unification on Cuba. However, to date Cuban demands remain unanswered;[26] the European Commission, in collaboration with German authorities, is still investigating the contracts Cuba had with the former GDR.

Cuba occupied a very small place in German foreign policy during the Cold War. Because of a lack of cultural and historical links with the region, West Germany's activities in the Caribbean Basin had generally been quite modest. So-called mormal relations with the Cuban government were hindered by ideological conflicts between the two Germanies and Cuba's close relationship with the GDR. In reaction to the establishment of formal diplomatic relations between the two socialist countries in 1963, West Germany broke off diplomatic ties with Cuba. Relations between Cuba and West Germany during the 1960s can be characterized as hostile and frozen.

Diplomatic ties between both countries were formally reestablished under the Social Democratic German government in 1975. Nevertheless, in the context of the bipolar system, the Federal Republic was one of the Western nations most strongly opposed to Cuba's intervention in Angola and, consequently, banned aid to Cuba in 1978. When Christian Democrats took power in October 1982, bilateral relations suffered a new setback, edging the German government closer to U.S. policy postures.

In accordance with the general trend of a gradual deterioration of European-Cuban relations, German criticism of the Cuban regime and the human rights situation on the island increased in the 1990s. One month following the summer 1990 asylum crisis, the German minister for economic cooperation, Jürgen Warnke, stated that democratization in Cuba was a precondition for aid.[27] Given this posture, it can be assumed that German contribution to Cuban development, as well as the reestablishment of political contacts with the island, will depend on the implementation of internal political changes.

While Cuba and the German Christian Democrats never held friendly relations, links with the German Social Democratic Party and its former leader, Willy Brandt, were rather strong. During Brandt's October 14, 1984, visit to Cuba as president of the Socialist International (SI), during which he discussed the Central American crisis with Fidel Castro, he established informal ties between the international party organization and Cuba.

Although German political foundations[28] have traditionally had a strong influence in Latin America, Cuba seems to be a special case. With the exception of the Friedrich Ebert Foundation (FES), German political foundations hold few official contacts in Cuba. More recently, the foundations closely related to the Christian Democratic Union, the Christian Social Union, and the Liberal Party have established relations with Cuban opposition parties—namely, the Cuban Democratic Platform in Madrid and the Cuban Christian Democrats in Miami. Their activities in Cuba are strongly dependent on political changes on the island. As long as democratic reforms fail, these German political foundations see the external support of democratic parties in exile as the only possibility to pressure for political change in Cuba. The social-democratic-oriented Friedrich Ebert Foundation has a different political standpoint. In its opinion, political dialogue with reform-willing political forces within the Cuban government, as well as cooperation and debates on social democratic policies, are more appropriate strategies for democratic reform in Cuba than strategies of political confrontation and trade embargoes.

Although the FES is not directly represented in Cuba, it has established a series of institutional and official contacts there. Particularly strong are the links with the Center for European Studies in Havana, institutionalized by the cooperation agreement of 1983. In collaboration with the Center for European Studies, the FES organizes seminars in Cuba and Germany on different issues in the framework of European–Latin American relations. High-ranking German politicians—such as Oscar Lafontaine, Hans Ulrich Klose, and Hans Matthöfer—participated in these seminars. Moreover, the FES is an important supplier of European literature to Cuba, substituting for the suspended deliveries from the former GDR.

Additionally, despite ideological differences, German enterprises have continued to operate in Cuba in the 1990s, and Germany became one of the most important Cuban markets within the European Community. For Cuba, the importation of German machinery, technical know-how, and credits have been of major importance. The end of subsidized economic ties with the East stimulated German activity in Cuban markets. The chemical giants Hoechst and Bayer, as well as Siemens, have opened offices in Cuba; they supply the Cuban market with medicine and chemical products. Moreover, Cuban promotion of foreign direct investment has sparked new cooperation projects—notably, Siemens's recent entry into the Cuban nuclear sector and joint ventures with enterprises like Hoechst and Degussa in the chemical sector.

Know-how and investments in the service sector, mainly tourism, are increasingly important. Among EC countries, German tourists form the largest group of visitors to Cuba. More recently, German enterprises have started to participate in different projects within the framework of the newly established Cuban joint venture diplomacy with market economy countries.

France: Independent Globalist Approach and the African Conflict

Cuba's third most important partner in Europe has traditionally been France, with the French-Cuban relationship being political rather than commercial. Both countries have also maintained strong cultural links, strengthened by the Agreement on Cultural Cooperation and the establishment of mutual intergovernmental commissions.

While economic cooperation with France was important at the beginning of the Cuban regime, bilateral trade relations became less significant in the 1980s. Even during the more intense trade exchange periods, in the mid-1980s, the French position in Cuban total trade never exceeded the average value of 1–1.5 percent.[29]

Within the framework of political cooperation, France was one of the few countries to establish substantial contact with the Cuban government. The maintenance of French diplomatic relations with Cuba was motivated by its historical and military presence in the Caribbean[30] and, above all, by the need to stress its independence from Washington. France refused to participate in the U.S. embargo and maintained diplomatic and economic ties with Cuba under the de Gaulle presidency in part as a demonstration of France's independent, multipolar political orientation. More than a profound political strategy, the French stance on Cuba reflects its traditional Latin American policy, often characterized as rich in symbolic gestures and political rhetoric.

Relations improved considerably under the socialist presidency of François Mitterrand from 1981 onward, when Mitterrand presented France, and in part the EC, as a third alternative to the U.S. and Soviet ideological influences. Relations were formally strengthened in August 1983 when Cuba was visited by Foreign Minister Claude Cheysson, a defender of an independent French policy in Central America and the Caribbean. Cheysson, EC commissioner for North-South relations from 1984 to 1988, became one of the few European politicians with sympathy for the Cuban regime.

After Foreign Minister Roland Dumas took office in December 1984, the French policy toward Cuba began to more closely resemble U.S. policy. The French Communists—one of the few remaining non-perestroika-influenced European Communist parties—are the only loyal French pro-Cuban group.

However, the somewhat strong Cuban-French political relationship was shadowed by Cuban involvement in two traditional French zones of influence: the French Caribbean and the former French colonies in Africa. The French government viewed the presence of Cuban troops in Africa as a threat to stability in the African region, as well as a threat to its own political and commercial interests in Africa (see Chapter 4). The region thus became a permanent stage of bilateral conflict and competition.

Cuba's withdrawal from Africa, especially after troops left Angola in 1989, contributed to the easing of mutual relations. However, France has now joined the group of European nations appealing for greater respect of human rights, as well as greater political freedom on the island.

EC-CUBAN RELATIONS IN THE 1990s:
PRECARIOUS STATUS QUO OR BIRTH OF A DIALOGUE?

Given Cuba's geographic position and sugar-based economic structure, EC economic cooperation with the Caribbean island has not been very notable. At a political level, during the initial period of the Revolution, Cuba offered the opportunity to emphasize the EC's own political strategies in Latin America, often opposed to the U.S. Latin American policy. In the 1990s, the focus of political relations has been grounded on human rights policy and internal changes in Cuba. From the EC perspective, without real Cuban efforts for democratic reforms, EC-Cuban relations will remain at a low, almost nonexistent, level. The same argument can be applied to bilateral European-Cuban relations.

The Cuban perception, however, is quite different than that of the EC. In the context of its international isolation, Cuba is looking for new political and economic partners, especially in the noncommunist world. Moreover, Cuba views its differences with the EC as stemming from the North-South conflict and the special problems of EC–Latin American relations, rather than from ideological differences.

The future nature of the triangular relationship among the United States, Cuba, and Europe depends mainly on the evolution of internal changes in Cuba. Most analysts agree that the Castro regime's survivability is highly dependent on external factors, the most important being the end of Castro's international isolation. An essential element for the survival of the regime is the maintenance of social living standards, impossible without external support.

In spite of Cuba's international isolation and social crisis, general expectations that Cuba will be the next example of an inverse of the domino theory seem improbable. Despite the serious economic situation in Cuba today,[31] the Castro regime has not yet demonstrated signs of imminent collapse. Yet Cuba's future is still an open question. Regardless of whether international pressure on the Cuban regime in combination with Cuban isolation will trigger a democratization effect, most analysts agree that market-oriented reforms are the only realistic option for the economic survival of the island.[32] At present, the Cuban government seems to have adopted a two-track course combining economic opening with political indoctrination, comparable with the Chinese development strategy.

Though the final outcome of the current Cuban crisis is still unpredictable, the future of the island can be viewed in the context of three options: (1) the end of Castro and a transition to democracy; (2) U.S. invasion; and (3) a kind of Spanish democratization model after the death of the caudillo. The first option is considered by most analysts as the most realistic.

The collapse of the Cuban regime could be provoked by three political events, all of them with different consequences for the relations between Europe and Cuba: (1) elections and the replacement of Fidel Castro, as in the case of the Sandinista regime in Nicaragua; (2) violent democratic transition; or (3) the death of Fidel Castro. In any event, it will be practically impossible for the EC-Cuban relationship to be more than a normal one.

The first scenario involving the end of Castro envisages a pacific democratic process from within. Political actors in this case are fundamental, though the military or the Cuban Communist Party are the only institutionalized forces of the Cuban regime. Since the execution of General Ochoa and other military officials in 1989, there are no signs of an opposition movement in the army, and reform-willing elements within the party are still controlled by Castro. An opposition democratic movement that could assume the role of a political vanguard, as in the case of the former East Germany, is not in the offing at the present time. Nevertheless, it can be expected that the current economic crisis in Cuba will encourage internal opposition forces.

The second scenario envisages a violent democratic transition of the type that occurred in Romania, with armed conflicts between regime supporters and opponents.[33] Internal opposition forces could be supported by exile groups in Miami. The fundamental problem with this scenario lies in the different approaches of the internal and exiled opposition forces. While the first group seems to suggest a peaceful and slow transition, the Miami group would vote for external support and a radical, even violent replacement of the current regime.

The third scenario leading to a democratic transition is a kind of Spanish democratization model. In this case, transition would be sparked by the death of Fidel Castro.

The second suggested option about the future of the island is a U.S. invasion of Cuba in order to overthrow the "dictatorial regime," following the Grenada and Panama examples. This option seems to be out of fashion in the new political context of the 1990s. A U.S. invasion would be too risky, and recent surveys indicate that U.S. public opinion favors improving bilateral relations with Cuba. A peaceful transition to democracy forced by economic crisis[34] seems to be the preferred option of U.S. policymakers.[35] Any invasion would provoke a harsh reaction from Europe.

A third option is the midterm maintenance of the current political situation, probably with some reform elements in the economic sphere. This would permit a partial reinsertion of the Cuban economy into international market relations. Given that the Cuban economy is dependent on the outside world, and considering the refusal of Fidel Castro to introduce political reform, the end of Castroism seems to be a question of time and opportunities. In the long term, Cuba cannot ignore regional and international trends. The recent positive economic trend in Latin America, combined with political freedom, makes complete reintegration into the Latin American community more attractive for the Cubans. On the other hand, elements like geographic isolation, the particular national revolutionary model based on Castro's caudillismo, and the original-leader syndrome[36] do not indicate an imminent regime transformation. Unlike the Eastern European countries where nationalism was a strong factor for destabilization, Cuban nationalism and the fear of becoming a new U.S. dependency are strong arguments for regime legitimation. The lack of attractive alternative political models is another factor contributing to the longevity of the Cuban government. There is little likelihood that European-Cuban relations will improve unless there is some sort of regime change in Cuba. European-Cuban relations will probably continue to be an expression of a "policy without illusions."[37]

NOTES

Special thanks are owed to Susanne Gartius for her research and María-Eugenia Marín for her editing assistance.

1. One of the more recent overviews of Cuba's international relations is published by Georges Fauriol and Eva Looser, eds., *Cuba, the International Dimension* (New Brunswick and London: Transaction Publishers, 1990).

2. European Parliament, Resolution 158.954, on the execution and human rights violations in Cuba, adopted on February 13, 1992.

3. For a discussion on European interests in Central America and support for the Contadora initiative see also Wolf Grabendorff, "Mexico and the European Community: Toward a New Relationship?" in Riordan Roett, ed., *Mexico's External Relations in the 1990s* (Boulder and London: Lynne Rienner, 1991), pp. 95–123.

4. The EP's Socialist Group last visited Cuba April 22–23, 1989.

5. On November 12, 1991 a group of European Parliamentarians requested the reestablishment of diplomatic links between the EC and Cuba.

6. For a discussion of European interests in the Caribbean Basin see Wolf Grabendorff, "The Role of Western Europe in the Caribbean Basin," in Alan Adelman and Reid Reading, eds., *Confrontation in the Caribbean Basin*, International Perspectives on Security, Sovereignty and Survival (Pittsburgh: University of Pittsburgh, 1984), pp. 275–292.

7. Scott MacDonald, "Cuba's Relations with Europe and Canada: Accommodation and Challenges," in Fauriol and Looser, *Cuba, the International Dimension*, pp. 233–254.

8. See "Cuba: The Challenge of Change," Institute of European–Latin American Relations (IRELA), dossier no. 27, Madrid, October 1990, p. 18.

9. One of the most internationally criticized actions against regime opponents has been the detention of the poet and president of the Criterio Alternativo group, María Elena Cruz Varela, on November 26, 1991.

10. *Agence Europe*, No. 5652, Bruxelles, 23.01.1992, p. 3.

11. See European Parliament, Resolution 149.145, on relations with countries of Central America, including Cuba, adopted on February 22, 1991.

12. Jorge I. Domínguez, *To Make a World Safe for Revolution: Cuba's Foreign Policy* (Cambridge: Harvard University Press, 1989), p. 186.

13. See Michael Erisman and John M. Kirk, "Cuba and the Struggle for Political Space in the 1990s," in Michael Erisman and John M. Kirk, eds., *Cuban Foreign Policy Confronts a New International Order* (Boulder: Lynne Rienner, 1991), pp. 1–21. In the 1980s, the EC and its member states absorbed more than half of Cuban commerce in freely convertible currency.

14. See Sistema Económico Latinoamericano (SELA), "Cuba y la Europa Comunitaria ante el mundo cambiante de los noventa," working document, no. 12 (unpublished), Caracas, March 1992, p. 14.

15. See Olga Álvarez, "Relaciones Cuba–Europa Occidental," *Revista de Estudios Europeos*, no. 11 (July–September 1989).

16. Gareth Jenkins, ed., *Cuba Business*, no. 6 (December 1991), p. 2.

17. INTUR, Estadísticas, in *Comité Estatal de Estadísticas*, Anuario Estadístico (1973–1989), Havana.

18. See the comment on p. 10 in Economic Intelligence Unit, *Country Report Cuba, Dominican Republic, Haiti, Puerto Rico* (London, 1992).

19. One of the few most recent analyses of European-Cuban relations is the article by Gareth Jenkins "Western Europe and Cuba's Development in the 1980s and Beyond," in Erisman and Kirk, *Cuban Foreign Policy*, pp. 183–223.

20. For a more detailed analysis of Spanish interests in the Caribbean Basin, see Jean Gurgel, "Spanish Foreign Policy in the Caribbean," *European Review of Latin American and Caribbean Studies*, no. 50 (June 1991), pp. 135–155.

21. See "El vínculo Iberoamérica, Comunidad Europea: planes, políticas y estrategias de desarrollo," Agencia Española de Cooperación International and Ministerio de Economía y Hacienda, Madrid, March 1992, p. 85.

22. See Frank Vera Cañete, "Relaciones Cuba-España en los 80. Consideraciones y perspectivas," *Revista de Estudios Europeos*, no. 12 (October–December 1989), pp. 118–134.

23. The negative effects of Spain and Portugal's entry into the European Community for Cuba are analyzed by Lázaro Peña, "El comercio bilateral Cuba-España y sus afectaciones luego del ingreso de España a la Comunidad Económica Europea," *Temas de la Economía Mundial*, no. 24 (1988), pp. 7–55.

24. See *ABC*, Madrid, July 7, 1990.

25. The first meeting between members of the Cuban Democratic Platform and Assistant Secretary of State Inocencio Arias took place in April 1991.

26. See "Cuba y la Europa Comunitaria ante el mundo," SELA, p. 23.

27. "Cuba: The Challenge of Change," IRELA, p. 18.

28. Four political foundations have been created in Germany: The Friedrich-Ebert Foundation (FES), close to the German Social Democratic Party; the Friedrich-Naumann Foundation (FNS) related to the German Liberal Party; the Konrad-Adenauer Stiftung (KAS), related to the Christian Democratic Union; and the conservative Hans-Seidel Stiftung, close to the Christian Social Union.

29. One of the few articles on French-Cuban relations was written by Eduardo Perera, "Cuba en la política exterior de Francia," *Revista de Estudios Europeos*, no. 12 (December 1989), pp. 91–118.

30. With seven thousand soldiers in its former colonies (Martinique, Guadeloupe, French Guiana), France has one of the largest military presences in the Caribbean.

31. In his most recent article on Cuba, Howard Wiarda mentioned seven different regime crises. See Howard Wiarda, "Is Cuba Next? Crisis of the Castro Regime," *Problems of Communism*, no. 1/2 (January–April 1991), pp. 84–93.

32. Carmelo Mesa-Lago, "Is There Life After USSR?" *Hemisfile* 3, no. 1 (January 1992), pp. 10–13.

33. For an evaluation of the current internal situation in Cuba, see Saul Landau, "Resucitar el debate sobre Cuba," *Papeles para la Paz*, No. 44 (1992), pp. 75–85.

34. In April 1992, the U.S. government tightened its long-standing embargo on Cuba, and on October 3, 1992, Congress passed the Torricelli Bill, which penalizes U.S. subsidiary enterprises selling to Cuba.

35. See the recent analysis by Susan Kaufman Purcell, "Collapsing Cuba," *Foreign Affairs* 71, no. 1 (1992), pp. 130–146.

36. Irving Louis Horowitz, "Cuba's Revolutionary Holdout: Insular Revolution," *Hemisphere* 2, no. 3 (Summer 1990), pp. 22–24.

37. See Wolf Grabendorff, "European Community Relations with Latin America: Policy Without Illusions," *Journal of Interamerican Studies and World Affairs* 19, no. 4 (Winter 1987/1988), pp. 69–87.

7

Trade Relations
Between Britain and Cuba

GARETH JENKINS

In view of the "special relationship" that has existed between Britain and the United States in the half-century since the end of the World War II, one might have expected the British government to have complied with the U.S. blockade of Cuba, or at least to have discouraged the active involvement of British companies in trade with Cuba. Although Britain has been of diminishing relative importance to the United States in recent years, throughout the postwar period Britain was that country's most reliable political ally in Europe.

There is no doubt that the U.S. government did try on a number of occasions to exert direct pressure on Britain to comply with its policy toward Cuba and continues to do so. But by and large Britain went its own way, unimpressed by U.S. arguments. This was not the result of any ideological affinity with Cuba but rather because it did not see Cuba as a threat to its interests and could see no particular reason to forego a trading relationship that, while fairly marginal, was of considerable importance to some individual companies. This approach was shared by the Conservative and Labour parties alike.

There may also have been an element of satisfaction in the British attitude of taking an independent line when on so many of the big issues Britain had no choice but to do the bidding of the United States. This was no doubt combined with the pragmatic view that drawing a line against U.S. interference on Cuba could only strengthen British trade policy in general.

Resentment at the trade dominance of the United States has never been as strong in British political circles as it has in, for instance, France or Italy. But it always has the potential to emerge as an important issue, as it did, for example, when Michael Haseltine resigned from Margaret Thatcher's Conservative government over the sale of Westland Helicopters to a U.S. company.

In February 1987, the British Conservative government faced opposition from within its own ranks—including, reportedly, Attorney General

Michael Havers—for agreeing to allow U.S. trade inspectors to examine the books of British manufacturing companies importing U.S. parts. The decision was taken to clear the way for the contract with Boeing to buy the AWACS early-warning radar plane, and it was the first time that U.S. trade law was permitted to be applied directly to British firms. The legal basis for the decision was the 1985 U.S. Export Administration Act, which has subsequently been used in a number of cases to prevent non-U.S. firms exporting products containing U.S. components to Cuba.[1]

More recently, attempts by Sen. Connie Mack and Congressman Robert Torricelli to introduce legislation in the U.S. Congress to tighten the blockade of Cuba have drawn strong opposition from the British government, as they have from the European Community and the Canadian government, among others. When Sam Gibbons, U.S. House of Representatives trade subcommittee chair, visited London in September 1991 to discuss the issue, Trade Secretary Peter Lilley told him that he would use Britain's Protection of Trading Interests Act to block the effects of the proposed Mack Amendment. Lilley told a press conference that "it is for the British government, not the U.S. Congress, to determine the UK's policy on trade with Cuba. We will not accept any attempt to superimpose U.S. law on UK companies."[2]

Whereas some other European countries with similar levels of trade with Cuba—such as West Germany—never established government-level cooperation agreements, Britain has had such an agreement with Cuba since 1975. Vice President Carlos Rafael Rodríguez of Cuba visited London in that year to sign the Anglo-Cuban Economic and Industrial Cooperation Agreement, which provided for a joint commission that would meet annually. (In fact, it has met approximately once every two years.) A few months later, then–trade secretary Peter Shore visited Havana, the first member of a British cabinet to do so since 1959.[3]

Apart from having government-level relations with Britain, Cuba has from time to time been visited by senior British political figures. Edward Heath, Conservative prime minister from 1970 to 1974 and a prominent member of the Brandt Commission on North-South relations in the 1970s, paid his third visit to Cuba within a decade in March 1988, during which he met with Foreign Minister Isidoro Malmierca and Vice President Rodríguez. This was shortly after the defeat of a U.S. motion condemning the Cuban government at the UN Human Rights Commission. Mr. Heath made clear his support for that outcome in an interview published in the Cuban national newspaper, *Granma*.[4]

The essential stability of British-Cuban relations was apparent following an ill-explained incident in London in 1988, as a result of which two Cuban diplomats were expelled. On the afternoon of September 12 Carlos Medina Pérez, commercial attaché to the Cuban Embassy, was surprised outside his London apartment by the Cuban defector Florentino Azpillaga and four other people, widely reported by the British press to have been a female friend of Azpillaga and three members of the British and U.S. security services, MI5 and the CIA. Pérez drew a gun and shot Azpillaga in the stomach; the others bundled him into a car and drove off. Pérez was expelled within twenty-four hours for carrying and using a gun, and Ambassador Oscar Fernández Mell was expelled for refusing to apologize to British Foreign Office under secretary Timothy Eggar.

Whatever the motive for this apparent kidnap attempt, the subsequent response of the British and Cuban governments was instructive. In an article written for *Cuba Business*, George Foulkes, Labour Party spokesman on Latin America, criticized the expulsion of Mell, who, he said, has "been in the forefront of developing good relations between our two countries . . . since he led the first Cuban delegation to the Inter Parliamentary Union in London in 1984." Foulkes expressed his hope that Cuba would not respond in kind so that full relations could be restored quickly.[5] This is in fact what happened, and a year later a new Cuban ambassador was appointed to London.

Britain played a critical role in thwarting U.S. policy in the early days of the blockade against Cuba. In the opinion of George Lambie, "It was the success of the British company, Leyland Motors in winning a series of large contracts which, perhaps more than any other single case, opened the door to normal trade between Western Europe and the Castro government."[6] Leyland's first contract was in 1964 and was worth $12 million. It was backed by British government export credit guarantees, which prompted France and Japan, whose own bus companies had failed in their bids, to make export credits available for trade with Cuba. The Johnson administration was furious.[7]

Leyland set up a permanent office in Havana, which it kept open for ten years. A number of further contracts followed, which helped pave the way for other British companies to win contracts. The largest was a £10 million contract won by Simon Carves to build a fertilizer plant near Cienfuegos, which was again backed by British government credit. This was the largest single credit received by Cuba up to that date.[8]

Although Leyland did not obtain any contracts in Cuba after 1973, British trade with the island was buoyant throughout the 1970s. During that decade, exports to Cuba averaged $60 million a year, while imports averaged $24 million. Cuba became the seventh most important market for British goods in Latin America and the Caribbean. Britain's main exports were fertilizers, pesticides and herbicides, chemicals, milk products, motor vehicle tires, and spare parts.[9]

One of the most important British companies to trade with Cuba in this period was ICI, which began selling its products to the sugar, general agricultural, and public health sectors in 1966 and continues to do so today. It has been probably the most important Western supplier to the sugar industry. However, when the economy went into recession in the mid-1980s, Cuba began to fall behind with payments both to government lenders and commercial companies. By 1990 its debt to ICI agrochemicals had reached "several million pounds," according to John Clement, the company's commercial manager responsible for Latin America.[10]

Because this business was so important to Cuba, ICI was able to negotiate a rollover of the entire outstanding debt in October 1990, with guarantees on payment of all new debt tied to sugar futures contracts. As a result, ICI's agrochemical sales to Cuba—which grew steadily throughout the recession from 1987 to 1990—were expected to reach $10–12 million in 1991.[11]

The main growth area for ICI was herbicides, following four years of field trials in close cooperation with the Field Production and Technical Development departments of the Cuban Sugar Ministry (MINAZ). The herbicide program, known as the "trash blanket program," covered more than 50 percent of Cuban cane in 1991. It generated an increase in herbicide exports for ICI from $3.2 million in 1988 to $5.2 million in 1990. The company has been working to develop a similar program of technical advice and investment to support the Cuban Ministry of Agriculture's Food Program.[12]

Another British company that managed to continue trading with Cuba despite a large outstanding debt was the chemical company Technical and Manufacturing Services (TAMS). It had been supplying a range of industrial organic chemicals to the medical trade enterprise MediCuba and the chemicals trade enterprise Quimimport since the early 1980s. By 1988, however, its cash flow system could no longer cover the mounting commercial debt owed to it by Cuba, and trade dwindled to virtually nothing. In October 1991, though, TAMS was able to roll over the outstanding debt of $486,000 by agreeing to establish a joint venture based on a debt-for-equity swap, the first such agreement between a British company and a Cuban enterprise. The agreement is for the joint production, with Quimimport, of a chemical cleanser, with the Cuban partner providing the manufacturing capacity, work force, and some nationally produced inputs and TAMS providing new finance, advanced technology, and export marketing.[13]

The Pig Improvement Company, a subsidiary of the British firm Dalgety, became interested in Cuba in 1988 when it learned that Cuba planned to double pig meat availability by the year 2000. It was able to initiate a successful business despite Cuba's payment problems by negotiation of a pigs-for-sugar countertrade deal. The company supplies "super" pigs as part of a genetic improvement plan—at a value of $335,000 in 1989 and $448,000 in 1990—and sells the sugar it receives in return on the sugar-trading house Gill and Duffus.[14]

During 1991 Cuba's economic crisis became acute following the political and economic collapse of the Soviet Union and Cuba's other main trading partners in Eastern Europe. The sharp reduction in the price that Russia was prepared to pay for Cuban sugar, combined with the general problems of economic dislocation, led to a reduction in Cuba's import capability by nearly one-half. As a result, production in many Cuban facilities was either reduced or completely stopped. Machinery could not function for lack of spare parts and raw material inputs, and many trade contracts had to be canceled.

One British company to suffer acutely from this crisis was Holland Enterprises, which had for ten years been importing children's coloring books printed by Ediciones Cubanas from final film supplied by the British partner. This business had been expanding strongly, from $.72 million in 1988 to $1.8 million in 1990, the latter figure representing 3.2 percent of all British imports from Cuba in that year. But Ediciones Cubanas announced that it would not be able to accept any new contracts from the company for 1991/92, nor would it be able to fulfill about $2.5 million of outstanding contracts because of shortage of paper, raw materials, fuel, and spare parts.[15]

Schemes put forward by Holland Enterprises to salvage the business by retaining a percentage of each letter of credit to be used for purchases of materials and parts on the open market as needed were rejected. The main problem, according to Ediciones Cubanas's sales manager, is that while 70 percent of the raw material used in Cuba's paper factories is sugarcane bagasse, the other 30 percent has been very inexpensive wood pulp from Eastern Europe. Purchasing pulp on the open market has increased costs substantially; thus, without new technology and a reorganization of production, Ediciones Cubanas can no longer supply at the prices Holland Enterprises requires.

Nor is Holland Enterprises in a financial position to invest in a joint venture to modernize the plant that produces its books, as was suggested at one point. A Finnish company has taken over management of a 5,000-tons-per-year paper plant in Palma Soriano, Oriente Province, and is investing in new technology, but this will not help Holland Enterprises because all production will go to Finland.[16]

Trade between Britain and Cuba has nevertheless held up fairly well. Total UK imports from Cuba between 1988 and 1990 amounted to $51.3 million, $61.9 million, and $54.5 million in the three years respectively. This compares with UK imports of about $14.4 million per year in the mid-1980s, before the recession developed.

The corresponding figures for total UK exports to Cuba were $55.8 million, $95.8 million, and $67.5 million. But if exceptional sales of cereals from London of $46.1 million in 1989 and $19.3 million in 1990 are excluded, exports in those two years held up at about $48.6 million, only a little below the 1988 figure. These figures represent a sharp decline in UK export levels of nearly $108 million in the mid-1980s.[17]

The main UK import from Cuba in 1988–1990 was petroleum oils, at over $39.6 million each year. Cigars came second, with steady imports of $6.3 million. Other imports were children's coloring books, molasses, honey, raw tobacco, paper and board, coffee, and metals. Apart from cereals, the main UK export to Cuba over the same three-year period was agricultural and other chemicals, which averaged $14.4 million per year. Scientific instruments and medical equipment averaged $4.68 million per year; vaccines and medicines, $3.06 million; and paints and varnishes, $2.88 million. Machinery and transport equipment averaged $13.14 million per year and metal and mineral products amounted to $5.94 million annually.

Cuba's sudden need to reorient trade away from Eastern Europe has increased the importance of Cuban-owned and joint venture trading companies in Western countries. A number of these have been operating since the 1960s and 1970s, such as the Dutch metal trading joint venture Curef; the chemicals company Quiminter, in Vienna; Yamaru in the Far East; Coprova in Paris; and in London, ETCO, which trades a wide range of Cuban commodities in Europe and elsewhere.

The Cuban tobacco enterprise Cubatabaco has always geared its cigar exports to hard currency markets on account of the high prices its products fetch and their ready acceptability. Traditionally, its export trade had been in the hands of long-established distributors. However, in 1988, even before the general reorientation of Cuban trade, Cubatabaco decided to move into distribution to benefit from the large profits to be made there. Accordingly, it forced the main distributors to negotiate joint venture agreements.

In London, for instance, Cubatabaco first took over Knight Brothers, which had been importing Havana cigars since 1860, and soon after merged with the other main importer, Hunters and Frankau. In most cases the distributors felt they had to comply with Cubatabaco's wishes. In one notable case, however, the Swiss company Davidoff decided to resist. As a result, it found itself without Havana cigars to sell and has had to look instead to the Dominican Republic for supplies. Davidoff claimed it had broken with Cuba because the quality of the cigars had declined, but the real reason for the break was that it had refused to play ball with its monopoly supplier.

In the spring of 1992, Cubanacán S.A., the Cuban tourism development and general trading corporation, set up an office just outside London to promote tourism from Britain and to market Cuban products. This move was prompted by the launch of the first direct flight between Britain and Cuba in April 1992, a biweekly charter run by Cubana de Aviación, from London's Stansted Airport. Thomson Travel was the main tour operator behind establishing this flight, together with several small tour operators.

The trade figures discussed above refer mainly to goods. In addition, there is a certain amount of business activity in services such as shipping, banking, and insurance. The autonomous Cuban insurance company Esicuba S.A., for instance, reinsures its policies in the London market through Lloyds. Anglo-Caribbean Shipping, a London-registered company, acts as shipping agent for Cuba in Western Europe. The Cuban national bank has one of its most important foreign branches in London, the Havana International Bank. Moreover, since 1991 Cuban sugar has been traded on the London Futures and Options Exchange (FOX).

In the fall of 1988 the Cuban shipping company Mambisa was involved in discussions that might have led to the largest single contract ever between the two countries. This was a potential order worth $100 million from NESL, a near-bankrupt subsidiary of British shipbuilders. Mambisa's interest even extended to the possibility of joining a consortium to bid for private ownership of NESL.[18] However, NESL went out of business.

Cuban-British trade was achieved in the absence of British government export credit guarantees and often required considerable ingenuity to develop. It did, however, benefit from active encouragement from the Foreign Office, the Department of Trade and Industry, and quasi-governmental entities. Cuba was not treated as a special case: larger hard currency markets in Latin America were naturally given higher priority by British companies. Despite a tightening of the U.S. blockade, it was business as usual for British companies.

Before leaving to take up his new appointment as British ambassador to Cuba in March 1991, Leycester Coltman gave an interview in which he explained Britain's attitude toward trade with Cuba. He said he would like to see a situation in which the British Embassy would actively encourage British companies to develop trade with Cuba. For this to happen, Cuba would have to expand its hard currency earnings. Coltman said he was interested in learning of opportunities for Cuba to increase exports such as citrus, to expand tourism, and to form joint ventures in tourism and other sectors.[19]

Coltman emphasized the British government's opposition to any U.S. attempt to extraterritorially extend the U.S. embargo by preventing third-country subsidiaries of U.S. companies from trading with Cuba. He said that while Britain did not seek a special political relationship with Cuba, as perhaps Spain had in the past, it wished to maintain a political dialogue.

It would appear that the British government sees relations with Cuba as quite important at a time of potentially greater regional integration. In the 1991 interview, Coltman remarked on the importance of the December 1990 meeting in Rome of Rio Group and European Community foreign ministers, suggesting that Latin American integration could mirror the moves toward political union with the EC.

Certainly, British firms approaching the Foreign Office in London for advice on doing business with Cuba have been actively encouraged to pursue their interests. The most important potential contract recently pursued by a British company was for the modernization of Cuba's international telecommunications. (The contract, a $41 million joint venture, was in fact won by the Italian state communications company Italcable in December 1991.) The British company, Cable and Wireless, had spent more than a year preparing a bid for this project, despite worries about U.S. pressures both through official channels and from AT&T, a close business partner in the Caribbean. It was only after careful consideration at the highest levels in the company that a decision had been taken to pursue the contract. This is significant because Cable and Wireless's chairman, Lord Young, was at one time trade and industry secretary under Thatcher and strongly associated with her free-trade and pro-U.S. wing of the Conservative Party. In any event, it is surprising that they did not win the contract, as they were widely recognized as the most qualified company in the running. Perhaps, after all, worries about U.S. pressure made them hold back from bidding as strongly as they might have.

Another major British company with substantial interests in the United States certainly did hold back from getting involved in Cuba. British Petroleum (BP) became interested in prospecting for oil off the Cuban coast in the late 1980s. In August 1991, it sent a team of a dozen senior geologists to Cuba. It was strongly rumored that BP would receive prime prospecting rights north of Ciego de Àvila Province, which had previously been allocated to the Brazilian state company Petrobras. Subsequently, however, BP executives responded to press inquiries by denying its interest in Cuba.

Throughout the 1980s and early 1990s British trade missions sponsored by the Department of Trade and Industry visited Cuba. The Association of British Health Care Industries, for instance, organizes delegations to the biennial Health for All trade fair. Twenty-nine British companies participated in 1987, twenty-two in 1989, and twelve in 1991. The companies represented included major players such as Wellcome, Amersham International, Fisons, Boots, and Philips. Others, such as Beecham Research (now part of the U.S. company Smith Kline Beecham) and Glaxo, conduct significant trade with Cuba without participating in trade fairs. The decline in numbers attending Health for All since 1987 reflects payment problems even in this high-priority sector.

In recent years, missions have also been organized by the quasi-governmental Caribbean Trade Advisory Group (CARITAG) and by regional chambers of commerce and industry—London, Manchester, Birmingham, and Nottingham. To date the most recent mission has been pursued by the London Chamber, in October 1991. Apart from prompting normal company-to-company discussions, mission leader Merilyn Potter emphasized the Chamber's interest in helping to promote Cuban exports to Britain to generate the basis for expanding trade and in providing training and marketing.[20]

David Jessop, director of the London-based West India Committee, put forward proposals for larger companies to take equity stakes in joint ventures in exchange for forgiving outstanding debts. He subsequently expanded this approach in a report prepared for CARITAG that pointed to the "unusual opportunities for companies wishing to sell into the new autonomous state sector, a sector not burdened by a lack of convertible currency or by the restraints imposed by the Banco Nacional de Cuba or other state mechanisms. It also offers companies the opportunity to get in at the ground floor in establishing joint ventures or other previously impossible commercial relationships."[21]

CARITAG subsequently organized a delegation of London investment bankers to visit Cuba in April 1992 to explore the scope of developing debt-for-equity swaps and other financial mechanisms. This followed a Foreign Office–sponsored visit to London in 1991 by Abraham Maciques, director general of Cubanacán. During this visit, Maciques held discussions with banks such as Morgan Grenfell, Midland Montague, and S. G. Warburg; the hotel groups Hilton and Inter-Continental; and airline companies Virgin Atlantic, Booker Tate Engineering, Lonhro, and British Aerospace.

The future of British trade relations with Cuba is closely linked with Cuba's ability to surmount its economic problems and reorient its trade toward Western economies. While some slow improvement may be possible, Cuba's long-term economic future depends critically on when it reestablishes relations with the United States, and on what conditions. This, then, will to a great extent also determine the course of British relations with Cuba.

NOTES

1. *Cuba Business* pilot issue (April 1987), p. 4.

2. *Financial Times*, September 11, 1991.

3. George Lambie, "Trade Relations in the '70s," *Cuba Business* 3, no. 5, p. 6, 1989.

4. Heath noted the important role other Latin American governments had played in the defeat of the motion: "The outcome is historic because it shows the will of Cuba and other Latin American countries to work together, not just on this issue but also on others in the international sphere. . . . The United States has seen that its anti-Cuba strategy is not making gains and they must therefore consider improving their relations with this Caribbean country. Perhaps a new administration will do that."

5. *Cuba Business* 2, no. 3 (June 1988), p. 5.

6. George Lambie, "British Contracts in the '60s," *Cuba Business* 4, no. 1 (February 1990), p. 3.

7. *Cuba Business* 4, no. 1 (February 1990), p. 5.
8. Ibid.
9. Lambie, "Trade Relations in the '70s," p. 6.
10. *Cuba Business* 5, no. 1 (February 1991), p. 5.
11. *Cuba Business* 5, no. 3 (June 1991), p. 5.
12. *Cuba Business* 5, no. 1 (February 1991), p. 5.
13. *Cuba Business* 5, no. 6 (December 1991), p. 5.
14. *Cuba Business* 5, no. 5 (June 1991), p. 5
15. *Cuba Business* 5, no. 4 (August 1991), p. 5.
16. *Cuba Business* 6, no. 2 (June 1992), p. 5.
17. *Cuba Business* 5, no. 1 (February 1991), pp. 6–7.
18. *Cuba Business* 2, no. 4 (August 1988), p. 3.
19. *Cuba Business* 5, no. 1 (February 1991), pp. 5–6.
20. *Cuba Business* 5, no. 6 (December 1991), p. 5.
21. *Cuba: New Opportunities for British Business*, Caribbean Trade Advisory Group (London, 1992).

8

Cuba and the Soviet Union, Cuba and Russia

WAYNE S. SMITH

Cuba's alliance with the Soviet Union often placed the island at center stage in the Cold War. The two superpowers never came so close to nuclear war as during the 1962 Cuban missile crisis. The Soviet Union and Cuba and their clients clashed head-on with the United States and its allies in Angola and again in the Horn of Africa during the 1970s. It was the Carter administration's incredibly inept handling of the question of the Soviet brigade in Cuba in 1979 that put a new SALT treaty on the shelf. Cuban involvement in the Central American imbroglio, albeit greatly exaggerated by the United States, was one of the East-West flashpoints during the Reagan years. And for a time in the late 1980s, at the dawn of the post–Cold War era, continued Soviet assistance to Cuba almost derailed a promising new relationship between the two superpowers.

As an ally of the Soviet Union, Cuba often seemed to play a role on the world stage out of all proportion to its size. How it did so is rather a mystery, relying upon the charisma of its leader and on Soviet assistance for its resource base. But as the Soviet Union has disintegrated, with it has gone the Soviet-Cuban alliance and Cuba's capacity to project its influence internationally. Cuba is in the process of adjusting to that new reality and working out a new relationship with Russia and the other republics of the former Soviet Union. This essay will review how the Soviet-Cuban alliance began and how it evolved over the years; it will also discuss how well (or poorly) Cuba is adjusting to a postalliance situation, what the future of Cuba's relationship with Russia and the other republics may be, and what Soviet-Cuban relations mean for the United States.

EVOLUTION OF THE SOVIET-CUBAN ALLIANCE UNTIL GORBACHEV

It is important to remember that Fidel Castro was not a Marxist-Leninist when he first came to power. After he had made his decision to enter into

127

a close relationship with the Soviet Union and convert Cuba to a Marxist-Leninist state, it served his purpose to suggest that he had all along been a convinced Marxist and that the decision was part of a continuum rather than the sharp divergence it in fact was. His interest in rewriting history is clear, but the historical record cannot be undone. Prior to 1961, Castro himself not only denied that he was a communist but scathingly denounced the Soviet Union as a class dictatorship. "We are against all kinds of dictatorships," he said in 1959, "whether of a man, of a country, or a class, or an oligarchy, or of the military. That is why we're against Communism."[1]

Had Castro simply been biding his time before revealing his true allegiances, it seems unlikely that he would have attacked the very forces to which he owed that allegiance. The U.S. intelligence community took that and a good deal of other evidence into account in concluding that as of 1959, Castro was not a communist. In testimony before a Senate subcommittee in November 1959, CIA deputy director C. P. Cabell stated that ". . . the Cuban Communists do not consider him a Communist party member or even a pro-Communist."[2]

Confirmation of Cabell's assessment comes from no less a source than Sergo Mikoyan, who accompanied his father, Anastas, on the latter's first visit to Cuba in February 1960, the visit that was in effect the first step toward the formation of a Moscow-Havana alliance. According to Mikoyan, the Soviets knew very little about Castro. What they'd learned of him prior to 1959 had been through the Cuban Communist Party, which had been highly suspicious of him. By 1960, Moscow had come to see certain advantages in encouraging him but did not think that he was or ever would be a Marxist-Leninist. That assessment was confirmed during Anastas Mikoyan's visit, according to his son—that is, that Castro was the leader of a national liberation movement whose views coincided in part with Moscow's and whose principal adversary was the United States; hence it might serve Moscow's purposes to assist him. But a communist he was not. "No one who knew the first thing about Marxist-Leninist doctrine could have listened to Castro's views and positions in February of 1960 and come away with the conclusion that he qualified as an adherent," Mikoyan has noted.[3]

Why then did Castro turn to the Soviet Union? Almost certainly for protection against the United States so that he might pursue his international objectives. In his own words, Castro said he intended to do nothing less than turn the Andes into the Sierra Maestra of Latin America and to free Latin America of U.S. economic domination. He did not expect Washington to sit idly by and watch that happen; rather, he expected that it would lead to a confrontation. Initially, however, he anticipated that the Cuban Revolution would almost immediately spark revolutions in many other Latin American countries. The United States would be less likely to

attack Cuba if the latter were supported by other revolutionary governments throughout the hemisphere. But it soon became apparent that the
other revolutions would not take place soon enough, if indeed at all. Cuba
would stand alone. By early 1960, it was clear that the United States was
beginning to think of ousting Castro as it had ousted Jacobo Arbenz in
Guatemala in 1954. Castro thus began shifting toward the Soviets and by
April 16, 1961, announced that the Cuban Revolution was indeed a socialist one. It is no coincidence that he made that declaration on the day before
the Bay of Pigs invasion, which he already knew was on the way. It was a
transparent effort on his part to say to the Soviets, "This is a communist
revolution and you must therefore come to its assistance."[4]

The Soviets did not rise immediately to the bait. It was obvious that
they would not have come to Cuba's defense even if the United States had
landed marine divisions rather than the brigade of exiles. And given that
recognition of Cuba as a Marxist-Leninist state implied increased costs
and risks for Moscow, the latter had to weigh those factors carefully before making a decision. Nonetheless, by mid-1962, Moscow had accepted
Cuba's Marxist-Leninist credentials and was planning the emplacement of
nuclear missiles on the island. Castro, meanwhile, had embarked upon a
program of transforming the island into a Marxist-Leninist state. The
Soviet-Cuban alliance had become a reality.

Given the genesis of the alliance, and given that Castro was not a
Marxist-Leninist to begin with, it is indeed ironic that he is now left, as of
1993, as one of the few remaining Marxist-Leninist leaders in the world.
Also, it was ironic that his principal reason for throwing in with Moscow
(i.e., so that he could continue his efforts to extend revolution to the rest
of Latin America) immediately led to sharp differences with his new pro-
tectors. Castro pushed for guerrilla warfare throughout the hemisphere,
and he advocated instant confrontation with the imperialists. Moscow favored more cautious, popular-front tactics. During most of the 1960s,
Cuba and the Soviet Union were at odds, often bitterly so. Ernesto ("Che")
Guevara accused the Soviets of being "Marxist revisionists"[5] and in their
dealings with developing countries little more than "accomplices of imperialist exploitation."[6] Castro also heaped scorn on Soviet caution. "For us,"
he said, "liberation is not a matter of demagogy, but something we have
always truly believed in."[7]

By the end of the decade, however, Castro's revolutionary tactics had
produced not a single victory. Guerrilla movements throughout the hemisphere had either been defeated outright or were on the run. Guevara's efforts to open a guerrilla front in Bolivia had ended with his capture and
execution in 1967. Thus, with his own tactics in shambles and under constant pressure from Moscow, Castro began to shift away from support of
armed revolution and toward the popular-front tactics favored by Moscow.
He not only dropped his hostile rhetoric toward the Soviets but actually

began to press the idea that other Third World countries ought to follow the Soviet model, that indeed there was a natural alliance between the socialist countries and the developing countries. If the decade of the 1960s had been one of conflict between Havana and Moscow, the decade of the 1970s was one of great harmony. The two saw eye-to-eye on tactics and objectives. They cooperated effectively in Angola in 1975 and again in the Horn of Africa in 1978, and they worked hand-in-glove in such forums as the United Nations and the Nonaligned Movement (NAM). Cuba, moreover, increasingly accepted Soviet advice as how to best organize and direct the Cuban economy.

Two events converged in 1979 to bring an end to this most harmonious ten-year period. First, Castro became the chairman of the Nonaligned Movement and, in the process of discussing positions with the other leaders, realized there was too much opposition to his "natural alliance" thesis for it ever to be adopted. He realized that he was expending his own precious political capital for a lost cause. From that point forward, Castro never again suggested that other developing countries ought to follow the Soviet model or seek a special relationship with Moscow.

The second event was the Soviet invasion of Afghanistan, a founding member of NAM. Moscow embarrassed Havana with this action and did not even bother to inform Cuba of its intentions. Further, reaction among the other nonaligned countries put Cuba on the defensive. Rather than being in a position to use its four-year chairmanship of NAM to consolidate a preeminent leadership position, Cuba found that, if anything, its influence in NAM declined, precisely because of its relationship with the Soviet Union.

It is no wonder that from 1980 on, Castro not only dropped from his speeches before NAM any reference to the natural-alliance thesis, he also dropped references to the Soviet Union. During the 1970s, Castro had often attributed the gains of the developing countries to the increasing strength of the Soviet Union, which, he said, had so changed the correlation of forces in the world that the imperialists were no longer able to impose their wills on their former colonies. After 1980, however, the gains of the developing countries became, in Castro's eyes, strictly their own. No more did he thank Moscow for having made them possible.[8]

That Castro chose an increasingly low-key relationship with Moscow did not mean Soviet-Cuban relations had returned to the tensions and disagreements of the 1960s. If anything, economic relations actually increased, as did military ties, in response to the Reagan administration's threatening attitude toward Cuba after 1981. But it had become clear to Castro that painful losses as well as useful gains could result from his alliance with Moscow and that, in prudence, he should manage the relationship with greater discretion and reticence. After a decade of trying to bridge the contradiction between his role as Soviet partner and his leadership aspirations in NAM, Castro now concluded it was unbridgeable. He would continue to pursue both, but in discrete contexts.

If the period 1979–1985 saw growing Cuban awareness of the costs implicit in being tied to Moscow (at the same time the Cubans recognized the continued, perhaps even increased, importance of Soviet economic and military assistance), the Soviets also were beginning to see declining returns from their investment in Cuba. Except for a brief burst of enthusiasm immediately following the 1979 victory of the Sandinistas in Nicaragua (an enthusiasm dashed by the defeat of the guerrilla offensive in El Salvador in January 1981), Moscow had soured on the prospects for socialist victory in Latin America. Initially, Cuba had been valuable as a model, a showcase of socialist success that others might wish to emulate. By 1981, however, Moscow was more interested in costs and less in world revolution. It held out little hope that other countries, with the possible exception of Nicaragua, would go the way of Cuba; and as it made clear in the case of Nicaragua, it was unwilling to foot the bills even if they did.[9] Cuba's value was thus significantly reduced, if not dissipated altogether.

Cuba remained of some importance, however, as an advance base in Moscow's strategic competition with the United States. Because of the limitations imposed by the Kennedy-Khrushchev understandings of 1962, Moscow could not position offensive weapons in Cuba or even use the island to service its nuclear missile submarines on station off the U.S. coast. It could, however, deploy naval reconnaissance planes to Cuba, thus enabling them to remain longer over surveillance targets in the Atlantic; and it had by then constructed a huge electronic surveillance station at Lourdes, just east of Havana, which monitored millions of radio and telephone messages on the U.S. East Coast.

The truth was, however, that the fire had gone out of Moscow's revolutionary ethos. In the years before Gorbachev's rise to power, the country had been ruled by men who were far more concerned over their positions in the power structure at home than in extending socialism abroad. Moscow's perceived need for an advance base began to dwindle, and with it the value Moscow placed on Cuba as an asset. There was still much that held them together, but the realization on both sides during 1979–1985 that their alliance might be one of diminishing returns set the stage for what was to come under Mikhail Gorbachev.

SOVIET-CUBAN RELATIONS UNDER GORBACHEV

Initially, the Cubans greeted Mikhail Gorbachev's rise to power in 1985 with relief. Better a younger, more vigorous, and more politically attuned leader in the Kremlin, they reasoned, than the senile old men who'd been there during the first half of the decade.[10] But their relief was short lived.

As Gorbachev began his sweeping reforms, Cuban concerns grew. It was all very well for Gorbachev to take the position that it was up to each Communist Party to interpret and apply Marxism-Leninism in accordance with the particular conditions of its particular country. That had been Castro's message back in the 1960s when he'd said that there should be no pope and no Rome for the international Marxist movement and that each party should choose its own path.[11] But Gorbachev had now gone further. He was saying that it was up to the people of each state to decide which system they wanted, and that if the Communist Party did not have the support of the people, it would have to give up power. He made it clear that in Eastern Europe the ruling parties could no longer count on Soviet tanks to maintain themselves in office.

To some extent, the Cubans agreed with the underlying principle of Gorbachev's position. They had often said that one of the reasons for dissatisfaction in Eastern Europe was that a number of the parties there had lost touch with the people in a way that would never be possible in Cuba. But they also understood full well that the ultimate consequence of this position would likely be the collapse of communist governments in Eastern Europe—a consequence that could only prove damaging to Cuban interests. For one thing, it was certain to disrupt Cuban trade with the area.

Perestroika was not a major irritant between Moscow and Havana. The Cubans had no intention of emulating the kind of economic and societal restructuring initiated by Gorbachev in the Soviet Union. But as this was a matter of internal arrangement entirely within the jurisdiction of the Soviet government, they could only stand on the sidelines, occasionally expressing disbelief and predicting dire consequences if the reforms were carried too far. The same was true of glasnost. Castro was not about to allow more openness in Cuba, but if Gorbachev wished to be so foolish, that was his affair.

For its part, noting these disagreements between Moscow and Havana, the United States began pressing the former to break, or at least reduce, its ties with the latter. After all, U.S. officials asked, if the Soviet Union really wanted détente with the United States, shouldn't it cease to bail out this Caribbean ally that was so painful an irritant to the United States and that publicly took issue with the new thinking in the Soviet Union itself?[12] Vice Pres. Dan Quayle suggested that the Soviet Union ought to pressure Cuba to follow its lead.[13] For a time, U.S. officials even suggested that halting aid to Cuba would be one of the key preconditions to improved U.S.-Soviet relations.[14]

Bemused Soviet officials noted that their government was now out of the business of pressuring smaller states to do its bidding, something they had thought the United States would applaud. Thus, it could encourage Cuba to move toward a more open system but could not force compliance.[15] Soviet officials also insisted that there be no double standard. As of 1988, for example, they had halted all arms shipments to Nicaragua and voiced full support for the Central American peace plan launched by Pres. Oscar Arias Sánchez of Costa Rica. They called on the United States to follow suit. Gorbachev suggested that the United States halt its military aid to the contras in Nicaragua and withdraw military advisers from Honduras and El Salvador. "We believe symmetry is the best approach," said Victor Komplektov, one of Gorbachev's key advisers.[16] Soviet officials insisted that reciprocity was needed toward Cuba as well. If the Soviet Union was adjusting its relationship with Cuba to fit the post–Cold War context, the United States should do the same, principally by beginning a dialogue with Cuban leaders.[17]

The United States, of course, demurred.

Meanwhile, as Gorbachev's "new thinking" put an end to the concept of world revolution, as Moscow began to lay the groundwork for withdrawal from Afghanistan to encourage resolution of other regional conflicts (as in Central America) and to pursue détente with the West ever more vigorously, Cuba's strategic worth plummeted. Of what real value was an advance base in the West's backyard if East-West struggle was coming to an end? Of what value was a socialist foothold in Latin America if there was no further interest in the extension of socialism?

Still, trade between the two remained mutually beneficial. The Soviet Union needed Cuban sugar, nickel, and citrus. Cuba needed Soviet petroleum and manufactured products. And though frayed, ideological ties remained intact. Both were communist countries still committed to the same doctrine, however differently they might interpret it. And there was no denying the emotional and personal links that had been forged over more than a quarter of a century. Tens of thousands of Soviet technicians and military men had spent years in Cuba. Tens of thousands of Cubans had lived and studied in the Soviet Union. Bonds of friendship had formed.

By the time Mikhail Gorbachev visited Havana in April 1989, the two governments seemed to have worked out a modus vivendi. They would pursue their different paths of internal reform and simply agree to disagree about what best served the interests of Marxism-Leninism. Trade would continue and possibly even increase but would shift toward a more commercial basis. The Soviets wanted better use made of their technical assistance projects, but such assistance, as well as military aid, would continue. A new treaty of friendship and cooperation was thus signed before Gorbachev left Havana; and, in the months that followed, a new trade agreement was worked out that projected an increase in 1990 commercial exchanges between the two countries.

Contrary to the perception in the United States, Moscow and Havana were also on essentially the same foreign-policy wavelength. If the former was no longer interested in underwriting foreign adventures (such as the 1975 intervention in Angola or Cuban support for revolutionary movements in Latin America), Havana was no longer in any position to carry them out, and in any event realized that the time for that had passed. In 1988, Havana had sent a clear message to Washington that it was prepared to sit down and discuss such issues as outside arms supply to Central America in the same constructive context in which the talks on Southern Africa had been conducted—talks that resulted in December 1988 in a tripartite agreement under which, among other things, Cuban troops began to withdraw from Angola. The United States, through its failure to respond, in effect rebuffed the Cuban overture.[18]

In late 1989, moreover, the Cubans indicated that they would be guided by the wishes of the Sandinistas in suspending military shipments to Nicaragua in the period prior to the elections. Beyond that, Cuban officials stressed that while they considered it a duty to help Nicaragua meet its defense needs so long as that was necessary, they were perfectly prepared to help work out security arrangements in Central America that would be satisfactory to all sides. As a Cuban Foreign Ministry official summed it up in November 1989: "We have indicated to the US our willingness to hold substantive discussions on the arms-supply question, but we have received no reply from the Bush administration."[19]

Nor did they ever receive a reply. The issue became largely moot in February 1990, however, when the Sandinistas lost the elections in Nicaragua (elections arranged by the Central American presidents, initially against the opposition of the United States). With that, it can be said, the whole era of the romantic revolution that had opened with Castro's victory in 1959 now came to an end. Fighting would continue for a time in El Salvador and Guatemala; but even there, there was movement, encouraged by the Cubans, toward peace talks.

Thus, while Moscow and Havana might debate the pace of international détente and the limits to which it ought to be carried, they were not in basic disagreement on the general policy lines. In November 1990 Valery Nikolayenko, then the director of the Latin American division in the Soviet Foreign Ministry, summed up Soviet-Cuban relations in the following way:

> Regarding relations with Cuba—we value our friendship with this country and we plan to develop further our historically established links with it. The Soviet-Cuban summit in Havana in April of 1989 and the Soviet-Cuban treaty of friendship and cooperation signed there provided new impetus to these links. The treaty, of course, does not jeopardize the interests of any third countries.
>
> Concerning the US trade and economic blockade of Cuba, already an anachronism and practically the last outcry of the Cold War, the Soviets continue to be the main support for the Cuban people in the area of economic development, although there have been miscalculations and mistakes in that regard. At the same time, we openly speak of our intention to move this cooperation to a new level, adequate to the imperatives

of today. Our economic relations with Cuba will be streamlined to ensure maximum mutual benefits for both parties. This should not be taken as the consequence of attempts to exert influence on us from outside.

Soviet military cooperation with Cuba is a consequence of the external threat to the security of that country. That is why the nature and the scope of our military assistance to Havana will depend on the degree to which this threat will decrease—on whether the normalization of Cuban-US relations will begin.

Our relations with Cuba are, in fact, undergoing a complicated process of adapting to new conditions, but it would be completely wrong to say that some kind of crisis is breeding in them.[20]

As though to give substance to Nikolayenko's assurances of normality and continuity in the relationship, in December 1990 a trade agreement projecting exchanges for 1991 was signed between Cuban and Soviet negotiators. Prices were to be calculated in dollars and at near-world-market levels, but no money was actually to change hands; rather, trade was to continue on a barter basis. While it was to receive several million tons less petroleum than had been supplied the previous year, Cuba was assured sufficient supplies for its basic needs. Prices of various Soviet products—such as tires, spare parts for trucks and buses, fertilizers, and grains—were left to be fixed in subsequent negotiations.

Cubans collectively breathed a sigh of relief. Their trade ties with Moscow, though altered, remained viable and intact. "We are all in a more optimistic mood now," a high-ranking Cuban official commented to U.S. interlocutors during an international conference in January 1991. "The terms of trade with the Soviets are not so favorable as they used to be, but they remain advantageous. With things as they are now, we can get by."[21]

There were complications in establishing those prices not fixed by the December 1990 agreement. This resulted in a hiatus in the supply of tires and badly needed spare parts, with a negative impact on the transportation system. By 1991, however, agreement had been reached and the Cubans expected the flow of these goods to resume immediately.[22]

In August, moreover, Cuba had hosted the Pan-American Games and had done so quite successfully. There had been a good deal of speculation in the Western media that Cuba did not have enough food and other resources to handle such a large influx of visitors, that the game sites would not be finished on time, and that everything would be poorly organized. None of those fears proved well founded. The games were the most successful in history and almost all participants acknowledged that Cuba had been a gracious and effective host. Cuba's image abroad also improved, as viewers saw thousands of enthusiastic Cuban fans enjoying themselves and expressing pride in their national teams and in their country. A Cuban official summed up the hopes of many others in August when he said: "We've definitely turned a corner, in our economic ties with the Soviet Union, and in our image abroad. The Soviets will soon again be supplying all the commodities we need, and the world will now see that Cuba can cope with the difficulties it faces. The worst is over."[23]

However, the worst was yet to come. The Pan-American Games ended on August 18. The next day, a hard-line coup to depose Gorbachev and reverse the reform process began in Moscow. Any good feeling toward Cuba was immediately erased by the perception that the Castro government had sided with the hard-liners. (In an otherwise carefully calibrated August 20 news conference, for example, President Bush scornfully described Cuba as one of the renegade nations that had welcomed the coup.)

In fact, the Cuban government had not made—nor did it subsequently make—a single statement or gesture to welcome the coup. On the contrary, in a statement released on August 20, it expressed its "profound concern" but also its faith that the Soviet people would overcome their difficulties peacefully.[24]

The cause of Cuban concern was not difficult to fathom. Perhaps the Cubans silently yearned for the good old days and the return of the hard-liners to power. But international politics are not built on nostalgic dreams. Realistically, the Cubans understood that the hard-line coup would either fail quickly or lead to cataclysmic upheaval in the Soviet Union, even to a full-scale civil war that could only have disastrous consequences for Cuba. Given those options, the Cubans, whatever their sympathies for the hard-liners, hoped for the coup's quick defeat. As a Cuban diplomat in Washington put it at the time:

> This cannot work in our favor. It could lead to civil war, or at least to far more unsettled conditions in the Soviet Union. Our trade with the Soviets would thus become even more problematical—just as we were hoping the uncertainties had been dispelled. What we would like to see in the Soviet Union is stability, not upheaval. And despite some differences of opinion, we have excellent relations with both Gorbachev and [Boris] Yeltsin.[25]

Cuba had nothing to do with the hard-line coup, but it suffered the consequences. Reaction in the Soviet Union against the conservatives and against the Communist Party itself was swift and furious. Cuba was caught up in the reaction. This author visited Moscow in the month after the coup and found two distinct views regarding Cuba. If one spoke to knowledgeable officials or academics, those who really knew the history and details of Soviet-Cuban relations, one found a pragmatic view of how those relations ought to develop under the changed situation in the Soviet Union. Essentially, such people believed that trade was beneficial to both and should continue; that military ties should be reduced only gradually, and at a pace determined by the elimination of the threat posed by the United States; and, finally, that given their long-standing ties of friendship, the Soviet Union and Cuba should maintain a "special relationship," however it might be restructured and reduced.

Contrary to that minority view, however, was that of the average Russian, the man in the street. He was outraged by the hard-line coup and convinced that his government had squandered billions on the faraway island and that no matter what government officials might say about trade being mutually beneficial, in fact it would cost the Soviet Union dearly. Further, he now fiercely repudiated anything that had to do with the communist system and with the past, and Cuba was identified with both. The popular view held that the Soviet Union should simply wash its hands of Cuba. As one Moscow cab driver put it, "If Castro is so blind that he insists on following the communist system, then we should have nothing to do with him."

The view in favor of a reduction in ties was not an informed one, but it is one that any Soviet (or Russian) government must take into account. It was perhaps in response to that popular mood that Boris Pankin, the Soviet Union's new foreign minister, announced in early September 1991, in the immediate wake of the coup, that Soviet-Cuban relations would be reviewed and henceforth based less on ideological considerations than in the past.[26] Two steps in the review process were announced a few days later by President Gorbachev. Trade, he said, would henceforth be conducted strictly on the basis of world market prices. This was almost certainly meant for internal consumption; it implied little change in the existing situation, as most Soviet subsidies had already been phased out. The second step, however, was more meaningful: all Soviet combat forces were to be gradually withdrawn from Cuba.[27]

Havana immediately expressed anger that the announcement of troop withdrawals had been made without consultations with the Cuban government. The anger may have been premature, however, for Gorbachev followed up by saying that the drawdown would begin only after negotiations between the Soviet and Cuban governments. Subsequently, some troops were indeed pulled out; but as of July 1992, a timetable satisfactory to the Cuban government and the new Russian government still had not been established. The Russians, moreover, have made it clear that they have no intention of closing the Lourdes surveillance facility.

Further, the Soviet announcement of a gradual troop withdrawal came only after Moscow had gotten assurances from Washington concerning Cuba's security. Gorbachev had said that security arrangements had to be mutual. In July 1991, Assistant Secretary of State Bernard Aronson stated categorically that the United States would not attack Cuba militarily. The Aronson statement was given so that the Soviets would have no excuses to continue aid to Cuba; the purpose was to isolate the island rather than to relax tensions with it.[28] Even so, the results were the same as far as the Soviets were concerned. They asked for guarantees and received them. They could now begin their troop reduction with a good conscience.

Discussion on Soviet withdrawal of troops from Cuba was virtually the last major development in Soviet-Cuban relations. The abortive August coup had fatally undermined not only the communist system but the single foundation upon which the various ethnic republics stood. By the end of 1991, the Communist Party had been abolished, the whole communist system was scrapped, and the Soviet Union itself had for all practical purposes disintegrated. The fifteen republics had become fifteen independent nations.

CUBA'S RELATIONS WITH RUSSIA
AND THE OTHER REPUBLICS

As of this writing, Cuba is struggling to adjust to the loss of its special relationship with Moscow. The preferential terms of trade are gone. The two are no longer ideological allies. Russia and the other republics have repudiated communism; Havana still holds to it. The two are not even political allies. Russia voted against Cuba in the UN Human Rights Commission, and the two have been at odds frequently in the United Nations itself. Russia, for example, did not back Cuba's bid to have the Security Council take up the issue of the U.S. embargo against Cuba.

Still, remnants of the old ties remain. The Lourdes surveillance facility remains open, for example, and the Russians have indicated that it will remain so "until the situation with the United States is clarified."[29] They apparently mean that given that the United States has closed none of its surveillance stations around the borders of the former Soviet Union, they see no need to rush into closing Lourdes.

Cuba, moreover, has established diplomatic relations with virtually all the republics and signed trade agreements not only with Russia but with Kazakhstan, Ukraine, the Baltic republics, Georgia, Armenia, Azerbaijan, Tajikistan, and Kyrgyzstan. The most important by far is that with Russia. Because of chaotic conditions in Russia itself, the government of Boris Yeltsin is in no position to project levels of trade much beyond a three-month period. Hence, rather than signing annual trade agreements, Moscow and Havana are opting for a series of agreements to cover periods of three to four months. Assuming that the quantities of oil and sugar swapped during the first half of the year are maintained throughout 1992, Russia will have imported some 2.5 million tons of sugar and shipped to Cuba some 4 million tons of petroleum. Cuba will also swap sugar for petroleum with Kazakhstan and perhaps with Azerbaijan. Still, as the Cubans calculate that they must have 7 million tons of oil for their basic needs, they will have to look elsewhere to pick up the remainder.

Cuba must find new trade partners. It can no longer count even on its residual links with Russia. Russia and the other republics are in such uncertain situations themselves, and with such economic difficulties, that no matter what they undertake in short-term trade agreements, they cannot guarantee delivery. If the new Russian economic system cannot even get bread into the stores in Moscow, much less can it assure delivery of petroleum to an island ten thousand miles away.

Cuba has had only limited success in linking with new partners. It will trade sugar for oil with Iran this year and has discussed the possibility of doing so with the Algerians and presumably the Libyans. It has tripled its trade with China and increased its exports of biotechnological products to other Latin American countries. It has also mounted intensive efforts to construct a major tourist industry (expected to bring in at least half as much hard currency as used to be brought in from sugar sales) and to attract foreign private investment for everything from tourist hotels to textiles to exploration for oil.

In his public speeches, Fidel Castro is vowing not to retreat a step from Cuba's socialist economy. In fact, however, the Cubans are moving toward a mixed economy. One might criticize them for not moving faster and more energetically, but the Cubans say that they have seen in Eastern Europe and the former Soviet Union the results of uncontrolled change and they want none of it. They prefer to go slowly, lest their system unravel as did the others. And given the economic distress in those areas and the breakup of the Soviet Union, Yugoslavia, and Czechoslovakia, usually accompanied by horrendous bloodshed, who can blame them?

CUBA IN THE POST–COLD WAR WORLD: IMPLICATIONS FOR THE UNITED STATES

Cuba stands virtually alone. China, Vietnam, and North Korea are still communist countries, but they are on the other side of the world—and Vietnam at least is moving in the same direction as the Eastern European countries. Cuba's adjustments will almost certainly carry the country toward a mixed economy and a more open political system, no matter how much Fidel Castro may demur.

Meanwhile, Cuba's foreign policy has undergone sweeping change. Cuba is no longer a Soviet ally. Its troops are out of Africa. As January 1992, Fidel Castro announced that there would no longer be Cuban support for revolutionary movements in Latin America and elsewhere. Cuba now seeks again to become a more integral part of the Latin American family of nations and, to compensate for the loss of its ties with the former communist world, to broaden its relationships with countries throughout the world.

Implicit in U.S. policy statements over the years had been the point that the Cuban-Soviet alliance was at the core of Washington's concern; if the alliance could somehow be erased or even significantly reduced, the way might then be open for dramatically improved relations between the United States and Cuba. Beyond Washington's wildest dreams, the Soviet Union has disintegrated, and with it, the alliance. One would expect, then, a relaxation on the part of the United States and improvement in U.S.-Cuban relations.

What we have seen, however, is quite the opposite. With the end of the Cold War, the United States has raised tensions with Cuba to a level not seen since the 1960s. It is now even trying to pressure such friends and trading partners as Canada and Great Britain to reduce their own economic relations with the island. Further, it has moved the goalposts by issuing a new set of preconditions for improving relations: (1) Cuba must first have a market economy—that is, it must totally abandon even residual manifestations of a socialist economic system; and (2) it must hold fully democratic, internationally supervised elections.

U.S. demands, in other words, now have nothing to do with Cuba's foreign policy or relations with Moscow but everything to do with Cuba's internal arrangements. Does this mean the United States was never in fact concerned over the Soviet factor in the equation, that its expressions of concern were but a subterfuge? Probably not. What seems to have happened is that concerns related to the Soviet presence in Cuba have been rendered obsolete so suddenly and under such circumstances that the U.S. government is now tempted to make greater demands. The United States is raising pressures in hopes of bringing about the elimination of communism in Cuba.

This effort, however, is likely to be counterproductive in at least two ways. (1) By stirring up nationalist sentiment in Cuba in defense of sovereignty, the United States helps Castro rally the Cuban people behind him and thus assists him more than it hinders him. (2) U.S. efforts could create serious problems between the United States and Canada, Great Britain, and a series of other important trading partners, none of whom are likely to accede to demands at this point; if they would not reduce their trade with Cuba at the height of the Cold War, they certainly will not do so now. If anything, then, the present U.S. policy toward Cuba isolates Washington more than it does Cuba and causes Washington more problems than it does Havana. Western Europeans and Canadians have always regarded the U.S. obsession with Cuba as slightly irrational. At this point, they find it simply inexplicable.

Beyond that, the inability of the United States to adjust its Cuba policy to the post–Cold War period undermines confidence in its ability to provide international leadership. If it is so obsessed with insignificant problems of the past, how can it be relied upon to focus intelligently on the truly critical problems that endanger the future of all humankind?

NOTES

1. Quoted in Herbert Dinerstein, *The Making of a Missile Crisis* (Baltimore: Johns Hopkins University Press, 1976), p. 41.

2. "Communist Threat to the United States Through the Caribbean," hearings before the Senate Subcommittee to Investigate the Administration of the Internal Security Act and Other Internal Security Laws, Eighty-Sixth Congress, First session, pp. 164–166. Testimony of C. P. Cabell, deputy director of the CIA, November 5, 1959.

3. As stated by Sergo Mikoyan on a number of occasions, most recently at a lunch with the author in Washington on June 25, 1992.

4. For an excellent discussion of Castro's calculations, see Jacques Levesque, *The USSR and the Cuban Revolution* (New York: Praeger, 1978), pp. 20–38.

5. In the Egyptian leftist weekly *Akher Saa*, as quoted in Daniel James, *Che Guevara: A Biography* (New York: Stein and Day, 1970), p. 134.

6. *Revolución* (Havana), February 26, 1965.

7. *Revolución*, March 14, 1965.

8. For a full discussion, see Wayne Smith, *Castro's Cuba: Soviet Partner or Non-Aligned?* (Washington: Woodrow Wilson Center, 1984), pp. 22–28, 30–38.

9. See a statement on the part of Valery Nikolayenko, then-Soviet ambassador to Nicaragua, who in 1988 made it clear that Moscow's responsibilities in Nicaragua were limited and that it had no interest in drawing the country closer to the Socialist bloc. Quoted in the *Washington Post*, November 6, 1988, p. 42A.

10. Statements of a number of Cuban officials to the author during a visit to Cuba in early 1986.

11. Quoted in Maurice Halperin, *The Taming of Fidel Castro* (Berkeley: University of California Press, 1981), pp. 178–179.

12. Martin McReynolds, "Soviet Support for Cuba Still an Irritant for the US," *Miami Herald*, April 10, 1990, p. 8A.

13. *Miami Herald*, June 5, 1990, p. 6A.

14. Warren Strobel and Karen Riley, "U.S. Support for Soviets Seen Tied to Cuba Aid Cut," *Washington Times*, June 7, 1990, p. 9A.

15. See, for example, Sergo Mikoyan, "The Future of the Soviet-Cuban Relationship," in Wayne Smith, ed., *The Russians Aren't Coming: New Soviet Policy in Latin America* (Boulder: Lynne Rienner, 1992), pp. 130–134.

16. Alfonso Chardy, "Soviets Hint at Latin Shift," *Miami Herald*, April 1, 1989, pp. 1A, 11A.

17. See Wayne Smith, "Conflict Management in the Caribbean Basin," in Thomas Weiss and James Blight, eds., *The Suffering Grass: Superpowers and Regional Conflict in Southern Africa and the Caribbean* (Boulder: Lynne Rienner, 1992), pp. 116–120.

18. The author was informed of this Cuban overture during the African talks by members of both the Cuban and the U.S. delegations.

19. As stated to the author by an official of the Cuban Foreign Ministry who asked not to be identified.

20. Valery Nikolayenko address at the Johns Hopkins University Paul H. Nitze School of Advanced International Studies. As quoted in "An Official Statement of the New Soviet Policy in Latin America," in Wayne Smith, ed., *The Russians Aren't Coming: New Soviet Policy in Latin America* (Boulder: Lynne Rienner, 1992), p. 61.

21. Statements of Cuban official to the author during the Missile Crisis Conference in Antigua, January 1991.

22. Statement of a member of the Central Committee to the author in early August 1991.

23. Ibid.

24. Press release distributed by Cuban Interests Section, Washington, August 20, 1991.

25. As stated to the author by an official of Cuban Interests Section, Washington, who asked not to be identified.

26. Alfonso Chardy, "Soviets Rethink Ties with Cuba," *Miami Herald*, September 6, 1991, p. 1A.

27. Juan Tamayo, "Soviets to Recall Cuba Troops," *Miami Herald*, September 12, 1991, p. 1A.

28. Christopher Marquis, "US Assures Soviets It Will Not Attack Cuba," *Miami Herald*, July 12, 1991, pp. 1A, 12A.

29. As stated to the author on June 5, 1992, by a senior diplomat at the Russian Embassy in Washington who asked not to be identified.

PART 3

CUBA'S RELATIONS WITH LATIN AMERICA AND THE CARIBBEAN

9

Cuba and the CARICOM States: The Last Decade

JOHN WALTON COTMAN

We must integrate, or we will disintegrate.   —Fidel Castro

This chapter examines Cuba's political and economic ties to the English-speaking Caribbean. Emphasis is on the period after the collapse of the Grenada Revolution. To be examined in turn are: (1) Cuban perspectives on regional integration; (2) multilateral relations; (3) bilateral relations; and (4) the anglophone Caribbean's place in Cuban policy since the Fourth Congress of the Cuban Communist Party (PCC) in October 1991.

CUBAN VIEWS ON CARIBBEAN INTEGRATION

The Cuban foreign-policy establishment's support of regional integration has a long history and was reaffirmed in autumn 1991. One pundit in Havana has bemoaned the limited scope of its realization:

> In Cuba's opinion, it will not be possible to advance seriously toward the continent's greater economic integration—a condition for survival in the face of the world centers of economic power—without the political will of the region's governments. This will has barely shown itself beyond statements of intent and glimmerings of coordination. Thus, a greater degree of economic integration does not appear feasible absent greater political integration.[1]

As Havana's ties to the Council for Mutual Economic Assistance (CMEA, or COMECON) began to disintegrate, the Cuban Foreign Ministry admitted that it too had suffered a lack of political will. This was evident in Cuba's "low diplomatic profile" in the anglophone Caribbean during the 1980s. Deputy Foreign Minister for American Affairs Ramón Sánchez Parodi addressed this in a December 1989 interview:

Washington's hostile policy against the Cuban government has been a very important factor in the links with countries that are economically dependent on the United States. But we must also acknowledge that there was a lack of diplomatic work and our foreign-policy didn't give the area adequate priority. . . . The priority now is to place Caribbean integration in the Latin American context, given the growing economic and political polarization of the present world.[2]

MULTILATERAL RELATIONS

Despite suspended membership in the Organization of American States (OAS) since 1962, Cuba wields considerable and expanding influence on intergovernmental organizations operating in the English-speaking Caribbean. To be examined, in turn, are Havana's relations with nine such organizations.

CARICOM. Cuba's desire for closer ties to the Caribbean evident during the late 1980s was reflected in its press coverage of the Caribbean Community and Common Market (CARICOM), the premier regional grouping of anglophone states. In an analysis of the year 1989 the PCC noted, "In political terms, the subregion's most important event of the year was the 10th CARICOM Summit of Heads of State or Government, [m]eeting in July at the beautiful resort of Grand Anse in Grenada." There CARICOM decided to accelerate the integration of its thirteen member states in an attempt to soften anticipated negative regional economic repercussions of the upcoming EC single market.[3]

Meeting in Jamaica in August 1990, the Eleventh CARICOM Summit opted to send a mission to Havana to explore greater political and economic ties. Three months later CARICOM secretary-general Roderick Rainford met with President Castro while attending the fourth meeting of Chambers of Commerce and Industry of the Group of 77 held in Havana. In March 1991 Cuban deputy foreign minister Ramón Sánchez Parodi addressed a CARICOM conference in Trinidad, indicating Cuba's continued support of regional integration in the Caribbean and Latin America.[4]

On April 27–May 5, 1991, Cuban foreign trade minister Ricardo Cabrisas hosted CARICOM's first mission to Cuba. It was led by Byron Blake, director of economics and industry of the CARICOM Secretariat. The two sides hammered out proposals for technical cooperation in biotechnology, genetic engineering, cane sugar and its by-products, agriculture, cattle breeding, fishing, and tourism. Trade talks examined two Cuban requests: (1) to be linked to the Caribbean Trade Information System and (2) for CARICOM to participate in the Havana International Trade Fairs. Preliminary discussions were held on preferential tariffs and joint ventures. Havana voiced its interest in joining the Caribbean Tourism Organization. The negotiations held much promise. But as became evident in a May 1991 meeting of CARICOM foreign ministers, deeper state-to-state ties under the CARICOM umbrella would be premised on Havana's full recognition of Grenada's government.[5]

The issue of Cuba's diplomatic relations with the Spice Isle—suspended in the aftermath of Washington's invasion of October 1983—was again raised during the July 1991 Twelfth CARICOM Summit on St. Kitts-Nevis. Summit guest Sánchez Parodi was immersed in negotiations to resolve this crucial diplomatic logjam.[6] He also led Cuba's informal delegation to a February 1992 CARICOM conference in Kingston, Jamaica, seeking to firm up ties. An observer of the event noted, "After years of wariness toward Cuba, at least in part for fear of invoking Washington's displeasure, many of the Caribbean's leaders are tentatively reciprocating Havana's interest." However, in the words of CARICOM leader Shridath Ramphal of Guyana, "If it were [in] a transition to a market economy and liberal democracy, I think CARICOM would be very eager to help Cuba. But right now I don't quite see how we could."[7]

A CARICOM delegation led by Ramphal visited Havana in March 1992. (Ramphal is president of the Independent West Indies Commission, formed by CARICOM in 1989 to promote strategies for regional integration.) Talks were held on the feared marginalization of the Caribbean as the world is restructured into EC, U.S.-Canada-Mexico, and Japan-Pacific trade blocs. Ramphal indicated a desire to strengthen Caribbean solidarity, noted Cuba's key role in any process of regional unity, and voiced CARICOM's opposition to the U.S. embargo of Cuba. In a dramatic turn of events, which bodes well for deeper Cuba-CARICOM relations, the government of Grenada released a statement in early May 1992 indicating that diplomatic relations between St. George's and Havana had been normalized. Although it appears CARICOM will not accept Cuba as a member in the short term, by spring 1992 Cuba had diplomatic relations with ten of thirteen CARICOM states. Only Antigua-Barbuda, Dominica, and St. Kitts-Nevis had yet to establish formal links with Havana. After ties were formalized with St. Vincent and the Grenadines in late spring 1992, Havana expected diplomatic relations with the three remaining CARICOM members to "soon be concretized."[8]

CDB. Indicative of Cuba's recent improvement in regional ties was the October 1991 arrival in Havana of a Caribbean Development Bank (CDB) delegation to examine the sugarcane derivatives industry. The mission, led by CDB president Neville Nichols, was motivated by the chronic lack of stable sugar export earnings in most of the sixteen nations served by the bank. One promising area for future collaboration involves the use of Cuban techniques for making animal feed from sugarcane. Of importance to Havana was Nichols's indication that the majority of CARICOM was interested not only in Caribbean but also Latin American economic integration. Firming up relations between the CDB and the National Bank of Cuba was also on the agenda.[9]

Table 9.1 Membership in Regional Organizations, 1991

	CARICOM	CDB	CDU[a]	CSA	ECLAC	GLACSEC	NAM	OECS	OLADE	SELA
Antigua-Barbuda	yes	yes	no	yes	yes	no	yes[b]	yes	no	no
Bahamas	yes	yes	no	yes	yes	no	yes	no	no	no
Barbados	yes	yes	no	yes	yes	yes	yes	no	yes	yes
Belize	yes	yes	yes	yes	yes	—	yes	no	no	no
Bermuda	no	—	no	yes	no	no	no	no	no	no
Cayman Islands	no	yes	no	no	no	no	no	no	no	no
Cuba	no[c]	no	yes	d	yes	yes	yes	no	yes	yes
Dominica	yes	yes	yes	no	yes	no	no	yes	yes	no
Grenada	yes	yes	yes	yes	yes	no	yes	yes	yes	yes
Guyana	yes	yes	no	yes	yes	yes	yes	no	yes	yes
Jamaica	yes	yes	yes	no	no	yes	yes	no	yes	yes
Montserrat	yes	yes	no	no	yes	no	no	yes	no	no
St. Kitts-Nevis	yes	yes	yes	no	yes	—	no	yes	no	no
St. Lucia	yes	yes	yes	yes	yes	no	yes	yes	no	no
St. Vincent	yes	yes	yes	no	yes	no	no	yes	no	no
Suriname	e	—	no	yes	yes	—	yes	no	yes	yes
Trinidad-Tobago	yes	yes	no	yes	yes	yes	yes	no	yes	yes

Sources: Peter Ashdown, *Caribbean History in Maps* (Harlow, England: Longwood Group UK Ltd., 1979), p. 45; Phil Gunson, Greg Chamberlain, and Andrew Thompson, eds., *The Dictionary of Contemporary Politics of Central America and the Caribbean* (New York: Simon & Schuster, 1991), pp. 62–264 passim; Jorge Heine, "A Letter from the President," *Caribbean Studies Newsletter* 18, no. 3 (Summer 1991), p. 11; Steven L. Reed, "Participation in Multinational Organizations and Programs in the Hemisphere," in Cole Blasier and Carmelo Mesa-Lago, eds., *Cuba in the World* (Pittsburgh: University of Pittsburgh Press, 1979), p. 311.

Notes: CARICOM: Caribbean Community and Common Market; CDB: Caribbean Development Bank; CDU: Caribbean Democratic Union; CSA: Caribbean Studies Association; ECLAC: Economic Commission for Latin America and the Caribbean; GLACSEC: Group of Latin American and Caribbean Sugar Exporting Countries; NAM: Nonaligned Movement; OECS: Organization of Eastern Caribbean States; OLADE: Latin American Energy Organization; SELA: Latin American Economic System.

Notes: a. Circa 1988. b. Permanent observer. c. Has participated as guest since 1973.
d. Acting members because of lack of foreign exchange. e. Has requested membership.
— = status unknown.

CDU. The lack of interaction between Cuba and the Caribbean Democratic Union (CDU), an eight-member conservative, anticommunist alliance, should come as no surprise. The CDU was founded in 1986 under the leadership of Jamaican prime minister Edward Seaga with the support of the Reagan administration. Four of its member states (Jamaica, Dominica, St. Lucia, and St. Vincent) directly participated in the U.S. occupation of Grenada—an act vehemently opposed by Havana.[10]

CTO. Cuba's heightened interest in regional tourism cooperation was evident in 1983 when it joined the Latin American Confederation of Tourism Press (CLAPTUR), which was founded in Caracas in 1973 to promote Latin American integration via tourism. Comprising eighteen national associations of tourism journalists, it held its eleventh congress in Havana in 1984. However, participation in CLAPTUR does not give access to the immense regional tourism market that membership in the Caribbean Tourism Organization (CTO) allows. Because of opposition from Grenada, Cuba's 1989 bid to join CTO was rejected; this impasse was overcome with Havana's formal recognition of the Grenada government in 1992. Cuba's membership was reconsidered at the June 1992 CTO board meeting, and the island is now a full member of the organization.[11]

ECLAC. The UN-sponsored Economic Commission for Latin America and the Caribbean (ECLAC) currently provides Cuba the most comprehensive regional forum for pursuing its relations in the Caribbean Basin. Cuba has been a central and respected leader of ECLAC since May 1975 when the commission launched the Caribbean Development and Cooperation Committee (CDCC) in Havana. The CDCC was the first attempt at regional economic collaboration and integration encompassing all independent Caribbean states.[12]

GLACSEC. Havana has been a major player in the Group of Latin American and Caribbean Sugar Exporting Countries (GLACSEC) since its founding in 1974. Charter members include Barbados, Guyana, Jamaica, and Trinidad-Tobago. Initially GLACSEC served as an advisory and coordinating center for raw cane sugar production and marketing. In 1991 GLACSEC's twenty-two members accounted for 45 percent of world sugar production. Current activity focuses on securing profitable sugar prices and regional economic integration of the industry via technical cooperation and product diversification. In a February 1988 visit to Havana, GLACSEC's executive secretary commented, "We must stress Cuba's pioneering role in a number of activities related to sugar agro-industry, for it is undoubtedly one of the most developed in the world."[13]

OECS. It is ironic that Grenada joined the Organization of Eastern Caribbean States (OECS) in 1981 when Maurice Bishop—the PCC's closest ally in the region—was prime minister. Its initial tasks were coordinating economic policy and diplomatic relations in the anglophone Lesser Antilles. Havana's relations with it deteriorated rapidly after OECS member states occupied Grenada and soon thereafter, with Washington's aid, launched a rapid deployment force to prevent the rise of leftist regimes.[14]

OLADE. Cuba, Guyana, Jamaica, and Trinidad-Tobago were among the initial signatories of the Lima Convention, which created the Latin American Energy Organization (OLADE) in 1974. Given its dependence on oil imports, Cuba has actively promoted regional cooperation in energy resource development under the aegis of OLADE.[15]

SELA. Cuba, Barbados, Grenada, Guyana, Jamaica, and Trinidad-Tobago were among the founders of the Latin American Economic System (SELA) in 1975. In 1985 the Latin American Council, SELA's highest executive body, elected Cuba as its president.[16] It also released the "Declaration of Caracas," which read in part:

SELA has made important progress in meeting its basic goals of promoting intra-regional cooperation and establishing a permanent consultation and coordination system to strengthen Latin America's joint action on the international scene. . . . *We are profoundly convinced* as to the need to increase regional cooperation and integration and to redouble our efforts to strengthen the region's economic system.[17]

BILATERAL RELATIONS

Commonwealth of the Bahamas

Lynden Pindling of the Progressive Liberal Party led the transition from British colonialism to independence in 1973 and has been prime minister since. Diplomatic relations between Nassau and Havana date back to November 1974. One year later, the Bahamas sent a representative to Havana for the first meeting of the Caribbean Development and Cooperation Committee. During the 1980s Cuba's ambassador to the Bahamas was based in Havana.[18]

Relations between the two isles reached their lowest ebb in May 1980 when an ongoing dispute over fishing rights tragically escalated. The Cuban air force, responding to the interdiction of two Cuban fishing boats in Bahamian waters by the Bahamian coast guard ship *Flamingo,* sank the *Flamingo.* Four of its crew perished. Initially Havana refused to apologize, believing Washington was somehow involved in stopping the Cuban ships. Soon Havana relented and apologized after Nassau moved to bring Cuba before the UN Security Council. Later the Castro government paid compensatory damages to the Bahamian regime and the dead sailors' families.

The Bishop government in Grenada played a behind-the-scenes role in these events. In September 1980 Grenada's ambassador to Cuba, W. Richard Jacobs, acted as intermediary between Havana and Nassau in an attempt to reduce tensions.[19]

Speaking before the OAS General Assembly in November 1983, Foreign Minister Paul Addarley of the Bahamas opposed the invasion of Grenada and asked that ideological pluralism be respected in the Caribbean. A thaw in relations was apparent when Clement Maynard, minister of foreign relations and tourism, met in Havana with Cuban foreign minister Isidoro Malmierca on August 15, 1985. According to a local press report, Maynard considered the talks to be "positive and satisfactory."[20]

In autumn 1990 Maynard returned to Havana on an official visit in his capacity as minister of tourism. During the cordial talks an accord was reached for a Cuban Institute for Tourism delegation to go to Nassau to further look into tourism cooperation. With over 1.5 million visitors in 1989, the Bahamas was the second most popular tourist destination in the Caribbean. (That year, Puerto Rico was the most popular, with over 2.5 million visitors; Cuba ranked tenth, with 340,000 guests.) Tapping this immense market is undoubtedly a high priority for Cuba. Two results of improved political ties were the securing of air links in 1991 and the visit in June 1990 of a prominent Bahamian entrepreneur to Cuba to explore business opportunities.[21]

Barbados

The drive for Barbadian independence from Britain was victorious in 1966, and Errol Barrow, leader of the Democratic Labor Party (DLP), became the first prime minister. He held that post initially until 1976. Barbados, along with Guyana, Jamaica, and Trinidad-Tobago, jointly established diplomatic ties with Cuba on December 8, 1972, after which Cuba's isolation in the Americas began to dissipate.[22]

Barrow wished to maintain some distance between Bridgetown and Havana, however. This was evident in the refusal to permit a Cuban diplomatic facility on Barbados. He approved the launching of regular Cubana Airlines flights between the two isles. A limited exchange of agricultural technicians also took place during the first DLP administration. Barrow solidified Barbados's links with regional intergovernmental organizations that were also a high priority for Havana—ECLAC, CDCC, SELA, GLACSEC, and OLADE. At the end of 1975 relations cooled considerably in reaction to Cuba's role in Angola. Barrow not only refused to allow Cuban planes to refuel in Barbados on their way to Angola but sharply rebuked Castro for "meddling" in Angola's internal affairs.[23]

Tom Adams's Barbados Labor Party (BLP) defeated Barrow in the 1976 elections. Until his death in March 1985, Adams cemented a firm alliance with Washington and campaigned against the Caribbean left. He was an outspoken opponent of the Grenada Revolution and the Castro-Bishop alliance. The BLP leader falsely charged that Cuba's ambassador to Grenada, Julian Torres Rizo, was a key policymaker within the Bishop cabinet.[24]

Despite profound political differences with Havana, Barbados's minister of foreign affairs, Louis Tull, paid an official visit in January 1983. He met with PCC Political Bureau members Armando Hart and Carlos Rafael Rodríguez. At that time President Castro chaired the Nonaligned Movement (NAM). Barbados was an observer in NAM and Tull discussed requesting full membership. Havana was keen on reaching a bilateral tourism agreement. A cultural accord was signed, providing for exchanges of artists, scientific literature, and information on literacy programs. In addition, Cuba offered scholarships to Barbadian students.[25]

The prospect of increased cooperation vaporized when Bridgetown backed the Grenada invasion. After Barbadian troops and police returned from the Spice Isle, the BLP government promoted the idea of hosting a joint military force for anglophone eastern Caribbean states. Adams lobbied within CARICOM for heightened political, economic, and military cooperation with Washington. After Adams's death in 1985, BLP leader Bernard St. John took power and—much to the chagrin of Havana—pursued the political trajectory of his predecessor.[26]

In the 1986 parliamentary elections, St. John was defeated by resurgent DLP leader Barrow. During his ten-year hiatus from power, Barrow had sharply criticized the Grenada invasion; however, his party supported it. While Barrow was off the island in October 1983, acting DLP head Erskine Sandiford backed Washington's move. Barrow traveled to Havana in July 1985 for the Continental Meeting on the Latin American and Caribbean Foreign Debt, chaired by President Castro. These acts by Barrow—coupled with his opposition to the militarization of the eastern Caribbean and his criticism of CARICOM leaders closely allied with the Reagan administration—were appreciated in Cuban foreign-policy circles.[27]

Barrow assumed office in June 1986. Havana anticipated improved ties, as the new BLP government seemed to be, in the words of a PCC analyst, "interested in greater regional cooperation, opposition to militarism, and the firm defense of national and regional sovereignty." But Barrow died in 1987; thereafter, Cuba's hopes of better relations hinged on its relationship with Prime Minister Erskine Sandiford.[28]

The paucity of coverage on Cuba-Barbados relations in *Granma* since 1987 hints that Sandiford prefers the cordial but distant relationship with Cuba characteristic of the period 1972 through early 1975. In 1989 Barbados was the seventh most popular Caribbean vacation spot, and Cuba's desire to launch joint tourism projects still awaits the nod of approval from Bridgetown.[29]

Belize

After decades of negotiations with Britain and a long-standing territorial dispute with Guatemala, Belize became a sovereign nation on September 21, 1981. A member of the Nonaligned Movement since 1976, Belize had Cuba's support in its struggle for nationhood. Founding member of the People's United Party (PUP) and self-described Christian Democrat George Price led Belize to independence and was its first prime minister (1981–1984).[30]

Parliamentary elections in 1984 gave the premiership to Manuel Esquivel, leader of the United Democratic Party (UDP). He upgraded ties with and received aid from the United States. Esquivel joined his conservative regional allies as a founding member of the Caribbean Democratic Union in 1986. Diplomatic relations between Belmopan and Havana continued, but there was no apparent desire on either side to expand areas of cooperation. Esquivel lost to George Price in the 1989 elections.[31]

It was during the second Price administration that links with Havana expanded considerably. On February 8, 1992, Belize and Cuba established trade and consular relations. This was an outgrowth of Price's support of CARICOM and regional integration. Cooperation between Belmopan and Havana involves (1) an investigation of long-term trade potential; (2) a signed memorandum of intent to collaborate in the sugar industry (sugar is Belize's largest export); (3) a Cuban medical brigade in Belize; and (4) a group of thirty-eight Belizean youth studying in Cuba. Also perhaps of interest to Havana are Belize's crude oil reserves.[32]

Grenada

Since the Spice Isle became independent in 1974, Cuba has faced seven different governments. This section will focus on bilateral relations after the collapse of the Grenada Revolution.[33] On November 1, 1983, U.S. troops surrounded the Cuban Embassy. Grenada governor general Paul Scoon (backed by the U.S. ambassador) ordered all Cuban diplomats off the isle in twenty-four hours. President Castro instructed them to remain until all Cubans—alive and dead—had headed home. The last Cuban to leave was chargé d'affaires Gastón Díaz González, on March 19, 1984.[34]

Chair of the Interim Advisory Council Nicholas Brathwaite took power on December 5, 1983, ten days before U.S. combat troops departed. He supported the expulsion of Cuban personnel and the cancellation of all collaboration programs, closed Grenada's embassy in Havana, and suspended—but did not break—diplomatic ties. Cuban foreign policymakers considered the regime to have been imposed by the United States and, therefore, illegitimate. According to Brathwaite, Havana was "very hostile" and tried to prevent the council's accreditation in diplomatic circles.[35]

Because there were two hundred or so Grenadian youth studying in Cuba, Brathwaite kept postal and telecommunication links open. Those who graduated in Cuba and returned home to work were seen as security risks and not considered for "sensitive positions." Controversy arose regarding a damaged Cubana Airlines plane and equipment Cuba had provided to build the Point Salines International Airport. In Brathwaite's words:

> [Cuba] wanted to have people come here to repair the aircraft and take it back. We were advised by the head of our security forces . . . and our Police Commissioner that the security situation was so delicate that we shouldn't give permission to any Cubans, engineers or otherwise, to come to Grenada. We indicated that we were prepared to get the aircraft out of here through a third country like Venezuela or Colombia. There was also the question of equipment which was, as far as I was concerned, donated to Grenada by Cuba.

Cuba filed suit August 20, 1984, in the Supreme Court of Grenada, charging the unlawful detention of its property and demanding U.S. $5.2 billion for the construction equipment and nearly two billion Cuban pesos (roughly equivalent to U.S. dollars) for the plane.[36]

A conservative veteran of turbulent local politics, Prime Minister Herbert Blaize took office on November 3, 1984, after receiving 66 percent of the vote. Concerning the continued chill in relations with Havana, he noted, "They take the absurd position that we are a planted government and not a government of the people of Grenada. When they started to become hostile to our representatives abroad, . . . we realized there was no point in making any attempt to have any better relations with their government." Blaize saw Cuba as a national security threat. According to his ambassador to the United States, "1983 was a serious blow and we don't expect Castro will accept that lying down. He'll be looking for an opportunity to reverse what's happened."[37]

The Grenadian government blocked Cuba's application to the Caribbean Tourism Organization, initially refused to grant licenses to practice medicine to ten Cuban-trained Grenadian physicians, and banned the writings of Fidel Castro and Che Guevara. Cuba's lawsuit against Grenada was dealt a setback when the Grenada High Court of Justice ruled that Havana had to pay a security fee for court costs. The enmity between the isles showed no signs of dissipating. In late 1989 Cuba reaffirmed its nonrecognition of the Blaize government but added, "Elections are scheduled for March in Grenada and a change of government could lead to better relations between the two countries."[38]

During Blaize's rule the Cuban Communist Party was openly aligned with the Maurice Bishop Patriotic Movement (MBPM), founded in 1984 by Bishop stalwarts who survived the October 1983 putsch. Havana continued its civilian aid program begun in 1979, albeit on a much smaller scale. It granted the MBPM up to five scholarships to Cuba per year, free medical care for Grenadians who could not be treated locally, and EC $30,000 (EC$1 = U.S. $2.70 in 1989) worth of dental equipment for a medical clinic in St. George's.[39]

Brathwaite returned to power in March 1990. Despite earlier conflicts with Havana, he was open to the possibility of a rapprochement: "Although I accept the reality that Cuba is part of the Caribbean, and in general Caribbean countries should establish ways in which they could collaborate with one another, I am not in any way an admirer of Castro or his policies."[40]

Cuba's hopes of increased trade within CARICOM and of CTO membership hinged on recognizing Grenada's government. In an apparent precondition for normalized relations, Cuba dropped its court suit in late 1991. By the first week of May 1992, St. George's had acknowledged its formal recognition by Havana, withdrawn its objection to Cuba's membership in CTO, and issued a statement verifying the resumption of diplomatic ties.[41]

Two areas of cooperation of interest to Havana may be tourism and agriculture. Grenada is a minor player in tourism, but it hosts the Caribbean Agricultural Research and Development Institute (CARDI), which has experimented in increasing the yields of regional root crops. As part of its crash program for food self-sufficiency, Cuba has initiated a research effort in *viandas* (root crops) and could benefit from CARDI's work.[42]

Republic of Guyana

Currently, Havana's strongest and longest-standing ally in the anglophone Caribbean is Guyana. Relations began in late 1972 under the reign of People's National Congress (PNC) chief Forbes Burnham. To show Cuba's appreciation to Guyana, President Castro traveled to Georgetown in 1973 to meet Prime Minister Burnham. Between 1974 and 1975 Guyana joined ECLAC, SELA, CDCC, GLACSEC, and OLADE.[43] In the spring of 1975 Burnham was awarded Cuba's José Martí National Order Medal, established "for heads of state and government and leaders of political parties and movements who have distinguished themselves for their international solidarity with the struggle against imperialism, colonialism and neo-colonialism and for their friendship with the Socialist Revolution of Cuba."[44]

Guyana's importance to PCC policy was again evident in late 1975. Despite vehement protest from the Ford administration, Burnham let Cuban aircraft refuel in Guyana on their way to Angola. Relations cooled briefly in 1980 when Guyanese intellectual and PNC opponent Walter Rodney was murdered; the media in Havana implied involvement by Burnham's regime. Ties improved in 1981 when Washington stymied an Inter-American Development Bank loan to Guyana and Burnham looked to Cuba for aid.[45]

Both nations were active in NAM. It was Guyana's UN representative who, on October 26, 1983, introduced a Security Council resolution condemning the Grenada invasion. Although vetoed by Washington, the parliament in Georgetown passed a similar measure. High-level meetings in both capitals led to the signing of two bilateral accords in late 1984. One provided for a three-year suspension of visas for state officials. The second was a PCC-PNC accord, the highest level of political relations with Havana. Upon President Burnham's death on August 6, 1985, Cuba declared three days of official mourning.[46]

Two weeks later, Pres. Desmond Hoyte confirmed to a high-level PCC delegation sent to Georgetown the continuity of PNC policy and the alliance with Cuba. Bilateral cooperation in NAM continued with the signing of the Georgetown Appeal at the March 1987 Nonaligned Ministerial Meeting on Latin America and the Caribbean. During an official state visit in January 1989, Presidents Hoyte and Castro toured Cuba. The Guyanese leader was awarded the José Martí National Order Medal. As Cuban foreign minister Isidoro Malmierca noted in July 1990, "There is identity of views between Cuba and Guyana on key foreign policy issues and we vote alike 97 percent of the time at the UN."[47]

Cuba's ongoing civilian aid program began in late 1972 with the arrival of fifteen doctors in Georgetown. By 1988 the number had reached fifty-four. In 1990 the Cuban medical brigade totaled 120 professionals serving six regions of the country. They were the backbone of the public health system. The fifteenth annual civilian aid accord signed in 1990 comprised four major areas: science and technology; education and culture; economy and industry; and a trade protocol. Gratis aid to Guyana included science, technology, and industry cooperation; university and technical education; medical teaching; and joint work in international scientific and professional events. Science and technology aid encompassed agriculture; basic, light, and food industries; iron, steel, and machine industries; fishing; construction; and sugar.[48]

In 1976 trade involved rice, timber, and cement. Cuban cement and salt and Guyanese rice and timber exchanged in 1987 were valued at nearly $7 million. By the mid-1980s, foreign exchange crises in both capitals led to annual barter trade accords. The 1990 trade protocol involved no convertible currency payments. Under it Guyana exported rice and "other products," while Cuba provided table salt, medicines, and tobacco. An agreement for a three-year trade protocol aimed at "improving planning for both countries" was signed in 1990.[49]

Jamaica

Jamaica, the most populous CARICOM country, won its independence in 1962. In 1971 Cuba's regional diplomatic ties were limited to a consulate in Kingston. By Christmas 1972 Prime Minister Michael Manley, leader of the People's National Party (PNP), had established full diplomatic and economic relations with Havana. The islands became close allies and collaborated in regional multilateral bodies. In early 1975 Manley was awarded the José Martí National Order Medal. In July of that year he led a 160–person Jamaican delegation to Cuba. Havana backed Manley's launching of the International Bauxite Association, and Fidel Castro welcomed Manley's unequivocal support of Cuban troops in Angola.[50]

Aid to Jamaica was highly visible. In 1976 it ranked second, after Angola, in the number of Cuban *internacionalistas* posted there. That year Cuba-Jamaica collaboration encompassed agriculture, fisheries, public health, transport, tourism, trade, and technical training. It is estimated that by 1981 Cuban medical brigades had treated one million patients; and one thousand Jamaicans had received university and technical training in Cuba.[51]

Cuba suffered a major foreign-policy defeat on October 30, 1980, when Manley fell at the polls to Edward Seaga, leader of the Jamaica Labor Party. The next day the new prime minister asked Cuba to withdraw its ambassador. One year later Seaga severed all ties.[52] PCC foreign-policy makers saw Manley's defeat in these terms:

> [The] fundamental cause of the PNP defeat . . . was the government's inability to solve the then existing crisis, whose roots were to be found in a spent neocolonial dependency model for economic accumulation and in hostile attempts at destabilization on the part of the US government on which Jamaica is so economically dependent.[53]

Relations became especially hostile after Seaga dispatched 130 troops to Grenada, as witnessed by the November 1983 arrest and expulsion of a Kingston-based *Prensa Latina* correspondent. Michael Manley, then–vice president of the Socialist International, demanded that foreign troops leave Grenadian soil. Cuba's disdain for the Seaga regime was coupled with open alliances with the opposition People's National Party and the smaller, pro-Moscow Workers' Party of Jamaica.[54]

The PCC was pleased by Seaga's electoral dethronement in early 1989 and Manley's return to power. However, it noted that PNP "political and economic projections apparently resembled those of conservative candidate Edward Seaga." Havana was concerned with the implications of Manley's improved ties with the United States and the jettisoning of "the populist and progressive stands that characterized the PNP as a left-wing political force in the 1970s." *Granma* took solace in other aspects of the foreign-policy enunciated in Kingston—the focus on "integration of the English-speaking Caribbean, relations with Latin America and South-South cooperation." On July 27, 1990, diplomatic ties were reestablished at the embassy level.[55]

In February 1992 Prime Minister Manley said, "There is quite a widespread view that we would like to see some measure of integration of Cuba. We are a democracy and they are not, but we have always felt it was good to cooperate in ways that do not compromise our principles." Manley stepped down in March 1992. Initial indications are that the new prime minister, PNP leader Percival J. Patterson, will not dramatically alter relations with Havana.[56] Current aid and trade pale in comparison with that of the 1970s. Economic relations currently focus on tourism, Jamaica's largest legitimate foreign-exchange earner. (In 1989 Jamaica had recorded the fourth highest tourist arrivals in the region, and in autumn 1990 Kingston supported Cuba's bid to become a full member of the Caribbean Tourism Organization.)

Trinidad-Tobago

Nationhood for Trinidad-Tobago was achieved in 1962 under the leadership of the People's National Movement (PNM), founded by Dr. Eric Williams in 1956; Prime Minister Williams held that office for twenty years. Williams initiated ties with Havana in December 1972. During the 1970s Cuban relations with Trinidad-Tobago were warm but never reached the range and level of those with Guyana and Jamaica. In June 1975 Williams received an honorary degree in history during an official visit to Cuba.[57]

PNM leader George Chambers took the helm after Williams's death in 1981. As prime minister, Chambers opposed the Grenada invasion. By 1983, agriculture, cattle raising, and industrial development were the focuses of economic cooperation between the isles. High-level bilateral talks in November 1983 dealt with "consolidating commercial, economic and cultural ties." By 1986 the PNM monopoly on state power had ended at the hands of an opposition alliance led by Arthur N. R. Robinson.[58]

Prime Minister Robinson took office in December 1986 as the head of the National Alliance for Reconstruction (NAR). Expanding relations with Havana was not high on his agenda. Nevertheless, Cuba's foreign-policy establishment was encouraged by NAR foreign-policy pronouncements:

> [Robinson] stressed his commitment to the Movement of Nonaligned Countries, the defense of national sovereignty and working towards a New International Economic Order. . . . [He] will develop friendly relations with all countries in the context of so-called South-South cooperation. . . . Ties with CARICOM countries will be further strengthened.[59]

Trinidad-Tobago minister of culture Jennifer Johnson visited Cuba in June 1990 and spoke of the possibility of expanded relations. Six months later, in an apparent attempt to curry favor, Cuba withdrew its candidacy for reelection to the UN Economic and Social Council (ECOSOC) in favor of Trinidad-Tobago, although it had obtained more votes than that country in two rounds of balloting. Connecting up with Trinidad-Tobago's tourism industry would be a boon for Cuba, but of qualitatively greater importance are pending trade negotiations between the two OLADE members for Trinidadian petroleum.[60]

CUBA AND THE CARICOM STATES
AFTER THE FOURTH CONGRESS

With the survival of its socialist experiment at stake, the PCC outlined an economic strategy in late 1991 that emphasized (1) achieving national food self-sufficiency as soon as possible; (2) gaining hard currency earnings through a dramatic expansion in tourism, traditional exports, and the export of biotechnology products, medicines, and sugar derivatives; and (3) securing a sufficient and reliable energy supply while drastically reducing the consumption of imported oil.[61]

Within the context of these policies, what role will the English-speaking Caribbean countries play? Food self-sufficiency is jeopardized by insufficient production of wheat, beans, and animal feed. No CARICOM nation can currently export to Cuba significant amounts of these items. However, barter trade for Guyanese rice will undoubtedly continue, and Grenada's research in root crops could prove valuable.[62]

The success of the economic plan hinges on generating foreign exchange, particularly via tourism. It is in this area that ties to the Caribbean are key. In 1989 the anglophone Caribbean (excluding the U.S. Virgin Islands) accounted for 38 percent of Caribbean tourist arrivals, with 3.6 million visitors. Cuba's plan to increase tourist arrivals from 340,000 in 1990 to 1.5 million annually by 1995 will require linking up to this market. The Bahamas, Jamaica, Barbados, Grand Cayman Island, and Trinidad-Tobago will continue to be targets of Cuban tourism expansion efforts.[63] Trinidadian oil could help Cuba resolve its current energy crunch. Another potential long-term source of oil is Belize.

Except for tourism and perhaps petroleum, CARICOM states will not be at the center of Cuba's immediate efforts to ward off economic collapse. Beyond the analysis presented here, it remains to be seen how relations between the English-speaking Caribbean countries and Cuba will evolve.

NOTES

The epigraph that opens this chapter is quoted from *Granma Weekly Review*, November 3, 1991, p. 1.

1. Communist Party of Cuba, "Programmatic Platform of the Communist Party of Cuba" (Havana, 1976), p. 125; "3rd Congress of the Communist Party of Cuba. Resolution on International Policy," *Granma Weekly Review*, February 23, 1986, p. 2; "Resolution on Foreign Policy," in Gail Reed, ed., *Island in the Storm: The Cuban Communist Party's Fourth Congress* (Melbourne, Australia: Ocean Press, 1992), p. 148; Juan Valdés Paz, "Cuba's Foreign Policy Toward Latin America and the Caribbean in the 1980s," in Jorge I. Domínguez and Rafael Hernández, eds., *US-Cuban Relations in the 1990s* (Boulder: Westview Press, 1989), pp. 185–186.

2. "Foreign Ministry Gives Priority to Caribbean Integration," *Granma Weekly Review*, December 10, 1989, p. 11.

3. "Caribbean 1989: No Solution to the Crisis," *Granma Weekly Review*, January 7, 1990, p. 11.

4. "Facing the Challenge of Integration: First CARICOM Mission to Havana; Areas of Interest Analyzed," *Granma Weekly Review*, May 26, 1991, p. 3; *Granma Weekly Review*, November 11, 1990, p. 9; "Cuba Favors Integration," *Granma Weekly Review*, March 24, 1991, p. 10.

5. *Granma Weekly Review*, May 26, 1991, p. 3; "CARICOM Talks," *Cuba Update* 12, no. 4 (November 1991), p. 16; Susan Kaufman Purcell, "Collapsing Cuba," *Foreign Affairs* 71, no. 1 (1992), p. 136.

6. "The CARICOM Summit: What the Future Holds," *Granma Weekly Review*, July 28, 1991, p. 16.

7. Howard W. French, "Cuba Seeks Friends and Tourists in Caribbean," *New York Times*, March 11, 1992, p. A9.

8. "Without Cuba There Is No Caribbean," *Granma Weekly Review*, March 15, 1992, p. 12; *Cubainfo* 4, no. 6 (May 18, 1992), p. 4; *Cubainfo* 4, no. 3 (March 9, 1992), pp. 2–3; "New Steps Toward Regional Integration," *Granma Weekly Review*, June 7, 1992, p. 13.

9. "Caribbean Bankers Seek Broader Relations with Havana," *Granma Weekly Review*, October 27, 1991, p. 3; "Inter-bank Relations," *Granma Weekly Review*, October 13, 1991, p. 4.

10. Phil Gunson, Greg Chamberlain, and Andrew Thompson, eds., *Dictionary of Contemporary Politics of Central America and the Caribbean* (New York: Simon & Schuster, 1991), p. 63; Jane Franklin, *The Cuban Revolution and the United States: A Chronological History* (Melbourne, Australia: Ocean Press, 1992), p. 183.

11. *Granma Weekly Review*, October 28, 1984, p. 4; "Puerto Rico to Host Travel Congress," *Granma Weekly Review*, May 7, 1989, p. 3; Rickey Singh, "Why Keep Cuba on Hold?" *Sunday Express* (Trinidad-Tobago), April 9, 1989, p. 21; "In Brief," *Cubainfo* 4, no. 5 (April 20, 1992) p. 7; "New Steps Toward Regional Integration," p. 13.

12. Gunson et al., *Dictionary*, p. 131; Steven L. Reed, "Participation in Multinational Organizations and Programs in the Hemisphere," in Cole Blasier and Carmelo Mesa-Lago, eds., *Cuba in the World* (Pittsburgh: University of Pittsburgh Press, 1979), pp. 303–304.

13. Reed, "Participation," pp. 305, 306, 311; "US, EC and Japan Cause Drop in Sugar Prices," *Granma Weekly Review*, September 8, 1991, p. 15; "International Sugar Market," *Granma Weekly Review*, February 15, 1988, p. 5.

14. Gunson et al., *Dictionary*, p. 264; "Antigua: US Navy 'Tourists'," *Granma Weekly Review*, January 26, 1986, p. 11; John Walton Cotman, "Cuba and the Grenada Revolution: The Impact and Limits of Cuban International Aid Programs" (Ph.D. diss., Boston University, 1992), pp. 436–491.

15. Gunson et al., *Dictionary*, p. 194.

16. Gunson et al., *Dictionary*, p. 193; Jorge I. Domínguez, *To Make a World Safe for Revolution: Cuba's Foreign Policy* (Cambridge: Harvard University Press, 1989), p. 238; "Declaration of Caracas," *Granma Weekly Review*, December 22, 1985, p. 2.

17. "Declaration of Caracas," p. 2.

18. Gunson et al., *Dictionary*, pp. 30, 282; Reed, "Participation," pp. 303, 311; U.S. Central Intelligence Agency, Directorate of Intelligence, *Directory of Officials of the Republic of Cuba, A Reference Aid*, LDA87–12438 (Springfield: National Technical Information Service, June 1987), p. 156.

19. Domínguez, *To Make a World Safe*, pp. 232–233; Cotman, "Cuba and the Grenada Revolution," p. 489.

20. *Granma Weekly Review*, November 27, 1983, p. 3; "Foreign Minister of Bahamas Calls Cuba Talks Positive and Satisfactory," *Granma Weekly Review*, August 25, 1985, p. 3; Jane Franklin, "Recent Developments: A Chronology," *Cuba Update* 6, no. 3 (Fall 1985), p. 18.

21. "Minister of Tourism Visits," *Granma Weekly Review*, October 14, 1990, p. 8; Orosman Quintero and Gustavo Gutiérrez, "Cuba's Tourism Revival: No Country Is an Island," interview by Gail Reed (Havana), *Cuba Update* 13, no. 1–2 (March/April 1992), p. 28; French, "Cuba Seeks Friends," p. A9; "International Notes," *Cuba Update* 11, no. 4 (Fall 1990), p. 36.

22. Gunson et al., *Dictionary*, pp. 30, 33–34; R. E. Jones, "Cuba and the English-Speaking Caribbean," in Cole Blasier and Carmelo Mesa-Lago, eds., *Cuba in the World* (Pittsburgh: University of Pittsburgh Press, 1979), p. 131; *Directory of Officials of the Republic of Cuba*, p. 156.

23. Anthony P. Maingot, "Cuba and the Commonwealth Caribbean: Playing the Cuban Card," in Barry B. Levine, ed., *The New Cuban Presence in the Caribbean* (Boulder: Westview Press, 1983), p. 20; Jones, "Cuba & Caribbean," p. 135; Gunson et al., *Dictionary*, pp. 131, 193, 194; Reed, "Participation," pp. 303, 311.

24. Gunson et al., *Dictionary*, p. 2; Cotman, "Cuba and the Grenada Revolution," p. 446.

25. *Granma Weekly Review*, February 6, 1983, p. 4.

26. Gunson et al., *Dictionary*, p. 2; *Granma Weekly Review*, November 27, 1983, p. 11; *Granma Weekly Review*, November 13, 1983, p. 9; "Barbados Elections: New Period in the English-Speaking Caribbean?" *Granma Weekly Review*, June 15, 1986, p. 9; "Barbados: Errol Barrow Is Back," *Granma Weekly Review*, June 22, 1986, p. 11; "Barbados: Rejection of Conservative Politics," *Granma Weekly Review*, June 8, 1986, p. 9; *Granma Weekly Review*, January 26, 1986, p. 11.

27. *Granma Weekly Review*, June 8, 1986, p. 9; Gunson et al., *Dictionary*, pp. 33, 34, 318; "Hundreds of Latin American and Caribbean Figures Arrive in Havana, *Granma Weekly Review*, August 4, 1985, p. 1; *Granma Weekly Review*, June 15, 1986, p. 9.

28. *Granma Weekly Review*, June 22, 1986, p. 11; Gunson et al., *Dictionary*, p. 318.

29. "Diplomatic Roundup," *Granma Weekly Review*, May 14, 1989, p. 4; "Diplomatic Roundup," *Granma Weekly Review*, September 29, 1991, p. 3; Quintero et al., "Cuba's Tourism Revival," p. 28.

30. Gunson et al., *Dictionary*, pp. 36–37, 288; "Cuba and Belize Establish Consular and Commercial Relations," *Granma Weekly Review*, February 16, 1992, p. 9; "Belize, Racial Melting Pot of the Caribbean," *Granma Weekly Review*, April 20, 1986, p. 2; "Belize Has Reason to Be Worried," *Granma Weekly Review*, February 13, 1983, p. 6.

31. Gunson et al., *Dictionary*, pp. 63, 135.

32. *Cubainfo* 4, no. 2 (February 18, 1992), p. 6; *Granma Weekly Review*, February 16, 1992, p. 9; "Cuban Doctors Are Praised Abroad," *Granma Weekly Review*, February 23, 1992, p. 12; Gunson et al., *Dictionary*, p. 36; *Granma Weekly Review*, February 13, 1983, p. 6.

33. *Feb. 1974–Mar. 1979*: Prime Minister Gairy, Grenada United Labor Party; *Mar. 1979–Oct. 1983*: Prime Minister Bishop, New JEWEL Movement; *Oct. 1983*: Gen. Austin/ B. Coard, Revolutionary Military Council; *Oct. 1983*: U.S. Amb. Gillespie/ Grenada Governor-General Scoon (during US/OECS occupation); *Dec. 1983–Dec. 1984*: N. Brathwaite, Interim Advisory Council; *Dec. 1984–Mar. 1990*: Prime Minister Blaize, New National Party; *Mar. 1990*: Prime Minister Brathwaite, National Democratic Congress. For an analysis of Cuba-Grenada relations before 1984 see Cotman, "Cuba and the Grenada Revolution."

34. Franklin, *The Cuban Revolution*, p. 183; "Arms Found in Cuban Embassy," *Newsline, A Publication of the Government Information Service Grenada*, April 21, 1984, p. 6; Governor-General Sir Paul Scoon, interview by author, April 20, 1989, St. George's, Grenada; Nicholas Brathwaite, interview by author, April 4, 1989, St. George's, Grenada.

35. Brathwaite interview; U.S. Department of State and Department of Defense, *Grenada: A Preliminary Report* (Washington, D.C.: USGPO, December 1983), p. 1; "Headed for Détente," *Granma Weekly Review*, August 4, 1991, p. 2; Osvaldo O. Cárdenas, "Grenada: 'Made in USA' Democracy in Crisis," *Granma Weekly Review*, November 12, 1989, p. 11.

36. "34 Students Return Home," *Newsline*, March 1–15, 1984, p. 2; Brathwaite interview; Solicitor General Denis Lambert, telephone interview by author, April 17, 1989, St. George's, Grenada; Grenada Supreme Court, *Supreme Court of Grenada (High Court of Justice), 1984 No. 271, Between the Government of the Republic of Cuba, Plaintiff and the Attorney General for Grenada, Defendant*, Writ of Summons, August 20, 1984; Grenada Supreme Court, *Supreme Court of Grenada (High Court of Justice), 1984 No. 271, Between the Government of the Republic of Cuba, Plaintiff and the Attorney General for Grenada, Defendant*.

37. Gunson et al., *Dictionary*, p. 63; "Fast Inauguration in Grenada for United States Candidate Herbert Blaize," *Granma Weekly Review*, December 16, 1984, p. 7; Prime Minister Blaize, interview by author, April 19, 1989, St. George's, Grenada; Lt. Col. Glenn Mignon, National Security Advisor to Herbert Blaize, interview by author, November 22, 1988, St. George's, Grenada; Albert O. Xavier, ambassador to the United States, interview by author, December 1, 1988, St. George's, Grenada.

38. Singh, "Why Keep Cuba on Hold?" p. 21; Maurice Bishop Patriotic Movement, *Eternal Flame for Liberation: To Die for One's Country Is to Live Forever* (San Fernando, Trinidad: Vanguard Publishing, 1986), p. 47; Leslie Pierre, "Personally Speaking: A Plea for Dr. Terry," *Grenadian Voice*, April 8, 1989, p. 4; Grenada, "S. R. & O. No. 6 of 1989: The Importation of Publications (Prohibition) Order, 1989," *Grenada Government Gazette (Extraordinary)* 107, no. 16 (April 14, 1989); Carol W. J. Bristol, attorney, telephone interviews, June 2, 1989, and April 29, 1992, St. George's, Grenada; *Granma Weekly Review*, December 10, 1989, p. 11. Note: Also banned were books by Malcolm X (whose mother was Grenadian) and Maurice Bishop's former press secretary Don Rojas.

39. Osvaldo O. Cárdenas, "Grenada: The Crisis of an Artificial Government," *Granma Weekly Review*, December 7, 1986, p. 2; "Students Off to Cuba," *Indies Times* (St. George's, Grenada), September 29, 1984, p. 2; Einstein Louison, MBPM, interviews by author, March 21, July 19, and August 24, 1989, St. George's, Grenada; Terence Marryshow, M.D., MBPM, interview by author,

March 21, 1989, St. George's, Grenada, and conversation with author, April 23, 1990.
40. Gunson et al., *Dictionary*, p. 153; Brathwaite interview.
41. Purcell, "Collapsing Cuba," p. 136; "CARICOM Talks," p. 16; *Granma Weekly Review*, August 4, 1991, p. 2; Bristol interviews; *Cubainfo* 4, no. 5 (April 20, 1992), p. 7; *Cubainfo* 4, no. 6 (May 18, 1992), p. 4.
42. Gunson et al., *Dictionary*, p. 153; Dr. Kenneth Buckmire, interview by author, March 17, 1989, CARDI, St. David's, Grenada; Carmen Diana Deere, "Cuba's Struggle for Self-Sufficiency," *Monthly Review* 43, no. 3 (July-August, 1991), p. 65; Communist Party of Cuba, "Resolution on the Country's Economic Development," in Gail Reed, ed., *Island in the Storm: The Cuban Communist Party's Fourth Congress* (Melbourne, Australia: Ocean Press, 1992), p. 133.
43. Clive Y. Thomas, "State Capitalism in Guyana: An Assessment of Burnham's Co-operative Socialist Republic," in Fitzroy Ambursley and Robin Cohen, eds., *Crisis in the Caribbean* (New York: Monthly Review Press, 1983), pp. 27–28; *Directory of Officials* (June 1987), p. 162; Jones, "Cuba and Caribbean," p. 131; Reed, "Participation," pp. 300, 303, 305, 311; Gunson et al., *Dictionary*, pp. 131, 193, 194.
44. Jones, "Cuba and Caribbean," p. 136.
45. Anthony Payne, Paul Sutton, and Tony Thorndike, *Grenada: Revolution and Invasion* (New York: St. Martin's Press, 1984), p. 75; Domínguez, *To Make the World Safe*, pp. 181, 237.
46. *Granma Weekly Review*, March 20, 1983, p. 2; *Granma Weekly Review*, November 6, 1983, p. 5; *Granma Weekly Review*, November 13, 1983, p. 10; *Granma Weekly Review*, November 18, 1984, p. 5; Franklin, *The Cuban Revolution*, p. 192; Franklin, "Recent Developments (Fall 1985)," p. 17; Thomas, "State Capitalism," pp. 41–42. Note: With the 1980 Constitution, Burnham became executive president of Guyana.
47. Franklin, "Recent Developments (Fall 1985)," p. 18; "President of Guyana Meets with Cuban Communist Party Delegation," *Granma Weekly Review*, September 1, 1985, p. 1; "Non-Aligned Countries to Consider Situation in Latin America," *Granma Weekly Review*, March 15, 1987, p. 1; "Georgetown Appeal by Non-Aligned Countries," *Granma Weekly Review*, March 29, 1987, p. 3; "Hoyte Stresses Cuban Solidarity with Africa," *Granma Weekly Review*, February 5, 1989, p. 1; "Malmierca Considers His Latin American Trip as an Expression of the Growth in Many-sided Relations and Greater Friendship and Cooperation," *Granma Weekly Review*, July 15, 1990, p. 11.
48. "Cooperation Without Dependency," *Granma Weekly Review*, November 13, 1988, p. 12; "Medical Cooperation with Guyana," *Granma Weekly Review*, November 4, 1990, p. 3; "Continuity and Development in Cuba-Guyana Cooperation," *Granma Weekly Review*, May 13, 1990, p. 5.
49. Payne et al., *Revolution and Invasion*, p. 75; "Growing Cuban Trade and Cooperation with Latin American Countries," *Granma Weekly Review*, March 12, 1989, p. 3; Julio Carranza Valdés, "The Current Situation in Cuba and the Process of Change," *Latin American Perspectives* 18, no. 2 (Spring 1991), p. 11; "Guyana Confirms Its Non-Aligned Status and Emphasizes Need for Greater South-South Cooperation," October 15, 1989, p. 9; *Granma Weekly Review*, May 13, 1990, p. 5.
50. Gunson et al., *Dictionary*, p. 181, 193, 194; Raymond W. Duncan, "Caribbean Leftism," *Problems of Communism* (Washington) (May–June 1978), p. 43; Jones, "Cuba and Caribbean," pp. 75–76, 131, 136; Reed, "Participation," pp. 303, 307, 311; Franklin, *Cuban Foreign Relations, A Chronology* (New York: Center for Cuban Studies, 1984), p. 23.

51. Jones, "Cuba and Caribbean," pp. 75–76; Franklin, *Cuban Foreign Relations*, p. 23; Domínguez, *To Make the World Safe*, p. 232.

52. Franklin, *The Cuban Revolution*, p. 153; Gunson et al., *Dictionary*, p. 323; *Directory of Officials of the Republic of Cuba* (1987), p. 64; *Granma Weekly Review*, "Jamaica, Wishful Thinking," December 23, 1984, p. 11.

53. Osvaldo O. Cárdenas, "Jamaica: Another U. S. Policy Bites the Dust?" *Granma Weekly Review*, August 17, 1986, p. 11.

54. *Granma Weekly Review*, November 6, 1983, p. 9; "Seaga, the Invader's Puppet," *Granma Weekly Review*, November 27, 1983, p. 10; *Granma Weekly Review*, November 13, 1983, pp. 9, 10; *Granma Weekly Review*, December 2, 1984, p. 3; *Granma Weekly Review*, November 25, 1984, p. 5.

55. "Jamaica: Manley's Victory Marks Failure of Reaganomics Model," *Granma Weekly Review*, February 19, 1989, pp. 1, 9; "Jamaica: The Opposition Puts on a New Face," *Granma Weekly Review*, January 27, 1991, p. 10; "Jamaica: New Foreign Minister Talks About Government Priorities," *Granma Weekly Review*, April 16, 1989, p. 11; "Jamaica and Cuba Reestablish Diplomatic Relations," *Granma Weekly Review*, August 5, 1990, p. 1; Franklin, *The Cuban Revolution*, p. 250.

56. French, "Cuba Seeks Friends," p. A9; "Tourism Cooperation," *Granma Weekly Review*, January 19, 1992, p. 12; "Cuban-Jamaican Relations," *Granma Weekly Review*, September 22, 1991, p. 2; "Cuba-Jamaica Tourism," *Granma Weekly Review*, February 17, 1991, p. 4; *Cubainfo* 4, no. 1 (January 27, 1992), p. 6; Quintero et al., "Cuba's Tourism Revival," p. 28; "International Notes," *Cuba Update* 11, no. 4 (Fall 1990), p. 36; "Jamaica Committed to Caribbean Integration," *Granma Weekly Review*, April 19, 1992, p. 14; "Patterson Sworn in as Prime Minister of Jamaica," *Granma Weekly Review*, April 12, 1992, p. 14.

57. Gunson et al., *Dictionary*, pp. 277–278, 341–342; Jones, "Cuba and Caribbean," pp. 135–136.

58. *Granma Weekly Review*, November 20, 1983, p. 6; "Trinidadian Acting Prime Minister Says His Country Acts in a Sovereign and Independent Manner and Is Pleased with Commercial and Economic Ties with Cuba," *Granma Weekly Review*, December 4, 1983, p. 3.

59. "Trinidad and Tobago: Robinson Celebrates His 60th Birthday as Prime Minister," *Granma Weekly Review*, January 11, 1987, p. 14.

60. "Trinidad and Tobago Minister Says Cuban Image Distorted Abroad," *Granma Weekly Review*, June 17, 1990, p. 9; "Bowing Out to Trinidad and Tobago," *Granma Weekly Review*, December 9, 1990, p. 3; Quintero et al., "Cuba's Tourism Revival," p. 28; Gunson et al., *Dictionary*, p. 194; "In Brief," *Cubainfo* 4, no. 4 (March 30, 1992), p. 4.

61. "Resolution on the Country's Economic Development," pp. 133–136; Purcell, "Collapsing Cuba," pp. 135–136.

62. Deere, "Cuba's Struggle for Self-Sufficiency," pp. 62–63.

63. Ibid., p. 66; Quintero et al., "Cuba's Tourism Revival," pp. 25, 28; French, "Cuba Seeks Friends," p. A9.

10

Central America on the Cuban Foreign-Policy Agenda: Where Does It Stand?

H. MICHAEL ERISMAN

Revolutionary Cuba and the Central American nations of Costa Rica, El Salvador, Guatemala, Honduras, and Nicaragua have long shared more than a mere geographic identity in their proximity to the Caribbean Sea. Rather, their histories and destinies have often been intimately intertwined. For example, the sociopolitical upheavals that convulsed Guatemala in the late 1940s and especially the early 1950s had a profound effect (at both the emotional and philosophical levels) on many of the young radicals who would later lead Cuba to the revolutionary forefront in the Caribbean. Che Guevara's sojourn there, where he experienced firsthand the rise and ultimate U.S.-orchestrated demise of the Jacobo Arbenz government, is perhaps the best-known illustration of this phenomenon. During the 1960s, Havana's relations with the region would be highly confrontational, with the Guatemalan and Nicaraguan governments becoming deeply involved in providing logistical support for the Bay of Pigs invasion, while Havana enthusiastically supported the armed struggles of various Central American pro-Castro guerrilla movements. In the 1980s, of course, Sandinista Nicaragua became one of the foremost recipients of Cuban military and developmental aid. Given the impact on Cuba of the recent changes in the international economic and political order, it has yet to be determined whether Central America will continue to occupy a prominent position on Havana's foreign-policy agenda. The basic thesis of this analysis, however, is that it will become a lower priority than in the past.

CUBA AND CENTRAL AMERICA: AN OVERVIEW

Cuba in most instances displays greater resources and higher levels of socioeconomic development than its Central American neighbors. It is, for example, clearly the leading country in terms of demographics and overall economic productivity; its only serious challenge in these areas is from Guatemala's population statistics (see Figures 10.1 and 10.2). Regarding more sophisticated measures of progress toward modernization, Cuba and Costa Rica emerge as the trendsetters. Both score well with regard to per capita GNP (see Figure 10.3) and are comparable with the most developed nations in such areas as the provision of health and educational services to their citizens (see Figures 10.4 and 10.5). Indeed, Cuba and Costa Rica have often been pinpointed as the two best Caribbean Basin examples for other LDCs (less-developed countries) of the Western liberal democratic and radical Marxist models of modernization.

The wide gap that separates Costa Rica and Cuba from the other Central American countries can be illustrated by their relative positions on the Human Development Index (HDI—an index created by the United Nations to compare socioeconomic progress on a global scale). The index uses three basic variables to produce a country's HDI score: life expectancy, adult literacy rate, and per capita GNP. All nations of the world (total = 130) are then ranked from the lowest quality of life to the highest, with the HDI rank minus the GNP rank providing a rough indication of how well a nation translates its wealth into developmental benefits for its citizens. Table 10.1 lists the Cuban and Central American results with those of other selected countries. Obviously, Costa Rica and Cuba fare quite well when measuring their HDI indexes not only against the other Central American countries but against the hemispheric community in general (Haiti being the lowest-ranked Latin American nation and Argentina the highest, HDI rank minus per capita GNP rank). Particularly impressive are their scores measuring the conversion of resources into benefits (which places them among the top ten countries in the world).

Table 10.1   Human Development Index

Rank	Country	HDI	GNP per Capita Rank, 1987	HDI Rank minus per Capita GNP Rank
29	Haiti	.356	34	-5
51	Honduras	.563	53	-2
55	Guatemala	.592	63	-8
59	El Salvador	.651	56	+3
71	Nicaragua	.743	54	+17
92	Cuba	.877	66	+26
99	Argentina	.910	89	+10
103	Costa Rica	.916	77	+26
112	United States	.961	129	-17
126	Canada	.983	124	+2
130	Japan	.996	126	+4

Source: Provided by Jon Harder and distributed via electronic mail by the "Technology Transfer in International Development" discussion list (DEVEL-L@AUVM.BITNET), October 1, 1991.

Figure 10.1   Cuban/Central American Population, 1991 (in thousands)

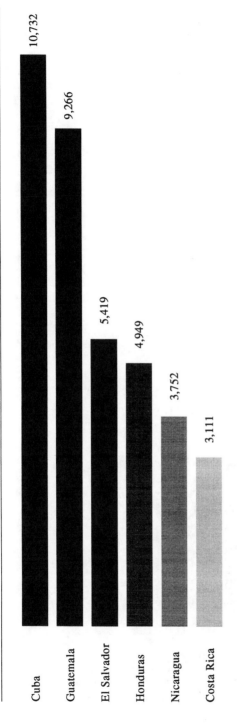

Source: Copyright © 1992 PC Globe, Inc. Tempe, Arizona. All rights reserved worldwide.

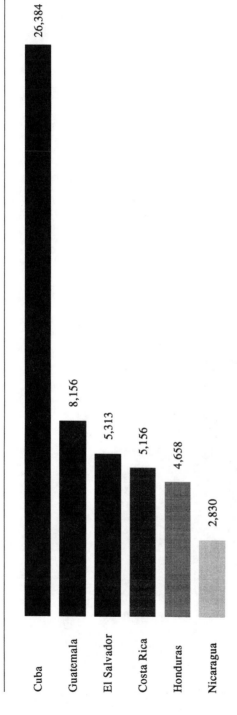

Figure 10.2   Cuban/Central American GNP, 1991 (in millions of U.S. $)

Figure 10.3   Cuban/Central American GNP per Capita (in U.S. $)

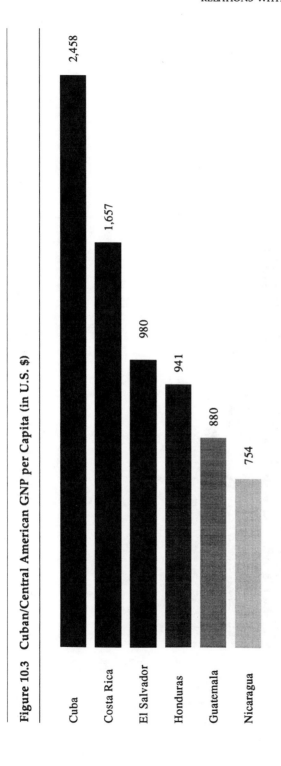

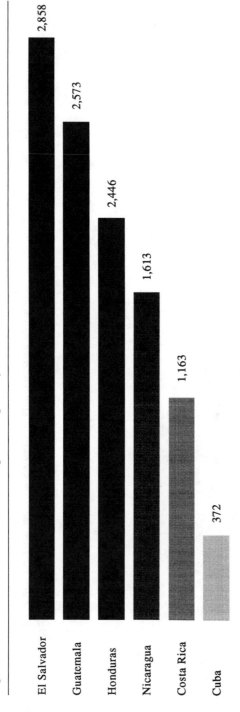

Figure 10.4   Cuban/Central American Population per Physician

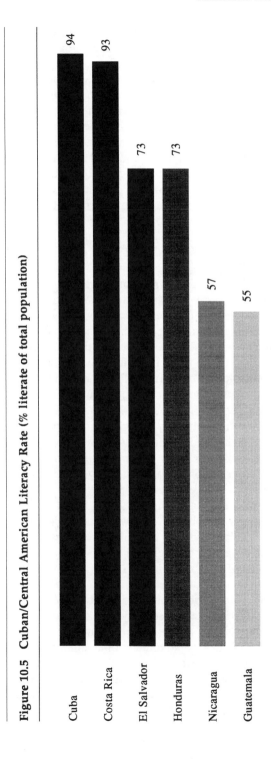

Figure 10.5   Cuban/Central American Literacy Rate (% literate of total population)

Cuba   94
Costa Rica   93
El Salvador   73
Honduras   73
Nicaragua   57
Guatemala   55

When the parameters of this performance equation are enlarged even further to include the resources and attention devoted to external activism, Cuba clearly stands out as the vanguard state. The Central American countries have for the most part behaved rather conventionally. In other words, like most small LDCs, they have tended to limit their major foreign-policy initiatives to their immediate region (e.g., Costa Rica's efforts under Pres. Oscar Arias Sánchez to promote the Contadora peace process) and otherwise have usually assumed a reactive stance to international developments. Revolutionary Cuba, on the other hand, quickly assumed an unusual role on the world stage by displaying not only an affinity for operating proactively on a global scale but also an ability to do so quite effectively. This audacity led Jorge Domínguez to his now-famous conclusion that "Cuba is a small country, but it has a big country's foreign policy"[1] and provided the raw material for an increasing number of studies (including this book) in which globalism on Havana's part is a key motif.[2]

Central America has traditionally been a top priority on the island's ambitious international agenda, with ideological considerations and security concerns being the two most important and often interrelated factors influencing its approach to the region. The ideological dimension of Cuban policy has been embodied in the mutually reinforcing concepts of proletarian internationalism and anti-imperialism. These two themes surfaced early in the Revolution and continue to be important in shaping the Fidelistas' perspective on their role in world affairs. Proletarian internationalism refers essentially to the contention that Marxists have an obligation to help their ideological brethren in other countries to seize power and to consolidate their revolutions. Such solidarity likewise implies, at least as far as the Cubans are concerned, a concomitant commitment to resist so-called Yankee imperialism—Washington's hegemonic pretensions are seen as one of the main obstacles not only to revolutionary change but also to the aspirations of countries to pursue policies of political and economic independence. Given Central America's long history of social upheaval and its location within the larger Caribbean Basin, which the United States has always considered its special sphere of influence, it was hardly surprising that the region soon became a battleground where Havana's sense of revolutionary mission clashed with Washington's eagerness to maintain a Pax Americana.

Although Cuba's decision to embrace proletarian internationalism is often explained in purely ideological terms, security considerations rooted in the island's evolving relations with the superpowers cannot be ignored. Havana's ties with the United States began to deteriorate almost immediately following Castro's triumph. Determined to rid the international and especially the Latin American scene of the Fidelista virus, Washington was increasingly able to isolate the Revolution by persuading (and sometimes browbeating) most of the countries of the Western Hemisphere and many others elsewhere to sever practically all of their ties with the island. Such Yankee hostility as well as other factors (e.g., philosophical affinity) spurred Havana to begin to establish its Kremlin connection in the early 1960s. Yet Castro had serious doubts (which the 1962 Cuban missile crisis served to verify) about Moscow's willingness to put its military power on the line to help defend the island against a U.S. assault. Compounding these misgivings were the serious ideological disputes that strained the Cuban-Soviet relationship throughout much of the 1960s.[3] Within this context, Havana's commitment to proletarian internationalism could be seen in part as having a significant security dimension, the basic idea being to force the United States to spread its counterrevolutionary efforts over as wide a front as possible and thereby promote a situation where Washington could not devote its attention solely to Cuba. The best-case scenario, of course, would entail Havana gaining new allies and new foreign-policy options as its compatriots succeeded in their attempts to seize power.

As with other Marxist (and indeed some non-Marxist) countries, the Revolution's foreign relations have always operated at two basic levels: (1) conventional state-to-state dealings and (2) party-to-party contacts (although the latter category is somewhat imprecise because the convergence of the party and the government within the Cuban political system can perhaps be more accurately characterized as a state-to-party link). Given this dualism, the island's attitude toward any particular country could be rather ambivalent—At the formal state level Havana could be maintaining correct and even cordial ties with an established regime while simultaneously supporting the efforts of indigenous rebels to overthrow it. In contrast to many other areas of the world where Havana has usually placed primary emphasis on improving its position at the state level, in Central America the tendency for many years was to concentrate on championing the fortunes of various revolutionary movements (one obvious reason being that the prospects for normal relations with the Central American governments were practically nil given their willingness to follow Washington's anti-Cuban impulses).[4] The focal points of such internationalism have been, as might be expected, the highly volatile situations in Guatemala, Nicaragua, and El Salvador. Honduras and Costa Rica have received little serious attention because of their lack of viable insurgent groups, although Havana has occasionally expressed moral support for the concept of armed struggle on the part of Honduran radicals.

What might be called the first wave of Cuban party-to-party internationalism in Central America occurred in the 1960s. At this time (1962–1968), Havana was deeply involved in promoting rebellion throughout the Western Hemisphere. The call to arms was sounded by Castro in his famous "Second Declaration of Havana," in which he eloquently pleaded the case for armed struggle. "The duty of every revolutionary," he proclaimed, is to make the revolution. It is known that the revolution will triumph in America and throughout the world, but it is not for revolutionaries to sit in the doorways of their houses waiting for the corpse of imperialism to pass by . . . [F]rom one end of the continent to another they [the common people] are signaling with clarity that the hour has come—the hour of their redemption. Now the anonymous mass . . . is beginning to enter conclusively into its own history, is beginning to write it with its own blood, is beginning to suffer and die for it.[5]

And, as Castro made clear, Havana intended to plunge into the thick of the fray. At a November 1964 conference of established Latin American Communist parties hosted by Cuba, the Guatemalan and Honduran contingents reaffirmed their commitment to armed struggle and therefore were officially designated the Central American organizations that most deserved solidarity. Subsequently, Havana carried through on its commitment to the Guatemalans (but not, apparently, to the Hondurans) by providing money, training, and other forms of assistance to the country's Revolutionary Movement of November 13 (MR-13).[6] In addition to such support for some of the region's more radical Communist parties, Havana likewise extended aid to various pro-Fidelista groups that were not associated with the established international Marxist networks traditionally having close ties to Moscow. Included in this category were the Guatemalan Revolutionary Armed Forces (FAR) commanded by Luís Augusto Turcios Lima and some of the individuals who would later emerge as the leaders of Nicaragua's Sandinista Front for National Liberation (FSLN).

Cuba's enthusiasm for party-to-party internationalism in Central America waned in the late 1960s and early 1970s. The major reasons for this turn of events were increased pessimism on Havana's part about the prospects for successful guerrilla warfare in Latin America as insurgents suffered one defeat after another, the most traumatic blow being the 1967 capture and murder of the legendary Che Guevara in Bolivia; the need for the Cuban leadership to devote more attention to questions of domestic development, especially after the economic dislocations caused by the unsuccessful 10-million-ton sugar campaign of 1970; Havana's efforts to strengthen its relations with the Soviet Union, which was not enthralled with the idea of promoting violent revolutionary upheaval in the Western Hemisphere; and increasing emphasis by Cuba on developing a more vigorous South-South dimension to its foreign policy by either normalizing or improving its state-to-state relations with as many Third World countries as possible. This retooling of the island's policy did indeed produce some diplomatic dividends in Central America. For example, in 1975 Honduras and El Salvador expressed their support for efforts that were under way (and which were ultimately successful) to lift the political and economic sanctions that the Organization of American States (OAS) had imposed on

Cuba in 1964. In a similar vein, Costa Rica reestablished full diplomatic relations with Havana in February 1977.

The second major wave of Cuban internationalism in Central America began in the late 1970s as the region—especially Guatemala, Nicaragua, and El Salvador—was once again racked by social upheaval. During this phase, however, Havana's party-to-party strategy shifted somewhat. In contrast to the 1960s when the Fidelistas tended to focus on extending material aid only to those radicals who shared their enthusiasm for the Guevara/Debray *foco* theory of guerrilla warfare,[7] the emphasis now shifted to functioning as a political broker whose top priority was to unify a country's various revolutionary factions into a comprehensive, flexible, popular-front organization. By adopting this more ecumenical, pragmatic stance, Cuba positioned itself to attack the problem of extreme fragmentation that had long plagued the Latin American left (and to which, it must be said, Havana's ideological puritanism during the 1960s had contributed). Speaking a babble of political tongues (e.g., Maoism, orthodox pro-Moscow Marxism, Trotskyism, anarchism, Fidelismo), these groups often spent more time and energy quarreling among themselves than mounting effective offensives. Consequently, they were extremely vulnerable to divide-and-conquer tactics (which were used with devastating results in the 1960s). With Cuban assistance, however, this weakness began to be rectified. For instance, in 1977 and early 1978, Armando Ulises Estrada, one of Havana's top Central American specialists, played a pivotal role in consolidating the three major wings of Nicaragua's Sandinista movement. Cuba also hosted a December 1979 meeting at which three of El Salvador's main guerrilla bands formed the Farabundo Martí Front for National Liberation (FMLN). A fourth organization, the Popular Revolutionary Army (ERP) joined the coalition in late May 1980 after more discussions in Havana. Finally, under Castro's prodding, four Guatemalan groups gathered in Managua in November 1980 and negotiated an arrangement establishing the National Revolutionary Union (with a central directorate called the General Revolutionary Command).[8] This new approach, noted Antonio Jorge, stressed the need to support

> . . . latitudinarian national liberation movements and [did] not insist on the ideological orthodoxy or purity of those collaborating in the political-military fronts engineered under Cuba's auspices. These vanguard movements receive[d] widespread cooperation and [were] carefully helped along in their revolutionary mission, in contrast to the simplistic *foco* approach to revolutionary struggle of the early and middle 1960s. [This] cohesive and more sophisticated Cuban model include[d] propaganda, technical assistance, training courses, ideological formulation, and logistical support, as well as other components, coalescing into a well-integrated aid package.[9]

These Cuban-brokered agreements, the main concern of which was to establish mechanisms for coordinating the political and military activities of radical leftists, generally succeeded in making the Central American revolutionaries much more formidable, as evidenced by the Sandinistas' victory in 1979 and the Salvadoran FMLN's ability to fight the government to a standstill throughout the 1980s, which ultimately led to a negotiated settlement of the conflict in early 1992.[10]

By the mid-1980s, Havana's approach to Central American affairs was once again revolving primarily around state-level relations. The principle of proletarian internationalism remained, of course, a key element in the Cuban-Nicaraguan connection, but it now operated in a government-to-government mode because the Sandinista Revolution was at this point well into its consolidation-of-power phase. To assist the Ortega government in this endeavor, Havana launched significant military and especially socioeconomic aid programs. It has been estimated that at the zenith of these efforts there were approximately fifty-three hundred Cubans involved in developmental projects (1984) and twenty-five hundred to thirty-five hundred serving as security advisers (early 1986).[11] A more mixed picture emerges with regard to El Salvador. It would appear that Havana extended significant (but not massive) material support to the FMLN guerrillas in the early 1980s[12] but subsequently embraced an essentially political, state-centric perspective centered on the Contadora peace process that most Latin American governments were advocating. This shift to a normalization strategy in Central America was consistent with the overall configuration of the island's international agenda as it entered the 1990s.

CUBA, CENTRAL AMERICA, AND THE NEW INTERNATIONAL ORDER

The relative tranquility that Havana enjoyed on its Soviet–Eastern European front for approximately two decades was shattered in the late 1980s and early 1990s as upheaval swept through the socialist camp. Communist governments with whom the Fidelistas had cultivated a complex web of beneficial relations were driven from power throughout most of Eastern Europe and replaced by regimes that displayed little sympathy for the Revolution and even less interest in helping it. The Council for Mutual Economic Assistance (CMEA, also known as COMECON), the Soviet bloc's rough counterpart of the European Economic Community, had been a lucrative source of developmental aid for the Cubans as well as providing them with privileged access to Eastern European markets. The CMEA gradually unraveled and finally was disbanded in June 1991. Standing at the epicenter of this turmoil is the former Soviet Union, which has undergone a process of partial disintegration and serious political and economic crisis. The shock waves of these convulsions have, of course, rippled through the larger global community and radically transformed the international order. Although all countries will have to adjust to this new reality, Cuba is a somewhat special case because of its traditionally close and in some respects unique links with the old Soviet bloc. As those relations have fallen further and further into disarray, Havana has been forced into a major reevaluation of its international priorities.

One outcome of this process has been an increasing proclivity on Havana's part to conceptualize its security requirements in economic as well as ideological and military terms. For many years, the island's basic developmental needs were essentially guaranteed via its special CMEA ties, involving preferential trade agreements and access to substantial amounts of assistance. One novel (and highly lucrative) aid program allowed Cuba to buy large amounts of Soviet oil on highly favorable terms (i.e., low prices with payment in rubles) and then, after its domestic demands had been met, sell on the open market whatever was left. This arrangement generated large amounts of hard currency that Havana then used to underwrite its purchase of Western goods and services (especially from the European Community and even from subsidiaries of U.S. corporations operating in third countries).

Such collaboration generated a ripple effect. In particular, it served to lessen Havana's vulnerability to the economic warfare that Washington was waging against the Revolution, while simultaneously enhancing the Fidelistas' capabilities to pursue an extremely audacious foreign policy. The 1970s were an especially active period for such globalism—Cuba made a generally successful bid to establish its credentials as a leader among Third World nations, was heavily involved in winning two wars in Africa (Angola and Ethiopia), and launched ambitious military and developmental aid programs.

This equation has, of course, changed radically as the Socialist bloc and the benefits that the island reaped from its existence have disappeared. No longer is Havana able to operate as it once did on the international scene, implementing a complex strategy of capitalizing upon its Soviet–Eastern European ties to help stabilize its economy and thereby putting itself in a better position to play a vigorous proactive role in world affairs. Indeed, as opposed to functioning as a major influence-wielder on the international scene, it must now concentrate on minimizing its potential vulnerability to hostile external forces (particularly those centered in Washington and Miami).

Few observers believe that Cuba faces a serious risk of military attack. Its armed forces remain among the most formidable in the Western Hemisphere, despite drastic reductions in Russian security assistance; they are relatively well equipped, extremely well trained, and in many cases battle hardened from their long involvement in the Angolan conflict. Moreover, for cases of invasion, the government has developed a comprehensive plan for protracted guerrilla warfare that includes the construction of an elaborate Vietnamese-style tunnel system throughout the country.[13]

The economic situation is, however, much more problematic. Havana was confronting significant difficulties here even before the Socialist bloc disintegrated—worker productivity was declining, export earnings were down, hard currency reserves were dwindling, the debts owed to Western creditors were becoming increasingly unmanageable, and unemployment was rearing its ugly head. In short, the country was in the grips of a recession that was then escalated to unprecedented crisis proportions by developments in Eastern Europe. The Fidelistas' enemies in Washington and elsewhere hope that these burdens, combined with increased external pressure, will bring about the Revolution's destruction. Within this context, foreign-policy concerns such as the implementation of internationalist principles and the quest for normalized state relations are apt to be viewed primarily in terms of their economic costs and benefits, with such calculations tending to be decisive in determining where Central America will stand on Havana's international agenda in the foreseeable future.

Proletarian internationalism, especially as it has been practiced in Central America, would seem to have little to offer Cuba with respect to immediate or even intermediate economic gains. On the other hand, the potential costs and especially the risks may be considerable. Generally, the support extended during the armed struggle phase of the process is not particularly burdensome; normally it has involved training, strategic advice, and perhaps some low-level logistical aid (including in some cases small arms and similar military equipment). The ante can, however, increase markedly if the insurgents triumph and Cuban internationalism assumes the form of assistance to consolidate their revolution. In Nicaragua, for example, Havana mounted a major campaign on behalf of the Sandinista government that represented a significant commitment of material and especially human resources. While there may very well be political and ideological assets associated with such ventures, there are also offsetting economic liabilities that must be taken into account. Commenting on this latter point, Serio Roca has noted that

> the [overseas] deployment of thousands of qualified technical personnel . . . has represented a heavy drain on the Cuban economy. Often because trained personnel were assigned to internationalist duties, domestic economic sectors suffered output losses and faced bottlenecks, and policy initiatives experienced delays in implementation.[14]

In short, Roca contends that domestic productivity and development, including activities with the potential to generate critical hard currency or to lessen Havana's need for it, may very well be adversely affected by diverting some of the island's most skilled people into these projects. Beyond such tangible costs, there is also the risk that established governments in the hemisphere or elsewhere might display their displeasure with Cuban internationalism by refusing to establish or maintain normal relations, thereby adversely impacting Havana's opportunities to expand its foreign-trade networks. Seen from this perspective, then, there is little to suggest that Cuba reaps any material rewards (in either the short run or the long run) from the pursuit of proletarian internationalism in Central America. There may even be grounds for concluding that there is red ink on the bottom line.

The above analysis leads to statecentric normalization as the theme most likely to be dominant in Havana's approach to its Central American relations. Here once again there may be some strategic and/or political benefits to be gained. It can, for instance, be assumed that as Cuba's acceptance and incorporation into the hemispheric community gains momentum, the probability (1) decreases that Washington would be tempted to launch military moves against the island and (2) increases that such South-South linkages will translate into multilateral bargaining power that Havana will find quite useful as it attempts to negotiate the terms of its new relationships with the more industrialized countries of the world.[15] The balance sheet becomes less optimistic, however, when one probes the potential economic interface between Cuba and the Central American countries. The basic problem, as indicated in Table 10.2, is that all these countries have tended to export and import similar products. Havana, recognizing that this is a pervasive problem and that the key to transforming its South-South trade into a vigorous growth sector is the development of new product lines, has targeted biotechnology, pharmaceuticals, and other health-related endeavors as particularly promising areas where it can provide goods and especially services to other LDCs as effectively and often more inexpensively than can the industrialized nations.[16] While the Central American countries might represent potential customers for these new Cuban exports, Havana is likely to concentrate on exploring the mass markets to be found in such countries as Mexico, Brazil, Argentina, India, and China.

In conclusion, Central America will not, at least in the foreseeable future, occupy as prominent a niche on the island's priority list as it has in the past. The need for Cuba to expand and diversify its economic relations, especially in such a manner as to compensate for the loss of its special ties with the Socialist bloc, suggests that the larger Latin American nations (along with the general process of hemispheric integration), the Far East, and Western Europe will attract most of its attention. Such a shift might be seen as a somewhat melancholy rite of passage, for it has been in Central America that Havana's foreign policy has maintained perhaps its strongest ties to the Fidelistas' heroic guerrilla heritage that was born and nurtured in the cradle of the Sierra Maestra. But to fail to adjust to the exigencies of

the world order emerging in the 1990s could jeopardize the Revolution's
very survival. The island's leadership will not take such risks.

Table 10.2   Cuban/Central American Trade Profile

	Major Exports	Major Imports
Costa Rica	Coffee	Petroleum
	Bananas	Machinery
	Textiles	Consumer durables
	Sugar	Chemicals
Cuba	Sugar	Capital goods
	Nickel ore	Industrial raw materials
	Citrus fruits	Food
	Fish products	Petroleum
El Salvador	Coffee	Petroleum products
	Sugar	Consumer goods
	Cotton	Foodstuffs
	Shrimp	Machinery
Guatemala	Coffee	Petroleum products
	Bananas	Machinery
	Sugar	Grain
	Cardamom	Fertilizers
Honduras	Bananas	Machinery
	Coffee	Chemical products
	Shrimp	Manufactured goods
	Lobsters	Petroleum products
Nicaragua	Coffee	Petroleum
	Cotton	Food
	Sugar	Chemicals
	Bananas	Machinery

Source: U.S. Central Intelligence Agency, *World Factbook 1990* (Washington, D.C.: Central Intelligence Agency, 1990).

NOTES

1. Jorge Domínguez, "Cuban Foreign Policy," *Foreign Affairs*, no. 57 (Fall 1978), p. 83.
2. See, for example, Jorge I. Domínguez, *To Make a World Safe for Revolution: Cuba's Foreign Policy* (Cambridge: Harvard University Press, 1989); H.

Michael Erisman, *Cuba's International Relations: The Anatomy of a Nationalistic Foreign Policy* (Boulder: Westview Press, 1985); H. Michael Erisman and John M. Kirk, eds., *Cuban Foreign Policy Confronts a New International Order* (Boulder: Lynne Rienner, 1991); Pamela S. Falk, *Cuban Foreign Policy: Caribbean Tempest* (Lexington: Lexington Books, 1986); and Carla Anne Robbins, *The Cuban Threat* (New York: McGraw-Hill, 1983).

3. Detailed discussions of the early ideological clashes that occurred between the Cubans and the Soviets can be found in Jacques Levesque, *The USSR and the Cuban Revolution* (New York: Praeger Special Series, 1978); and K. S. Karol, *Guerrillas in Power: The Course of the Cuban Revolution* (New York: Hill and Wang, 1970).

4. Domínguez, *To Make a World Safe*, p. 27, notes that by mid-1961 all of the Central American countries had lined up behind Washington's anti-Cuban policies and had broken diplomatic relations with the Castro government.

5. The entire "Second Declaration" can be found in Martin Kenner and James Petras, eds., *Fidel Castro Speaks* (New York: Grove Press, 1969), pp. 85–106. The quotes here are excerpted from pp. 104–106. The declaration provides an excellent sense of the revolutionary idealism that permeated Cuba's political culture during this period.

6. The Guatemalan revolutionary experience during the 1960s (including Cuba's involvement) is thoroughly examined in "Soldiers and Peasants in Guatemala," in Richard Gott, *Guerrilla Movements in Latin America* (New York: Anchor Books/Doubleday, 1972), pp. 37–118.

7. For details on the *foco* theory, see Che Guevara, *Guerrilla Warfare*, J. P. Morray, trans. (New York: Monthly Review Press, 1961); and Regis Debray, *Revolution in the Revolution?* (New York: Grove Press, 1967). Excellent critiques of the Debrayist formulation of the *foco* theory can be found in Leo Huberman and John M. Sweezy, eds., *Regis Debray and the Latin American Revolution* (New York: Monthly Review Press, 1968).

8. For more details regarding these matters, see U.S. Department of State, Special Report No. 90, "Cuba's Renewed Support for Violence in Latin America" (December 14, 1981), pp. 5–8, 10–11.

9. Antonio Jorge, "How Exportable Is the Cuban Model?" in Barry B. Levine, ed., *The New Cuban Presence in the Caribbean* (Boulder: Westview Press, 1983), p. 217.

10. Negotiations were also under way in 1992 between the Guatemalan insurgents and the government. However, no dramatic progress had occurred in the process up to that point and most observers were quite pessimistic about the prospects for any major breakthroughs in the near future.

11. These figures are cited in H. Michael Erisman, "Cuban Development Aid: South/South Diversification and Counterdependency Politics," in H. Michael Erisman and John M. Kirk, eds., *Cuban Foreign Policy Confronts a New International Order* (Boulder: Lynne Rienner, 1991), p. 153; and Rafael Fermoselle, *The Evolution of the Cuban Military, 1492–1986* (Miami: Ediciones Universal, 1987), p. 438.

12. For details, see Domínguez, *To Make a World Safe*, p. 136.

13. Associated Press report appearing as "In Cuba, Underground Tunnels are Part of a Defense Program," *Chicago Tribune*, May 10, 1992, sec. 1, p. 14.

14. Sergio Roca, "Economic Aspects of Cuban Involvement in Africa," in Carmelo Mesa-Lago and June S. Belkin, eds., *Cuba in Africa*, Latin American Monograph and Document Series, no. 3 (Pittsburgh: University of Pittsburgh Press, 1982), p. 175.

15. Discussion of the theoretical and practical aspects of employing a South-South diversification strategy to enhance one's North-South bargaining power can

be found in H. Michael Erisman, *Pursuing Post-Dependency Politics: South-South Relations in the Caribbean* (Boulder: Lynne Rienner, forthcoming 1992).

16. Some of Cuba's initiatives in developing new products (including the establishment of a world-class Center for Biotechnology and Genetic Engineering in Havana, which has already made important progress in creating several varieties of interferon and streptokinase) are reported in "Cuba Liberalizes Foreign Investment Policy," *CubaINFO* 2, no. 20 (December 14, 1990), p. 4.

11

The Limits and Possibilities of Cuban-Brazilian Relations

Luiz L. Vasconcelos

The natures of the Brazilian and Cuban regimes are quite different. Very different also are the dimensions of their GNPs and their economic development goals. Cuban society is more egalitarian, with fewer racial inequities, than is Brazilian society. Cuba has a better income distribution and a better higher education system, a better health care system, and less unemployment than does Brazil.

However, in other essential features, the two countries share many similarities. Their populations share a similar colonial heritage that has resulted in a strong cultural affinity. Cubans and Brazilians typically communicate easily and express themselves without reservation (other than reserve acquired under authoritarian pressure). Their music and dance have common features, marked by Iberian, African, and Indian roots. As well, *Moros y cristianos,* the popular dish of black beans and rice, may be prepared differently in each country but each style has a common background. (The movie theaters of Havana and other large cities regularly show Brazilian pictures, which are very popular on the island. Brazilian TV soap operas and records of varied musical trends have attracted unprecedented numbers of listeners and viewers in Cuba.)

THE EARLY YEARS

Three circumstances have shaped the economic and political relations between Brazil and Cuba: (1) Brazil's economy developed on the basis of import substitution industrialization. With the exception of a traditional exchange of wheat and fruits for Argentine pinewood for packaging, trade between Brazil and its neighbors south of the Rio Grande has been very modest. (2) Cuba is a small country whose basic production competes with traditional Brazilian products. This explains the past poor performance of Cuban sales to Brazil. (3) Since the Cuban Revolution of 1959, relations between Brazil and Cuba have suffered because of the profound political changes on the island; relations were complicated by allegations that Cuba was encouraging guerrilla movements in Brazil in the 1960s.

The Brazilian military dictatorship of 1964 broke relations with Cuba completely. During 1964–1981 there was a diplomatic "freeze" between the two countries. Contacts between citizens of Brazil and Cuba were limited to a few selected sports activities and fortuitous (if not furtive) visits of intellectuals, independent and left-wing politicians, and trade delegations tolerated since the late 1970s.

During the period before the military coup, Brazilian policy toward Cuba was based on an autonomous foreign policy vis-à-vis other countries, particularly the United States. For example, the Cuban delegation received a friendly reception at the FAO World Conference of 1961 in Rio de Janeiro a few months after the Bay of Pigs invasion. Che Guevara was decorated by Pres. Jânio Quadros several days before Quadros left his post in August 1961. Brazilian and Cuban representatives have often expressed similar viewpoints and voted together at many international meetings. And it is significant that Brazil never officially assumed a position against the presence of Cuban troops in Angola or anywhere else.

A straightforward, usually warm dialogue between artists, athletes, and intellectuals of both countries, despite the official restrictions imposed on them during the seventeen years of diplomatic freeze, played an important role in the development of official contacts that followed. Cuban citizens seldom visited Brazil during the freeze because Brazilian authorities strictly controlled their presence there and Cuban authorities limited exit visas. Brazilians traveling either on their own or on behalf of institutions encountered fewer hindrances in Cuba whether or not they were officially invited.

RESUMPTION OF DIPLOMATIC RELATIONS

A brief historical retrospective of the rapprochement between the Brazilian and Cuban governments begins in early 1977, when an aide to Pres. Fidel Castro, sociologist Sérgio Cervantes, further discreetly visited Brazil to attend a scientific symposium. Cervantes made further trips to Brazil under an aura of secrecy (he traveled under an assumed name and with fictitious objectives). Undoubtedly those visits were effective in developing informal contacts with authorities and representatives of the Brazilian government and society, particularly in business circles, who were pressing for the Brazilian National Security Council to waive, at least partially, the heavy restrictions imposed on Cuba at that time.[1] Finally, in 1985, Cervantes was granted an official visa to promote trade opportunities in Brazil and has lived as a Cuban diplomat there ever since. Four years earlier, a concrete step toward renewal of relations between the two countries was taken when a Cuban commercial mission visited São Paulo as the guest of Brazilian manufacturers of alcohol-distilling equipment. The Cuban delegation took advantage of the opportunity and contacted executives of other industrial sectors as well.

Meanwhile, diplomatic conversations between Brazil and Cuba continued at embassy level in Panama and France. The results of these discussions were consolidated after the 1981 "open-door policy" of Pres. João Batista Figueiredo and decisively grounded when his successor, José Sarney, was inaugurated in 1985. The negotiations evolved rapidly, clearing obstacles to a political understanding. The press closely followed the negotiations with encouraging articles about business prospects.[2] There were no further doubts about the goodwill of both governments. The only aspect still open to discussion within the Brazilian government was how to implement the recognition act: gradually or immediately.

This situation climaxed in 1986 at a conclusive meeting held in Paris at which it was finally decided that diplomatic relations would be fully resumed on June 25 of that year. Brazil appointed Italo Zappa, a career diplomat, to Havana. Zappa had been serving in Beijing at the time and was recognized for his specific interest in economic matters. Cuba appointed Jorge Bolaños, a vice minister of foreign trade, to head its diplomatic mission in Brasilia, where he continues in office at the present time. The Brazilian ambassador to France, Rubens Ricúpero, played a prominent role in the negotiations leading to the normalization of relations.

In November 1986, the Brazilian National Confederation of Industry (CNI) sent an important entrepreneurial mission to Havana headed by Luis Otávio Vieira, the vice president and director of the Foreign Trade Commission of CNI. The mission was received by vice ministers of foreign trade and other high-ranking representatives of the Cuban government, as well as by representatives of Cuban trading companies and several other institutions. Upon the mission's return to Brazil, the CNI issued a very favorable report, as optimistic as articles previously published by the Brazilian press. Drawing on a 1985 market study, the report forecasted extraordinary trade possibilities with Cuba and was enthusiastically received by entrepreneurs.[3] However, it took about two years for these high expectations to produce meaningful results—they were hindered by credit difficulties and other circumstances (including the U.S. embargo of Cuba), which continue today.

Brazilian ministers and governors paid repeated visits to Cuba, and though the missions were less ostentatious than CNI's original visit, they proved far more important. President Castro held long conversations with all visiting officials, including the governors of São Paulo and Rio de Janeiro. The ministers of communication, transportation, justice, public health, industry and trade, science and technology, and foreign affairs have all visited Cuba on different occasions.

From Cuba, the ministers of foreign trade and foreign affairs and other high-ranking officials, including Vice Pres. Carlos Rafael Rodríguez, visited Brazil. Castro attended the inauguration of President Collor de Mello in 1990. There were also visits of Cubans from universities, professional associations, and artistic circles, reciprocating calls by Brazilian counterparts.

Press interviews of visitors from both countries underline the commitment of all concerned to a long-lasting interchange. The hopeful prospects of the evolving business ties were repeated. Despite the optimism, in the early 1990s both the Brazilian and Cuban administrations were concerned with growing economic difficulties. In a climate of austerity aggravated by the heavy burden of foreign debt, the governments of both countries were intent upon increasing participation in international trade. Both countries attempted to diversify exports, paving the way for initiatives aimed at opening new markets.

Cuba faced a relatively greater balance-of-payments deficit than Brazil. In the late-1980s Cuba began carrying out a "rectification" of the national economic planning system; it also began diversifying its supplies of food and other necessities to ensure the effective implementation of its development programs.

Meanwhile, Brazil was consistently making substantial efforts to increase its export surpluses in order to comply with foreign debt commitments. Imports were curtailed, leading to complaints from trade partners who felt they were being compelled to bear undesirable imbalances; Cuba soon fell into this category. The reduction in Brazil's purchasing power for foreign goods had a less significant impact on the Brazilian economy than it did on the Cuban economy. Cuba's dependence on imports amounts to roughly 30 percent of the global social product, as compared with less than 5 percent of GNP for Brazil.

The 1986 renewal of political and economic relations between Brazil and Cuba, broken off in 1964, was the result of a slow but positive process that began at the end of the 1970s. During the first half of the 1980s, Brazilian products began to enter the Cuban market via Spain and Argentina. However, it was only after the reopening of embassies in Havana and Brasilia in June 1986 that Cuba entered noticeably in Brazilian statistical records.

Since 1986, relations between the two countries have rapidly expanded, particularly in the trade area. Delegations aimed at gathering information and discussing cooperation have been exchanged. However, high initial expectations of extensive cooperation were not met. Brazilian exports to Cuba jumped swiftly from $1.3 million in 1986 to about $85 million in 1990 and 1991, and then leveled off. Cuban exports to Brazil were much more modest and unsteady, though they reached an exceptional high of almost $100 million in 1990 because of the sale of immunobiological products; the figures for 1991, however, dropped sharply partly because of a Cuban balance-of-trade deficit of more than $100 million accumulated between 1988 and 1992, despite the 1990 high.

Two large-scale agreements have recently been signed between Cuba and Brazil, one related to trade and the other to science and technology (R&D). The former is not likely to bring about any substantial changes to bilateral trade relations. In the short run, Brazilian exports will continue to prevail over the limited competitiveness of Cuban products, except in certain internationally recognized biotechnological areas. Technological exchange, however, including joint participation of experts in applied scientific fields, appears very promising.

Observers from both countries agree that the projected economic growth in Brazil, combined with the economic and political adjustments being promoted on the island, is likely to strengthen Cuban-Brazilian ties. Such improvements will favor the development of South-South cooperation.

Contrary to initial expectations, the entente between the Brazilian and Cuban governments has not continued to improve. In the wake of the Ibero-American Conference in Guadalajara, Mexico, in July 1991, Francisco Rezek, then-Brazilian minister of foreign affairs, stated in a press release that his government "was not able to detect elements that would justify optimism with regard to the possibility of Cuba getting closer to the international community."[4] A similar feeling pervaded the Cartagena meeting of the presidents of the eleven-member Rio Group in November 1991 and the Buenos Aires summit of Rio Group foreign ministers in March 1992. It is interesting to note that on March 25, 1992, days before the Buenos Aires meeting, the Brazilian weekly magazine *Veja* published an interview with former Brazilian president Fernando Collor de Mello in which he commented sympathetically on Cuba's impressive social development. The press also commented favorably on the advanced negotiation of an important contract between the Brazilian and the Cuban oil companies for offshore drilling.

TRADE RELATIONS

The first direct Cuban imports after the renewal of diplomatic relations with Brazil in 1986 amounted to $1.8 million. These consisted mainly of 3,800 tons of cardboard for packaging, five vans, and different accessories for Volkswagen cars bought in previous years from other suppliers. Third-party operations, under whose cover several Brazilian companies had done business in the early 1980s, were drastically reduced; one of the Brazilian companies had sold $4.5 million worth of goods to Cuba in 1985 through such an operation.[5]

Before the breach of 1964, trade between the two countries was of little significance, and very unstable. Between 1958 and 1959, Brazilian sales to Cuba—consisting almost wholly of commodities—dropped from a level of about $560,000 to $230,000. On the other hand, Brazilian purchases rose unexpectedly from $700,000 to $5.3 million, including a surprising quantity of gasoline and diesel oil.

After a few years without any commercial exchange, Cuba bought $28 million worth of coffee in 1963, presumably for reexportation. Brazil purchased only $1,400 worth of exports from Cuba, mainly publications. The next year, Cuban imports of Brazilian coffee dropped to $484,000. The sale of publications continued at an insignificant level. Trade became negligible in the ensuing years. After 1966, Cuba did not enter into Brazilian trade records for a long time.

Trade was resumed in 1980, through the aforementioned third-party operations. Brazilian products were once again shipped to Cuban ports via Panama. This routing increased prices by about 25 percent. Nevertheless, through this method, Cuba bought a considerable quantity of prefabricated houses, galvanized steel frames, an alcohol distillery, canvas for lining, various durable goods, and different kinds of tools. Four large duty-free shops in tourist hotels were designed and fully equipped by Brazilian enterprises between 1981 and 1985.

Some Brazilian analysts predicted an enormous growth in trade between the two countries after relations were normalized. The Brazilian government and big business both were anxious to increase exports and contributed to the atmosphere of enthusiasm. The director of a well-known Brazilian trading company that was already doing business with the island did not hesitate to write, before the normalization, that "Cuba represents one of the most interesting challenges for Brazil."[6]

Some international analysts forecasted that Brazil could become, in the short term, Cuba's second most important trade partner among its nonsocialist associates. Excellent prospects for large sales of industrial products were heralded, with particular reference to utilitarian vehicles, machinery, whole factory facilities, thermoelectric works, and paper mills using sugarcane bagasse. Reference was also made to business opportunities in the modernization of ports, airports, and railroads. Finally, there was talk of joint ventures between Brazilian and Cuban companies. During his visit to Brazil in 1990, President Castro hinted at immediate joint venture possibilities in the field of biotechnology, with equally interesting prospects in other fields.

Limited access to specific and sufficient credits surfaced as the largest obstacle to improved trade almost immediately after diplomatic relations were renewed. Differences in bureaucratic management styles that regulate negotiations between Cuban state-owned companies and private foreign corporations have become another, although less important, difficulty. Moreover, Brazilian companies have close links with foreign, including multinational, firms and feel that they must comply with the U.S. embargo of Cuba, particularly after Pres. Ronald Reagan began an extraterritorial campaign to tighten the embargo in the late 1980s, which was signed into law by Pres. Bush in October 1992.

Whether a matter of credit limitations, high customs duties, or other reasons, Cuban products have been poorly received by Brazilian clients, relative to their potential purchasing power. Only biotechnological products purchased directly by the Brazilian government have been positively received so far. Sales of other products, such as processed ores, light electromechanical products, rum, and tobacco, have not yet fulfilled the expectations of Cuban exporters.

All in all, it is clear that Brazil gained more than did Cuba from the opening of commercial relations. Nevertheless, Cuba has positioned itself well for obtaining high-quality technological supplies. Furthermore, Brazilian tourism in Cuba has evolved as another important element in relations between the two countries. Since 1985, the number of Brazilian tourists in Cuba has grown steadily. About thirty-three thousand arriving either directly from Brazil or through Panama, Peru, or Mexico have already visited the island. In 1990 alone, 9,150 Brazilian tourists visited Cuba and spent approximately $15 million during their stay on the island, thus helping rectify the balance-of-payments deficit with Brazil.

As Table 11.1 shows, the initial optimistic forecasts on the development of the commercial flow from Brazil to Cuba were, to a certain extent, well founded. In 1987, Brazilian exports amounted to a modest $3 million, slightly below the level of imports from Cuba. In 1986 and 1987, the balance of trade favored Cuba. But the sale of Brazilian products to Cuba grew rapidly. In 1988 Brazilian sales to Cuba jumped to over $23.2 million; in 1989, to $76.7 million; and in 1990, to $84.6 million. The estimated total for 1991 will likely be close to $85 million. The total trade turnover reached about $105 million and $183.5 million in 1989 and 1990, respectively. Brazil had registered a cumulative surplus of $55 million in convertible currency by 1990.

Based on available data for 1991, it appears that Cuba's accumulated deficit with Brazil doubled to about $113 million. The drop in Cuban exports from $3.2 million in 1987 to only $18,000 in 1988 is symptomatic of the fragility of Cuban exports to Brazil. In 1991, after an increase to $99 million the previous years, exports barely reached a level of $28 million. Aside from vaccines and other immunobiological products whose sales increased steeply in 1989 and 1990, allowing Cuba to obtain a trade surplus of $14.4 million in 1991, the purchase of other goods by Brazilian enterprises amounted to very little. Biomedical sales brought Cuba's share of total Brazilian imports to 0.5 percent in 1990, an increase from 0.2 percent in 1989. Data for 1991 are not yet available. It is reported that in 1992 Brazil bought a considerable quantity of sugar to compensate for a bad harvest in Pernambuco State.

Table 11.1   Brazil: Trade with Cuba, 1986–1990

Year	Exports (in thousands of U.S. $)	Imports (in thousands of U.S. $)	Imports Coverage	Cuba's % Share of Brazil's Exports	Cuba's % Share of Brazil's Imports
1986	1,322	3,105	0.4	0.0	0.0
1987	3,012	3,242	0.9	0.0	0.0
1988	23,214	18	1,289.7	0.1	0.0
1989	76,656	28,321	2.7	0.2	0.2
1990	84,572	98,928	0.8	0.3	0.5
1991	85,000[a]	27,547	304.9	n.a.	n.a.

Sources: Bank of Brazil/DECEX; Brazil Ministry of Finance trade statistics.
Note: a. Estimated after January–September figures ($64.3 million).

Cuba's efforts to increase and diversify its trade with the rest of the world (as nonsocialist countries are referred to in the official Cuban statistics) may be inferred from Table 11.2. Brazil's participation in the totals for that particular area grew from 0.5 percent in 1986 to 2.6 percent in exports in 1989, and from 0.1 percent to 6.4 percent in imports, in spite of credit limitations, differences in bureaucratic management style, and the U.S. embargo.

Cuba's transactions with countries of the Latin American Integration Association (LAIA) increased by one-third in value in 1990, compared with the previous decade (see Table 11.3). Argentina, Mexico, and Venezuela stand out as top partners. However, judging from estimates, Brazil probably became Cuba's main client in Latin America in 1990.[7] Even so, this does not mean much. Regarding the overall value of Cuban foreign trade, transactions with Latin America and the Caribbean have fluctuated at about less than 5 percent.

One must keep in mind that the data under analysis is so affected by change that trends are impossible to identify. It is clear, however, that a single category of products has dominated Cuban exports to Brazil. Doubtless, Cuba and Brazil will have to concentrate their efforts to sustain the gains already attained, and further steps will be necessary to promote future exchange. The 1990 agreement detailed below may pave the way for more balanced trade.

Brazil is a large exporting country, whereas Cuba registers deficit balances year after year. (See Table 11.4.) Its exports—which in per capita terms are more than 2.5 times larger than Brazil's—correspond roughly to 20 percent of its global social product; imports claim about 30 percent of the same. Dominating the list of Cuban exports are a few selected commodities

Table 11.2   Cuban Foreign Trade with Brazil and Rest of World,
1986–1989

Year	Exports to Rest of World (in millions of pesos)	Brazil[a]	Imports from Rest of World (in millions of pesos)	Brazil[a]	Cuba Trade with Brazil as % of with World Exports	Imports
1986	622	3.1	1,152	1.3	0.5	0.1
1987	604	3.2	923	3.0	0.5	0.3
1988	753	0.0	954	23.2	0.0	2.4
1989	1,086[b]	28.3	1,191	76.7	2.6	6.4
1990	n.a.	98.9	n.a.	84.6	n.a.	n.a.

Sources: CEPAL Statistical Yearbooks; National Bank of Cuba; Bank of Brazil/DECEX.
Notes: a. At the rate of pesos 1.00 = U.S. $1.00.
b. Preliminary data.
"Rest of World" refers to nonsocialist countries.
n.a. = not available

Table 11.3   Cuba's Trade with Latin America
and the Caribbean, 1975/1980/1985–1990
(in millions of pesos at current prices)

Year	Economic Areas LAIA	CCCM	CARICOM	Other	LAIA Main Partners of Cuba Argentina	Mexico	Venezuela	Brazil[a]
1975	159.6	0.0	7.9	7.4	105.6	28.1	6.2	n.a.
1980	252.5	5.6	6.0	41.8	15.3	208.3	5.3	n.a.
1985	292.0	28.5	5.2	35.6	193.7	79.0	13.6	n.a.
1986	223.6	41.5	3.7	23.3	163.5	31.4	12.2	4.4
1987	234.8	38.3	6.7	26.6	125.6	74.0	20.6	6.3
1988	335.7	31.3	2.2	22.4	129.2	113.0	50.7	23.2
1989	515.0	34.0	4.0	18.0	n.a.	n.a.	n.a.	105.0
1990	600.0[b]	n.a.	n.a.	n.a.	n.a.	n.a.	n.a.	183.5

Sources: Statistical Yearbooks of Cuba; Bank of Brazil/DECEX.
Notes: n.a. = not available
LAIA: Latin American Integration Association; CCCM: Central American Common
Market; CARICOM: Caribbean Commonwealth.
a. At the rate of pesos 1.00 = U.S. $1.00.
b. Estimate.

such as sugar, citrus fruits, and nickel. Very promising achievements have been recorded in technological areas as well. Though a similar structural

Table 11.4   Total Foreign Trade of Brazil and Cuba, 1985–1990

Year	Brazil		Cuba		1:3	2:4
	1. Exports	2. Imports	3. Exports	4. Imports	Exports	Imports[a]
	(in millions of U.S. $)		(in millions of pesos)			
1985	25.639	13.154	5.983	7.983	4.3	1.7
1986	22.393	14.044	5.321	7.596	4.2	1.8
1987	26.213	15.052	5.402	7.584	4.9	2.0
1988	33.789	14.605	5.518	7.579	6.1	1.9
1989	34.389	18.255	5.392	8.124	6.4	2.2
1990	31.439	20.398	n.a.	n.a.	—	—

Sources: Bank of Brazil/DECEX; Statistical Yearbooks of Cuba.
Notes: In per capita terms, Cuban exports are roughly equivalent to U.S. $500, thus exceeding the average of U.S. $200 for Brazil.
a. The peso estimated at parity rate with the U.S. dollar.

rigidity is present in Cuba's trade with Brazil in relation to other export items, while Brazilian companies sell a range of 325 items Cuban sales involve only about 8 items.

Food products (mainly frozen chicken) rank first in Brazilian sales to Cuba, accounting for over one-third of total exports, followed by plastics of several kinds, machines and tools, spare parts for cars, and chemicals. Each category of these products varies in value between 5 percent and 15 percent of the total. Paper, rubber articles, iron, steel, aluminum, and textiles play a less important role. Publications, orthopedic prostheses, and traditional articles such as rum and cigars represent a small portion of Brazilian imports from Cuba. Vaccines and other biomedical products constitute the bulk. Brazilian biotechnological acquisitions are purchased through government-to-government agreements and serve as a basis for technology transfers. A recently proclaimed comprehensive agreement between the two countries involves 160 medical-pharmaceutical products from Cuba and a still-undefined number of products manufactured in Brazil.[8]

OFFICIAL AGREEMENTS

Two important agreements were signed by the governments of Brazil and Cuba to facilitate the expansion of commercial and scientific relations. To a certain extent, the first of the agreements was amplified in range to cover scientific and technological cooperation as well.

Trade Agreement

A trade agreement was signed in October 1989 in accordance with the 1980 Montevideo Treaty that created the LAIA. Brazil is a member, and Cuba presently has observer status in LAIA. A decree dated November 26, 1990, promulgates the agreement for an "undetermined duration." Composed of fifteen chapters and twenty-eight articles, ten of which are devoted to "safeguard clauses," the agreement plans for a significant reduction of duties and the gradual elimination of restrictions, charges, and taxes on trade. The preservation of preferences in relation to "original products" is included in an annex of the ten articles.[9] Other members of LAIA are welcome to join in this agreement.

Both parties agreed to exchange a wide range of products. Two hundred fifty-four Brazilian items were selected, of which many were already being sold to Cuba. One hundred sixty-two categories of Cuban products were selected, few of which have actually been exchanged with Brazil to date.

Like the trade agreements that Cuba has signed with six other LAIA members, the Brazilian trade accord does not include any reference to financial understandings. There are, however, no clauses impeding the managing bilateral commission—a commission composed of representatives of both the Brazilian National Committee to LAIA and the Cuban Ministry of Foreign Trade—to assist in financial matters aimed at improving the agreement. The creation of the bilateral commission will facilitate financing involved in the evolution of trade between the two countries.

There are several other measures yet to be considered that may improve trade relations. The opening of a regular shipping line, for example, would be helpful. A situation similar to that between the Cuban flag company and Argentine companies, which have established a joint administration of shipments and share freight revenues on a 50–50 percent basis, could be implemented. The same situation could apply to the establishment of regular passenger and cargo flights.[10] To date, Viação Aérea São Paulo (VASP) is the only Brazilian airline authorized to carry out weekly direct charter flights to Cuba. There is no reciprocity with Cubana Airlines. The VASP flights, which began in 1988, made it easier for Brazilian tourists to reach the island, avoiding stopovers on the way.

During the unofficial negotiations between government and private concerns that preceded the trade agreement, other flexible trade possibilities were discussed. The creation of joint ventures, the establishment of sectoral commissions at the enterprise level, and a closer cooperation between the chambers of commerce of the two countries are several such possibilities.

Despite the positive results so far attained, it is well recognized that direct and indirect political obstacles have hindered the development of more extensive trade. The U.S. embargo has greatly hindered exchange between Brazil and Cuba.[11] Nevertheless, the goodwill and mutual respect shown by Cuba and Brazil contribute to easing tensions in inter-American relations with regard to Cuba in general and its readmission into the OAS in particular.

Science and Technology Agreement

A science-technology (R&D) agreement was signed in March 1990 and became effective one year later without restrictions of any sort. The far-reaching agreement strengthens and develops lines of scientific, technical, and technological cooperation through the exchange or employment of experts, scholarships, joint research projects, seminars, symposia, conferences, and, finally, the mutual consent to use documents, information, and pieces of scientific experiments pertaining to the other party. Each country is under formal obligation to inform the other on the results of research and experiments in areas of common interest. Finally, the agreement provides for the expansion to additional forms of cooperation as they arise.

The agreement is coordinated, administered, and implemented by a joint commission formed by the Ministry of Foreign Affairs of Brazil and the Committee for Economic Cooperation of Cuba. The joint commission is charged with carrying out periodic evaluations of results achieved, making recommendations regarding modifications of the agreement, and discussing future programs. The commission also supervises the dissemination of documents and knowledge obtained under the agreement.

Besides the priority placed on biotechnology, the first meeting of the R&D joint commission chose to focus on agriculture and cattle raising, education, computer techniques, communications, heavy industry, fisheries, and transportation. Technology transfers are not limited to the prevention and treatment of diseases but include diagnosis and monitoring techniques as well. In the agriculture and livestock field, the cooperation covers genetics, citrus, rice, coffee, cocoa, and soil. Special attention is being paid to the sugar-production sector, including experiments on different sugarcane varieties and sucrose and alcohol production. In the transportation area, the programs concentrate on developing technology for manufacturing spare parts and on projects aimed at conserving fossil fuels.

Since 1985, about sixty semiofficial agreements, or statements of intent, between universities and research centers in both countries have been signed. It was under this type of understanding that the University of Havana signed an exchange agreement with several Brazilian entities, including the Federal University of Rio de Janeiro.

Thus began the frequent exchange of professors, researchers, and well-known personalities in the cultural world. The costs of such visits were covered either by the institutions concerned or on a private basis. At first, extensive study missions were planned, but few actually were completed because of lack of sufficient material support. However, even before the R&D agreement formally took effect, a number of Cuban technicians were able to visit Brazil to participate in programs at the Technological Research Institute of the State of São Paulo and at other institutions. The programs focused on civil architecture and construction, paper technology, and the utilization of sugarcane bagasse for multiple purposes. Other technicians collaborated in similar exchanges with Brazilian professionals in public health programs on tropical diseases.

From these initial steps, dozens of study missions have taken place between the two countries. Brazilian architects, engineers, biologists, filmmakers, tourism and telecommunication technicians, among others, have already worked or are currently working in Cuba; and Cuban engineers, health workers, geneticists, teachers, artists, and athletes have visited Brazil.

No outline of research exchange programs would be complete without mention of Brazil's participation in modernizing Cuban oil refineries, drilling for oil, and exploring deep-sea oil fields off the northern coast of Cuba. Negotiations initiated last year with Braspetro, a subsidiary of Petrobras, the powerful Brazilian state oil corporation, have almost been concluded. The final agreement is expected soon.

CONCLUSIONS

Many of the obstacles to the development of commercial, social, and political relations between Brazil and Cuba have been removed in recent years because of the dynamism of business interests in both countries spurred by the desire to expand foreign trade. Because of growing foreign debt problems, both countries have faced increasing economic difficulties since 1980. More recently, in the specific case of Cuba, the situation further deteriorated after the disintegration of the former Soviet Union and Eastern European socialist countries and the dissolution of the Council for Mutual Economic Assistance (CMEA). Trade, credit, and other forms of financial support from that area were suddenly and greatly reduced or simply cut off. The end of bilateral trade agreements with the Soviets, which accounted for most of Cuban foreign trade, has severely damaged the Cuban economy.

The doors for cooperation between Brazil and Cuba are now open. Substantial agreements in commercial and scientific-technological domains abound. Furthermore, prospects for future fruitful agreements are good. However, there is still a long way to go before the relations between the two countries are fully normalized. Differences in the regimes and anachronistic limitations inherited from the Cold War era still set limits on the relationship. Intensive efforts to overcome these limitations are necessary to achieve the full potential in commercial and diplomatic relations.

Given that both Brazil and Cuba are committed to finding solutions to such pressing problems, there is little doubt that commercial exchange will grow, especially after Brazil resumes its economic growth and Cuba successfully overcomes its current economic crisis. Most important, it is imperative that trade between the countries be balanced. Cuban exports must not continue to be dominated by products with a rather temporary demand. And beyond buttressing Cuban tourism, Brazil should purchase more Cuban products.

A wide range of new initiatives in the area of R&D appears to be within reach. There are indeed promising opportunities for expanding the transfer of technologies that will benefit large firms as well as small and medium-size enterprises.

Still, it should be noted that Brazil-Cuba relations have suffered several setbacks of late. The high-level political contacts optimistically carried out between the two countries did not yield as much as originally hoped. One conspicuous setback was the postponement of Brazilian foreign minister Francisco Rezek's trip to Cuba, originally planned for July 1991. Another setback occurred at the Guadalajara conference in July 1991 when it was widely expected that the Brazilian team was going to publicly support Cuba's readmission to the OAS. Although President Collor de Mello was one of the few heads of state to hold a private meeting with President Castro, no efforts were undertaken to support Cuba's readmission to the OAS. Moreover, the Brazilian foreign affairs minister stated with unusual impertinence that he "got tired of waiting for a political gesture from Havana."[12]

The Cuban government's resistance to change was stronger than anticipated by the Brazilian, Argentine, Mexican, and Venezuelan officials present in Guadalajara, and although the four governments generally agree that there are no juridical impediments to Cuba's readmission to the OAS, they all stressed that they do not consider it a priority. The press coverage of the Guadalajara meeting pointed out that U.S. pressure encouraged these governments to take the anti-Cuba position.

NOTES

1. Cervante's secret missions were dramatic in style; they are well summarized in the July 14, 1987, issue of the weekly newsletter *CACEX*, published by the Bank of Brazil. Cervantes remains very much at the center of attention.

2. Some articles expressed the opinion that, because of the delay in resuming official relations with Cuba, business opportunities involving hundreds of millions of dollars were being lost. The newspapers *Folha de São Paulo* (September 1, 1986) mentioned, for example, a contract for the building of eight hotels, which was signed with Argentine competitors who relied on credits provided by their government.

3. "Cuba—una nova alternative commercial para o Brasil (Cuba—a New Commercial Alternative for Brazil), published in 1985 by the board of RDC International, a consulting company.

4. *Jornal do Brasil*, September 29, 1991.

5. There is little available information on the third-party trade involving Brazil. Most of the operations were carried out through Argentine and Spanish companies and in some cases may have continued after 1986. Two trading companies from São Paulo stand out in this kind of business: Cominter and Servlease. The former may have sold $8–10 million a year until the mid-1980s; the latter, perhaps twice that amount. The Codistil group, linked to the Dedini enterprises, specialized in manufacturing equipment for sugar and alcohol plants and was also actively engaged in exploring possible business opportunities in the same period, but under the allegation of financing difficulties, it failed to bring about the large transactions it had in mind. The Cuban mission that visited São Paulo in 1981 came to Brazil at the invitation of Dedini.

6. Frederico Aflalo, director of Cominter, interviewed by *Gazeta Mercantil*, April 8, 1986, stressed the difficulties originating from the scarcity of export credits provided by Brazilian banks.

7. At the time of this writing, statistical data is not yet available on Cuban trade with the "rest of the world" after 1989. It is possible that the Brazilian participation in the results for that area did not decrease substantially in 1990. However, the fall in the sales of Cuban products in 1991 may have altered the picture.

8. At the beginning of 1991, there were discussions about the prospect of importing larger quantities of vaccines whose total value would exceed the sum registered in 1990, but this did not materialize. However, there are initiatives aimed at setting up a joint enterprise between Brazil and Cuba to produce vaccines and miscellaneous biotechnological products, such as the so-called epidermic factor for protection against burns, and medicines against vitiligo. Regarding the latter disease, a Brazil-Cuba medical center was set up in São Paulo with the participation of the Brazilian firm Servimed.

9. The definition of "original products," which is normal in these cases, attempted to avoid the re-exportation of surpluses from the CMEA area. The agreement stipulates that only products that undergo final stage processing in the territory of the exporting party are considered "original." The components supplied by third countries are not to exceed 50 percent of the FOB value of the final product.

10. Businessman Wagner Canhedo, owner of fifteen companies in different areas, and main shareholder of VASP (a Brazilian airline), showed great interest in establishing a joint venture with several Cuban companies. He was particularly interested in turning the present charter stopovers of VASP in Havana into regular flights. In May 1991, he began negotiating a joint venture between Cubana de Aviación and one of his enterprises to jointly operate all Cubana flights. In an interview in *Jornal do Brasil* on February 5, 1991, he said that he had already met President Castro on three occasions and had talked with him about these and other possible projects. Recently, the press announced that all negotiations, including that with Cubana, had been suspended because of pressure from the U.S. government. A few years ago, another Brazilian airline (VARIG) tried to obtain a stopover in

Havana within the framework of a bilateral, government-to-government agreement. As of today, no agreements have been signed.

11. A recent example is the Brazilian suspension of a contract for the purchase of Brazilian aircraft because they use U.S.-made aviation equipment, according to press reports.

12. Teodomiro Braga, *Jornal do Brasil*, September 29, 1991.

PART 4

CUBA'S RELATIONS WITH NORTH AMERICA

12

Mexico, Cuba, and the
United States: Myth Versus Reality

CARL MIGDAIL

For more than thirty years, the public posture adopted by Mexico toward Fidel Castro's Cuba fostered an international impression of understanding, sympathy, and friendship between the two countries. The reality was much different. Mexico's leaders privately recognized Castro's revolution as an immediate, serious threat to their country's continued internal political stability.

The presence of a profound revolution in nearby Cuba presented the Mexican leadership with a massive dilemma. Mexico enjoyed an international, highly cherished reputation as a revolutionary nation invulnerable to pressures from new revolutions elsewhere, while its leadership knew they were merely propagating a myth. There was a large, growing gap between rich and poor in Mexico, and the country's intelligent leaders understood that revolution in Cuba could perhaps produce similar uprisings at home.

Mexico's leaders were trapped by their history and revolutionary rhetoric. As the heirs of their country's own far-reaching revolution, they were compelled publicly to profess sympathy and support for the Castro Revolution, while privately they feared the new government in Havana and hoped it would somehow disappear.[1]

The Mexican dilemma created a neurotic policy toward Cuba. In its public stance, Mexico was a staunch defender of Cuba's independence and sovereignty and insisted that the United States comply with the principle of nonintervention toward the island. The principle of nonintervention had become the cornerstone of Mexican foreign policy after the United States either conquered or bought about half of Mexico's territory during the nineteenth century.

To shield their country from the unsettling political effects of the Castro Revolution, Mexico's leaders for more than thirty years carefully avoided decisions that might undermine unity at home, and they continue to do so today. While hoping that the United States would somehow solve the ongoing headache caused for them by Castro, Mexicans actively campaigned to prevent the Organization of American States (OAS) from acting decisively against Cuba. Since Mexican delegates were unable to sidetrack an anti-Castro resolution in the OAS, when the vote came Mexico preferred to abstain. The objective was to avoid a decision that might strain the unity of the ruling coalition at home.

MODERN MEXICAN POLITICAL HISTORY

Only an account of Mexico's modern political history can explain the crisis created for Mexico's leaders by the Castro Revolution and their erratic behavior in trying to insulate their country from what they considered could be Cuba's damaging effects. Mexico's revolution started in 1910 and ended in 1929. It was as traumatic as the Soviet Revolution of 1917 and probably equally as violent. The population of Mexico, fifteen million in 1910, dropped to fourteen million in 1920. The memory of their bloody revolution still haunts many Mexicans and remains a factor in their fervent desire to avoid factional confrontations that could precipitate a renewal of internal conflict.

With its call of "land for the peasants," the Mexican Revolution sparked a massive uprising against the country's feudal agricultural system. The cry of social justice for all Mexicans, which is still repeated constantly by Mexican politicians, led generations of workers to accept personal sacrifices in the conviction that the Revolution would at least bring a higher standard of living to their children.

By 1929, revolutionary violence and counterviolence had left Mexico exhausted. The country was more a framework of war-ravaged, mutually hostile regions than it was a nation. Whatever wealth was left in the ruined country was prey to the marauding and looting of local caudillos commanding well-armed, autonomous military gangs.

National order was restored when strongman Plutarco Elías Calles made a political pact with other leading caudillos. The coalition organized by Calles ended factional fighting, brought economic growth to Mexico, created a sturdy middle class, and developed a strong national consciousness among Mexicans. Calles's group became the forerunner of the governing coalition that still rules Mexico—the Institutional Revolutionary Party (PRI), in itself a contradiction in terms.

The PRI is not a political party in the usual meaning of the term. It is a governing coalition of almost all the major institutions in Mexico, ideologically from left to right. Conservatives and communists could feel at home in the PRI. Leftists moved freely between the left wing of the PRI and their own so-called independent political groups. Conservatives, when they were not members of the rightist National Action Party (PAN), inhabited the right wing of the PRI.

The primary task of PRI presidents of Mexico, who have governed the country since 1929, was to preserve Mexico's internal peace by keeping the ruling coalition intact. The president was expected to reconcile differences among coalition groups and distribute material rewards. Defections by major groups were regarded as crimes against the PRI and the nation, since divisions could rupture internal peace and lead to a renewal of violence.

By 1959, when Castro gained power, the Mexican government, despite its repeated use of revolutionary slogans, was in reality one of the more conservative regimes in Latin America. The revolutionary leaders and their children had become wealthy businessmen and politicians, while income distribution nationally was one of the worst in the Western Hemisphere. Many Mexicans became increasingly disillusioned and cynical about a government that was verbally committed to bringing them social justice but that left them impoverished with little real hope for improvement.

Among Mexico's leaders there was fear that the example of a new revolution in Cuba could fragment the ruling coalition. The left wing of the PRI might decide it had more to gain by mobilizing popular discontent and striking for ruling power for itself. Mexico's leaders saw a clear and present danger that the revolutionary Castro regime, unless carefully managed, might plunge Mexico into internal chaos.[2] The fulfillment of the primary task of Pres. Adolfo López Mateos's tenure (1958–1964) as chief executive of preserving domestic peace was made even more difficult by Mexico's traditional revolutionary reputation and the growing hostility of the United States to Castro's Cuba.

Because of its own revolutionary heritage, Mexico had become a haven for revolutionary exiles from other countries. Their presence in Mexico enhanced the country's international image, pleased the left wing of the PRI, and did not endanger domestic stability. After the fall of the Spanish republic to the armies of Gen. Francisco Franco, then-president Lázaro Cárdenas (1934–1940) brought about ten thousand Spaniards to Mexico. Leon Trotsky, hounded around the world by Josef Stalin, was also given refuge in Mexico. When Pres. Jacobo Arbenz of Guatemala was overthrown by a U.S.-organized coup in 1954, his followers fled to Mexico. Venezuelan exile groups waited in Mexico until governments they opposed at home were no longer in power and they could return.

After Pres. Fulgencio Batista released Castro—who in 1953 had tried to overthrow him—from prison, Castro also came to Mexico to plot his return to Cuba. In Mexico, Castro was befriended and supported by former president Cárdenas, a leader of the left wing of the ruling coalition. Castro trained his followers on one of Cárdenas's ranches, and it was from Mexico that Castro sailed to "invade" Cuba aboard the *Granma*. During his military struggle to defeat Batista, Castro maintained his close ties to the left wing of the Mexican ruling coalition.

MEXICO:
CAUGHT BETWEEN WASHINGTON AND HAVANA

President López Mateos

President López Mateos was acutely aware that Mexico was caught in and would be squeezed by the conflict between Washington and Havana. Mexico needed to maintain close political and economic ties with the United States but also desperately had to adopt policies that appeared consistent with Mexico's nineteenth-century territorial struggle with Washington. It was clear to López Mateos that while he was cultivating good relations with Washington, he had to protect Mexico's image of total independence from the United States to preserve unity in the ruling coalition. He also had to maneuver to give the impression that he was preserving Mexico's revolutionary traditions by appearing to cultivate a friendly policy toward Castro's Cuba.

López Mateos decided to neutralize the emergence of an active pro-Castro movement in the left wing of his ruling coalition by co-opting the political position of the left. The president stole the thunder of the left by declaring publicly that his administration was ideologically on the extreme left within the framework of the Mexican Constitution.

Mexicans were justifiably confused. López Mateos's public statements were deliberately so vague that opposing politicians within the ruling coalition and students at the universities who looked to Castro and Che Guevara as liberators came up with conflicting interpretations of his policies. Each faction assumed the president was its spokesman.

For the rest of his presidency after Castro came to power, López Mateos zigzagged to create the impression that he sided with all factions within the PRI. When López Mateos's successor was sworn in, Mexico was still politically unified despite the unsettling influence of the Cuban Revolution.[3]

In Washington, López Mateos's diplomats labored successfully to convince the United States not to pressure Mexico to take a decisive stand against Cuba in the OAS. U.S. officials, despite being irritated, were sympathetic to the Mexican argument that close cooperation between Mexico City and Washington against Castro would endanger Mexico's continued domestic peace. With a shared frontier of almost 2,000 miles, a tranquil Mexico has always been a high priority for U.S. foreign policy.

In 1960, an OAS foreign ministers' meeting was held in San José, Costa Rica, to consider, among other things, the problem of Cuban meddling in the internal affairs of Latin American countries. Before leaving Washington for the Costa Rican conference, Mexican diplomats convinced the U.S. State Department not to mention Cuba by name in the meeting's final resolution.[4]

At the foreign ministers' meeting, when asked if Cuba was going to be identified in the resolution condemning intervention, Roy R. Rubottom, Jr., the U.S. assistant secretary of state for inter-American affairs, replied, "If you are in a room with only one one-eyed man, you don't have to mention him by name for everybody to know whom you are talking about."[5] Cuba, by name, was not condemned at the San José conference.

The U.S.-organized 1961 Bay of Pigs invasion of Cuba aggravated the Mexican dilemma. The Mexican government publicly had to denounce all U.S. invasions of Latin American nations. The painful national memory of the loss of vast territories to the United States in the previous century demanded condemnation. Also, from the Mexican viewpoint, if approval were given to the United States to invade Cuba, it might set a precedent for an invasion of Mexico if Washington so desired.

It was inconceivable to Mexico's leaders that the United States would allow its Bay of Pigs invasion to fail. When it was clear that the exile fighters could not break out of the beachhead at the Bay of Pigs to overthrow Castro, Mexico's leaders reacted bitterly (albeit privately) against the United States. Foreign Minister Manuel Tello of Mexico, when told the invasion had failed, had difficulty understanding how the United States could have committed itself to an invasion of Cuba and then have allowed it to fail. Tello wondered how the United States could be so irresponsible. "Now we in Mexico will be cursed for the next twenty years by pressure from Castro's presence in Cuba."[6]

Since he was certain a U.S.-backed military effort to overthrow Castro would succeed, Tello had already written a statement for release after the expected victory of the invasion reaffirming Mexico's adherence to the principle of nonintervention. "Then I was going to go to church to offer up a prayer of thanksgiving to the United States for delivering us from the dangers of Castro," Tello said.

At the start of the Bay of Pigs invasion, former president Cárdenas precipitated an internal political crisis in Mexico. Cárdenas called on Mexicans to rally to the support of the Cuban Revolution and announced he was immediately flying to Havana to stand shoulder-to-shoulder with Castro against the U.S.-financed invasion. The prospect of Cárdenas in Havana to confront the United States moving to military confrontation with Cuba presented President López Mateos with a new headache caused by the Castro Revolution. But the Mexican government was equally anxious to avoid a direct confrontation with a former president respected internationally as a champion of leftist causes and supported at home by public opinion and his own faction in the ruling coalition.

López Mateos succeeded in avoiding a costly political showdown and in preventing Cárdenas from going to Cuba. During the week of the invasion, Cárdenas tried repeatedly but unsuccessfully to leave Mexico to go to Cuba. Even though commercial planes were landing and taking off without difficulty, every time the pilot of Cárdenas's chartered private plane asked for takeoff clearance, visibility suddenly became too dangerous for departure.

Cárdenas finally gave up. He held a mass demonstration in Mexico City's main square, the Zócalo, haranguing a pro-Castro crowd while standing on the hood of a car.[7] By then, the Bay of Pigs episode was over and pressure on the Mexican government had eased. With the United States proven inept in dealing decisively with Castro, Mexico became more energetic in trying to remain passive in the quarrel between the United States and Cuba.

In 1962 in Punta del Este, Uruguay, another OAS foreign ministers' meeting was held to consider the Cuba problem. Even though Mexico had tried to block the convocation of the meeting and did not want to get involved in any resolution or action that might cause domestic political difficulties, it was Foreign Minister Tello, who privately detested Castro, who suggested the solution at the conference for dealing with Cuba. Castro had by then declared, "I am a Marxist-Leninist." Tello suggested to the other foreign ministers that Castro's government, based on concepts of Marxism-Leninism, was "incompatible" with the basic principles of the inter-American system. The guidance of the Mexican foreign minister opened the way for the approval of final resolutions against Cuba.

Mexico voted for the paragraphs in the resolution that described the incompatibility of the Castro regime with the inter-American system. But Tello abstained in the vote on the final paragraph of the resolution, which excluded Cuba from further participation in the OAS.[8] The Mexican government was therefore able to contend at home that it had not taken any action against the government of another nation.

But the unwanted showdown of the United States over Cuba could not be avoided in October 1962 during the crisis over the deployment of Soviet nuclear missiles on the island. The United States insisted that Mexico vote, without equivocation, for the OAS action against communism because of the missile buildup in Cuba. President López Mateos and Foreign Minister Tello were on a tour of Asia at the time. Acting Foreign Minister José Gorostiza insisted that Mexico would adopt its customary position of abstention on any resolution that required action against Cuba.

This time the United States was not sympathetic to Mexico's potential domestic problems. Since a nuclear war was possible, the United States demanded a favorable vote. Gorostiza was warned bluntly that if the United States survived the nuclear crisis without Mexican support, favorable U.S.-Mexican relations would no longer exist.

López Mateos, then in Manila, authorized Gorostiza to vote with the United States at the OAS in the showdown on the missile crisis. When López Mateos returned to Mexico City, four former Mexican presidents called on him to express their approval of Mexico's vote against Castro; former president Cárdenas did not attend that meeting.[9]

At the next OAS foreign ministers' meeting called to deal once again with the continuing problem of Castro's interventions to overthrow Latin American governments, Mexico adopted a firm, isolated position that was applauded in Havana and the rest of the Third World and denounced in the United States as siding with communists in Cuba. The meeting was held in Washington in 1964. Venezuela accused Castro of having shipped arms to guerrillas fighting its government. With the exception of Mexico, the governments making up the OAS decided to break diplomatic relations with Cuba. Mexico, in what appeared to the world to be a defiant stance to show its total independence from outside pressures and its defense of the principle of nonintervention, continued after 1964 to maintain an embassy in Havana.

But several years later, the U.S. secretary of state Dean Rusk said in a private conversation that he had no quarrel whatsoever with the maintenance of diplomatic relations with Mexico and Cuba. "When we were discussing the breaking of relations at the foreign ministers' meeting," said Rusk, "we decided it would be in the best interests of all our countries if one country maintained relations with Cuba and acted as a listening post for all of us. That country was Mexico."[10]

López Mateos's personal anger toward Castro for having turned his presidency into an ongoing ordeal of maneuvering constantly to maintain domestic peace was directed also toward U.S. journalists. The president of Mexico was convinced that if U.S. journalists reporting in Cuba in 1958 had not written favorably about Castro, he would never have come to power, and Mexico, as a result, would have been spared the danger of domestic disruption because of the Cuban Revolution. López Mateos's successor, Pres. Gustavo Díaz Ordaz (1964–1970) fully shared his predecessor's belief that U.S. journalists had helped bring Castro to power and therefore were also to blame for Mexico's problems.[11]

President Gustavo Díaz Ordaz

President Díaz Ordaz, a fervent anticommunist, took office angered by the transformation of Cuba into a forward military base for the Soviet Union, the attempts by Castro to overthrow Latin American governments, and the problems caused for stability in Mexico by the Cuban Revolution. The new president of Mexico wanted to join the rest of the hemisphere in breaking relations with Cuba. His initial belief was that given a plausible excuse for doing so, Mexico would react by withdrawing its embassy from Havana.

By 1964, however, the Castro government had correctly concluded that no matter what it did, Mexico was locked into its policy of diplomatic recognition of Cuba. After having repeatedly sneered publicly at the rest of Latin America for vulnerability to Castro's revolution while it was supposedly immune, it would be too embarrassing for Mexico to admit its error. A break with Havana would also appear to the world as repudiation of Mexico's boast of unyielding adherence to a policy of nonintervention in the internal affairs of other nations. Castro and his aides, however, were under no illusions about the ideological orientation of Mexico's leaders. They distrusted the conservative Mexican leadership as much as Díaz Ordaz loathed them.[12]

It was important for Havana to continue normal diplomatic relations with Mexico City. Trade was a minor factor. Pressure from Washington forbade U.S. companies based in Mexico from shipping machinery and spare parts to Cuba. Castro depended economically on supplies from Canada, Europe, the Soviet Union, and secret Cuban-backed companies based in Panama.

Access to Latin America became the most important asset of continued relations with Mexico. Latin American revolutionaries traveled through Mexico on their way to Cuba to receive military training. Cuban diplomats used Mexico as their transit point to reach other countries to conduct covert operations.

With Díaz Ordaz inhibited from breaking relations with Cuba, Mexico became a mecca for spy activities during the late 1960s. It was understood that clandestine operations carried out by other governments on Mexican soil were supposed to be directed only against third countries. Mexico itself was not to be targeted. The oversized Soviet Embassy in Mexico City focused chiefly on debriefing its agents in the United States. With a free flow of tourists from the United States into Mexico, U.S. spies came to Mexico to report to their Soviet case officers and receive payment and instructions. The embassy also concentrated on supplying funds and maintaining contacts with local Communist parties in Latin America.

Mexico allowed the United States to counterbalance Soviet-Cuban communist activities. The CIA, working closely with Mexico's secret police, monitored arriving and departing Cuban and Soviet diplomats, U.S. spies reporting to their case officers in Mexico, and revolutionaries from Latin America passing through Mexico. Passengers bound for and arriving from Cuba were always carefully photographed at the Mexico City airport by the CIA.

Cuba's embassy in Mexico City expanded its operation carefully and slowly, until it was certain its covert activities would not result in a breaking of relations with Díaz Ordaz. The Cuban diplomats at first were careful to maintain correct diplomatic relations. But Mexico's leaders, even back in 1961, suspected that Castro's agents were involved in antigovernment uprisings—from villages on the frontier with Guatemala to Tijuana on the border with the United States—that were suppressed by the Mexican army. President López Mateos decided not to probe too deeply into the 1961 antigovernment conspiracy because of the possibility of provoking an even more serious rift in the ruling coalition.[13]

The Cubans then expanded their operations to include closer relations with the left wing of the ruling coalition; they also spied on activities of Cuban exiles in Mexico. The next step, tolerated by the Mexican government, was the use of Mexico as a base for subversion against Central America and Venezuela.

By 1966, the Cuban government, convinced it could violate Mexico's sovereignty with impunity, decided to target Mexico itself. The Mexican secret service in September 1966 arrested Julián López, the press secretary of the Cuban Embassy, as he walked into the hideout of a leftist group smuggling arms to Guatemalan guerrillas. López, who in 1979 handled the coordination in Costa Rica of Cuban arms made available to the Sandinistas, was carrying three hundred $20 bills for payment to the arms smugglers. The Mexican government feared that many of the four thousand rifles supposedly shipped to the Guatemalan guerrillas had, in reality, been diverted for use by peasants causing unrest in the countryside. Cuban diplomats had been identified by the Mexican police as having been in contact with rebellious peasant groups.

López was also linked to Victor Rico Galán, a naturalized Mexican from Spain, who was arrested for training two urban guerrilla groups in apartment buildings in Mexico City. Rico Galán was sentenced to several years in prison after conviction on charges of conspiracy to overthrow the Mexican government.[14]

Díaz Ordaz correctly interpreted the illegal activities of the Cuban Embassy in Mexico as contempt for himself and his government. His personal desire to get tough with Castro and bring López to trial in Mexico was tempered by the realization that publicity would be embarrassing to Mexico. It would prove to the Mexican people and the world that the government's policy of maintaining diplomatic relations with Cuba had been all wrong.

Castro's foreign minister, Raúl Roa, insisted that López was protected by diplomatic immunity. Díaz Ordaz surrendered. López was quietly sent back to Havana and the rift with the Cuban Embassy was hushed up.

During the Díaz Ordaz years, Mexican diplomats complained privately that while they and their government were being excoriated in the United States for being pro-Castro, they were in reality acting as Washington's surrogates in protecting U.S. interests in Cuba. U.S. congressmen discovered that when constituents complained of personal and property problems in Cuba, the State Department solved their problems by asking the Mexican foreign office to intervene.

Personal ties between senior U.S. and Mexican leaders were very close. When Mexican foreign minister Antonio Carrillo Flores suggested to U.S. secretary of state Rusk at a session of the UN General Assembly that he take the initiative to break the ongoing stalemate between Cuba and the United States, Rusk said that he couldn't start a negotiating process but that if Castro, for example, proposed freeing political prisoners, the United States would react positively.

Mexico acted as the go-between. Carrillo Flores notified Mexico City, which transmitted the message to Havana. As a result, Castro made a public offer to release political prisoners, which, however, did not change the impasse between Washington and Havana.[15]

By the end of the Díaz Ordaz era, failures of the Cuban Revolution had discredited it as a model for similar upheavals in Latin America. The danger of Castro to Mexico, as perceived by Mexico's leaders, lessened, and tensions between the two governments eased.

Presidents Luis Alvarez Echeverría and José López Portillo

The unwritten rules of the PRI assume that presidents of Mexico will govern within reasonable parameters that do not endanger the survival of the unwieldy ruling coalition. A PRI president who deviates by governing too sharply either to the left or to the right alienates factions within the ruling coalition and jeopardizes domestic peace.

Beginning with Pres. Luis Alvarez Echeverría (1970–1976), the political balance that had kept Mexico stable was fragmented. In the context of the Mexican political system, President Echeverría veered precipitously to the left. His successor, José López Portillo (1976–1982), continued the drift to the left. (Miguel de la Madrid (1982–1988) shifted back to the right, and the current president, Carlos Salinas de Gortari, has continued the rightist philosophy of his predecessor.)

Before he became president, Echeverría had earned the reputation of a lackluster bureaucrat. In office, his personality changed. He had always dreamed of becoming another Lázaro Cárdenas, esteemed internationally for championing revolutionary causes. During his six years as president, Echeverría tried to become the leader of the Third World; and he campaigned, albeit unsuccessfully, to become Secretary-General of the UN upon completion of his term.

The Echeverría period was a boon to the Castro Revolution. Since he considered himself also a revolutionary, Echeverría, to the dismay of major factions within his ruling coalition, sided openly with the Castro regime. He financed leftist organizations both in Mexico and abroad and diverted funds to the Castro regime. The Mexican president built a huge new embassy building in Mexico City for the Cuban government.[16]

In terms of policy toward Cuba, the López Portillo era divides into two equal periods. During his first three years as president, López Portillo had no interest in Cuba. His presidency was based on working out a long-term, close relationship with the United States, leading to a common market arrangement. With oil supplies from the Middle East precarious for the United States, López Portillo was convinced he could negotiate an equitable agreement with the giant United States, using Mexico's supply of petroleum as a bargaining chip.

The López Portillo pro-U.S. policy came to a crashing halt with the official visit to Mexico in 1979 of Pres. Jimmy Carter. It became apparent to the Mexican president that his vision of a U.S.-Mexico understanding was unreal—it was a vision not shared by the United States.

López Portillo reacted angrily. He gave up on the United States, reversed policy, and shifted to the left. The president invited Fidel Castro to make his first visit to Mexico since the late 1950s, when the Cuban revolutionary had used Mexico as the springboard from which to launch his invasion of Cuba. The invitation to Castro did not, however, imply personal support for the Cuban Revolution by López Portillo. The Mexican president was venting his bitterness toward the United States by appearing to befriend the principal enemy of the United States in Latin America.[17]

Presidents Miguel de la Madrid and Carlos Salinas de Gortari

President de la Madrid spent six years overwhelmed by economic problems inherited from the presidencies of Echeverría and López Portillo. The need to ease Mexico's massive foreign debt and to revive the business sector of the economy, depressed by the two previous PRI administrations, occupied almost all of his attention. Direct Cuba-Mexico relations were of little importance during the de la Madrid period. They became an indirect factor in nearby Central America where Cuba backed the Sandinistas who had taken power in Nicaragua and the guerrillas fighting to take power in El Salvador.

Friction between the United States and Mexico became acute when de la Madrid's foreign minister, Bernardo Sepúlveda, took the lead with other Latin American foreign ministers in trying to negotiate peace agreements in Central America. The United States contended that Foreign Minister Sepúlveda was anti-American and pro-Castro and that his efforts for peace were frustrating Washington's policies in Central America. Despite U.S. suggestions that de la Madrid fire his foreign minister, Sepúlveda remained in office during the six-year presidency.[18]

Salinas de Gortari came to office at the moment of the major turn in world history. Eastern Europe was freeing itself from Soviet domination, the Soviet Union was imploding, and Castro's Cuba was being isolated, cut off from Moscow's economic and political support. The president of Mexico, after realizing that Japan and Europe were forming trade blocs and that Mexico was in danger of being isolated as a trading partner, reversed the flow of Mexican history. He asked Pres. George Bush to negotiate a free-trade treaty that would imply an intimate, long-term relationship with a superpower now in possession of about half of Mexico's original territory. Until President Salinas de Gortari's term, Mexican foreign policy had been designed to stave off a too-close relationship with Washington. The new relationship with the United States is the overall objective of the Salinas de Gortari administration. Nothing will be permitted to place it at risk.

Policy regarding what is seen as the last days of the Castro Revolution differs in Washington and Mexico City. President Bush kept unchanged the U.S. hard-line policy toward the Castro regime. The United States is hoping for an anti-Castro explosion in Cuba that will sweep away the present government.

Salinas de Gortari joins other Latin American leaders who oppose political repression in Cuba and are pressuring Castro privately for democratic change. The Mexican president and the other Latin American leaders feel that since the Cuban experiment is finished, the agony should not be prolonged. They believe that the peaceful way to bring about democratic change is to start a dialogue now with Havana leading to Cuba's return to the inter-American system. President Salinas de Gortari is also concerned about the possibility of civil war in Cuba if opposition rises to the continuation of the Castro government. A spillover of refugees from turbulence in Cuba could involve Mexico once again as a haven for political exiles.

Mexico, however, vociferously opposes the U.S. Torricelli Bill. On September 30, 1992, the Mexican congress condemned the U.S. Congress's Torricelli Bill on trade with Cuba because "it is contrary to international law."[19]

But regardless of any doubts the president of Mexico has about the wisdom of the present U.S. policy toward Cuba, Salinas de Gortari will not say or do anything that endangers his objectives of a free-trade treaty with Washington.[20]

NOTES

1. I worked for United Press, Mexico, from 1951 to 1955; then I was in Washington for five years as chief of press for the Organization of American States; then I returned to Mexico as a correspondent for *US News & World Report*. I was present when President López Mateos maneuvered and zigzagged to contain the negative impact on the Mexican political system of the Castro Revolution.

2. Without a study of the PRI, there is no possibility of arriving at a realistic understanding of Mexican foreign policy of the last thirty years. This may not be as true in the future, since opposition leader Cuauhtémoc Cárdenas and Pres. Carlos Salinas de Gortari are changing the structure of the Mexican political system.

3. I am a great admirer of President López Mateos. I see him as one of Mexico's great presidents. He understood that his primary responsibilities as a PRI

president were to maintain internal unity and turn over power, completely intact, to his PRI successor. The next PRI president, Gustavo Díaz Ordaz, also understood his responsibilities as leader of the ruling coalition. Thereafter, as I indicate later, the PRI system began to break down.

4. This represents the conclusion of very senior Mexican diplomats after their private talks within the U.S. counterparts.

5. Rubottom said this to me in San José, Costa Rica, at the start of the foreign ministers' meeting.

6. Foreign Minister Tello, one of Mexico's very distinguished and competent diplomats, was bitter and depressed when he said this to me in a private conversation at the old Foreign Ministry building in Mexico City, the day after the beginning of the Bay of Pigs invasion, when it was clear the invading force was not going to be able to break out of its beachhead. We were alone in his private office.

7. The details of the frustrated Cárdenas attempt to join Fidel Castro in Cuba come from senior aides to President López Mateos who watched from the roof of the National Palace as the former president harangued the crowd.

8. Tello's contributions to the "incompatibility" resolution are part of the record of the OAS. Officials in the U.S. delegation to the foreign ministers' meeting have told me how grateful they were to the Mexican foreign minister for his diplomatic formula. The OAS has no provision for the expulsion of a member nation.

9. I reported on the U.S. insistence that Mexico publicly commit its vote against the Soviet missile buildup in Cuba. This time U.S. officials decided that a public policy of support by Mexico was more important than any possible adverse reaction to Mexican unity. The attitude of the four former Mexican presidents confirmed President López Mateos's decision of backing the United States.

10. Rusk's comments were made to me in Mexico City at the residence of the U.S. ambassador.

11. The conviction of López Mateos and Díaz Ordaz that U.S. journalists had played an important role in helping Castro come to power was said to me privately, in different years, by both presidents. I disputed their version of Cuban history.

12. The mutual distrust for each other was proven over and over again to me during this period, each time I visited Havana or spoke with senior aides to President Díaz Ordaz.

13. The 1961 uprising was reported (without explanation) fully in Mexican newspapers. The López Mateos government never provided the Mexican people with an explanation. It was hushed up and I would assume the Mexican government even today would prefer to forget about it. I reflect opinions expressed privately by senior government officials when I write that there was suspicion that Castro was involved. The last thing that President López Mateos wanted was confrontation within the ruling coalition.

14. In 1966, I used to lunch in Mexico City with Julián López and Victor Rico Galán. I followed very closely what they did and what finally happened to them. The information about the four thousand rifles came from a senior aide to President Díaz Ordaz, who showed me the Mexican intelligence file on the arms smuggling and was deeply concerned the weapons had not left Mexico.

15. Mexico's role as go-between was described to me in detail at lunch in Mexico City by Foreign Minister Carrillo Flores. I am prejudiced, since Carrillo Flores, now dead, was a dear friend but there is no doubt in my mind that he was one of the best foreign ministers ever produced by Latin America.

16. The material on Echeverría is based on personal contact with the president and his aides.

17. I had the same type of relationship with President López Portillo and his aides that I had with President Echeverría.

18. The friction between Mexican Foreign Minister Sepúlveda and, principally, U.S. secretary of state George Shultz was common knowledge in both Washington and Mexico City. I knew the details of the conflict and the unsuccessful effort by the United States to get Sepúlveda fired.

19. "Summary of World Broadcasts/The Monitoring Report," British Broadcasting Corporation, October 3, 1992.

20. Differing attitudes in Mexico City and Washington to what are seen as the last days of the Castro regime in Cuba reflect reporting in both countries. There is no doubt in the minds of Mexican officials about President Salinas de Gortari's priorities. As long as his dominant goal is an economic alliance with the United States, Cuba is just an irritant.

13

Canada and Cuba: Four and a Half Decades of Cordial Relations

RICHARD V. GORHAM

Canada did not begin to establish diplomatic relations with countries in Latin America until the early 1940s, although there had been substantial trading links with many of the countries of the region throughout several decades previously. Cuba was no exception to this general development, with Canadian-Cuban trading, business, and missionary contacts having been developed over many years. Cuba was also one of the countries in the region with which Canada early established formal diplomatic relations. The Canadian Embassy was opened in Havana on March 16, 1945, and it has been functioning there continuously ever since. During the subsequent forty-six years, Canada's relations with Cuba have been correct and as close and cordial as could be expected between two nations with very important differences on foreign-policy issues, security questions, social and economic structure and development, and political philosophy.

When I was in charge of the Latin American and Caribbean Bureau of the Canadian Department of External Affairs in the early 1980s, Cuban diplomatic representatives often told me that Fidel Castro had described the relations between Canada and Cuba as a model between nations of different social and political systems. I agreed with such a description but commented on the weight of those differences. I would remind my interlocutors that Canada was not a communist country nor a nonaligned nation; on the contrary, we were an ally of the United States in the military defense of North America against a possible threat by the Soviet Union. Furthermore, Canada was an ally of our NATO partners for the military defense of Western Europe also against such a threat. Cuba, on the other hand, claimed to be a nonaligned nation and was a close associate, if not formally a military ally, of the Soviet Union. It was also an active supporter of disruptive armed revolutionary causes in Central and South America and in Africa.

Thus in foreign-policy and security considerations there have been clear differences between the two countries that have always represented a barrier beyond which the development of closer bilateral relations has not been possible. Also, in terms of domestic political structures and respective domestic social, economic, and political policies, there have been fundamental differences that have impeded the type of close relations we have been able to enjoy with other Latin American nations of an ideological basis similar to our own. Both Canada and Cuba have always accepted these differences, notwithstanding which our relations have been correct and friendly up to the point where such differences have impeded further proximity.

The main element in Canada's relations with Cuba has been trade. Cuba has been a very substantial trading partner for Canada in the Caribbean region, and our bilateral trade relations have been favorable and to the benefit of both countries. In 1990 Canadian exports to Cuba totaled $170.5 million. In previous years this figure was higher, but Cuba's current financial resources have suffered limitations that have compelled a reduction in the volume of Cuban imports from Canada. Nevertheless, Canada's 1990 exports to Cuba represented a modest increase over the previous year. It is hoped that a positive change in Cuba's economic situation will be accompanied by a comparable increase in Cuban purchases from Canada.

Cuba's exports to Canada in 1990 more than doubled that of the previous year and amounted to $130.1 million. This has been an encouraging trend indicating that as Cuban goods become more competitive in price and quality they can find a place in the Canadian market. Cuba's major exports to Canada have been sugar, molasses, precious metals and stones, crustaceans, and clothing.

Canadian exports to Cuba are mostly agricultural products, such as wheat (much of which had been paid for by the Soviet Union), potatoes, and pulp and paper products. At one time Canada sold a considerable number of Holstein cattle to Cuba—most of Cuba's dairy stock can thus be traced to Canadian ancestry.

Canada-Cuba trade relations are carefully monitored by a joint committee on economic and trade relations, which meets regularly approximately every two years. In addition, there are periodic exchanges of visits in regard to our trade and cooperation in the fields of agriculture and fisheries.

Canada has consistently resisted pressure from the United States to impose a trade embargo on Cuba; at times this has created an element of strain in Canada-U.S. relations. We have undertaken, however, to prevent Canada from becoming a back door for the export of goods of U.S. origin to Cuba, which are prohibited by U.S. trade regulations. When violations of this restriction have been discovered, appropriate action has been taken by the Canadian authorities to prosecute the perpetrators. On the basis of the same undertaking, Canada also prevents the export to Cuba of Canadian goods that have substantial U.S. content; thus Canadian exports to Cuba consist mainly of agricultural products.

In the management of its trade relations with Cuba, Canada has always had to take carefully into account the state of Cuba-U.S. relations and the extent to which the state of that relationship could have a bearing on Canada-U.S. relations. Recently, strain in Canada-U.S. relations has occurred because of the Mack Amendment, as part of the U.S. Export Administration Act of 1990 and 1991, and the 1992 Torricelli Bill, the effect of which will restrict trade with Cuba by U.S.-owned subsidiaries in Canada.

Since 1963 Canada has rejected attempts by the United States to regulate such Canadian companies from trading with Cuba, and in 1984 Canada enacted the Foreign Extraterritorial Measures Act to deal with such matters. In response to the proposal of the Mack Amendment in 1990 Canadian secretary of state for external affairs Joe Clark wrote to U.S. secretary of state James Baker urging him to "weigh fully the impact that the 'Mack Amendment' will have on US-owned enterprises in Canada as well as on our bilateral relationship." At the same time, the government of Canada issued an order under the abovementioned Foreign Extraterritorial Measures Act to counter the Mack Amendment by prohibiting any individual or Canada-based corporation from complying with any U.S. measure to prevent trade between Canada and Cuba.

Pres. George Bush vetoed the 1990 attempt to enact the Mack Amendment, but the government of Canada was concerned by the renewed attempt to pass such legislation. On February 19, 1991, the Canadian secretary of state for external affairs expressed disappointment that this measure had been reintroduced and expressed the hope that "members of Congress will reflect on the unacceptable nature of this application of American law in Canada" and asserted, "Let there be no doubt that Canada intends to block compliance with this measure by Canadian firms." On October 3, 1992, however, both houses of the U.S. Congress passed the Torricelli Bill, which includes the extraterritorial subsidiary legislation. On October 23, 1992, the bill was signed into law by Pres. Bush. Canada remains firm in its opposition to this measure.

In other areas, such as cultural exchanges, Canada and Cuba have had a modest level of activity, which both sides would like to expand to the extent that resources permit. There have also been useful sports exchanges and some cooperation in the area of public health. In addition, over the past few years there has been a steady increase in the number of Canadian tourists who visit Cuba each winter—more than eighty thousand in 1990 alone. This will probably increase as Cuba's capacity to receive and accommodate tourists increases.

At the political level, exchanges between the two countries have generally been low key. In 1976 Prime Minister Pierre Trudeau visited Cuba, but the general public reaction in Canada to that visit was rather negative. Since then, no Canadian prime minister has visited Cuba, nor has there ever been a reciprocal Cuban visit to Canada (though Cuba would probably welcome one if there were an invitation). There have, however, been periodic exchanges of visits at the level of senior officials and occasionally ministers of specific portfolios such as fisheries, agriculture, and sports, including the August 1991 visit on the occasion of the Pan-American Games in Havana.

Although Canada-Cuba relations have been generally favorable, they have not been without strain, and there continue to be minor irritants. One such irritant was the occasional attempt by Cubans or their Canadian or U.S. associates to use Canada as a back door to circumvent U.S. trade regulations, as mentioned earlier. Another was the desire of the Cuban government to assign to Cuban diplomatic or consular offices in Canada personnel whom the Canadian authorities had reason to believe were active intelligence agents. When such assignments were not permitted, Cuba sometimes acknowledged that such individuals were not involved in intelligence activities against Canada but were involved against other countries unfriendly to Cuba. The Canadian response was that Cuban intelligence activity in Canada was not welcome, regardless of what country it was targeting.

At the time of the Cuban Revolution various properties of Canadian enterprises and of Canadian citizens were seized and nationalized. The question of compensation continued as an irritant in Cuba-Canada relations for several years. In the early 1980s, however, an agreement was reached and compensation promptly paid, thus removing that particular issue from the bilateral agenda.

Not surprisingly, given the fundamental differences between the two countries, foreign-policy and security considerations have always been the major problem in the Canada-Cuba relationship. The government of Canada—and indeed all Canadians—was very much concerned by Cuba's role in the Cuban missile crisis of 1962, and Canada has always been uncomfortable with Cuba's Soviet connection and its support of revolutionary movements in other countries. Canada was also uncomfortable with the Bay of Pigs operation and the subsequent basis of hostility and mutual antagonism in Cuba-U.S. relations.

In the early 1970s, Canada had a small economic development assistance program with Cuba—mainly in the agricultural and fisheries sectors—but this was terminated when Cuba sent its troops to Africa. The rationale for this decision was that if Cuba chose to devote its scarce resources to offshore military ventures, there could be no justification for the expenditure of Canadian taxpayer money on Cuba's economic development. In 1981 this restriction was broadened to terminate government subsidies to Canadian nongovernmental organizations with development assistance activities in Cuba.

Now that Cuba has reduced its military activities abroad, the rationale for the restriction has lost its validity. A case can therefore be made for a resumption of a modest economic assistance program, particularly if it would be of benefit to Canada as well. But higher priorities elsewhere and the current shortage of development assistance funds make it unlikely that any positive steps will be taken in that direction at the present time.

A current strain in Canada's relationship with Cuba involves the questions of human rights, treatment of dissidents, and family reunification. The government of Canada and the Canadian people are concerned about the situation of human rights in Cuba, and they deplore the treatment that the Cuban government accords to dissidents and human rights activists in that country. Canada does not accept that individual rights should be subject to those of a political party or the state. Canadian representatives have therefore taken every opportunity to raise human rights issues at the very highest levels, both bilaterally and in multilateral forums. Positive change in Cuban domestic policy could quickly ease Canadian-Cuban relations on this matter.

The question of family reunification has been an irritant in Canada-Cuba relations for a number of years, but it has recently shown encouraging signs of resolution. Over the past few years a number of Cubans on flights to or from Eastern Europe that have landed at Gander Airport in Newfoundland have defected and been granted refugee status in Canada. While the Cuban authorities have come to accept such situations with a grudging acquiescence, they have not been so forthcoming about allowing family members of refugees to leave Cuba and reunite with their relatives in Canada. This has been a very heartrending and poignant situation for the families involved, and they have the sympathy and support of the government of Canada. As a result of strong representations made to the Cuban authorities at every level, the last outstanding reunification cases were resolved in early 1991. It is hoped that the positive Cuban attitude in regard to these cases will encourage the swift resolution of possible future cases, all of which would have a salutary effect on the development of bilateral relations.

Canada attaches importance to its relations with Cuba and considers that Cuba is an important nation in the Americas that can play a role in the resolution of regional problems. Over the past several years we have seen positive trends of more pragmatism and less ideological rigidity in domestic policies and relations between different systems, including those in Latin America, indicating positive prospects for cooperation. In this regard the Canadian secretary for external affairs had the following to say to a parliamentary committee on November 8, 1989:

Cuba is in an increasingly interesting position in the world. Other countries with its system have changed their system more thoroughly than Cuba seems prepared to do. I think this is a time when it makes sense for Canada bilaterally to pay more rather than less attention to Cuba simply because Cuba seems to be sitting so far outside the stream of events. That is not in their interests and we do not think it is in the interest of the hemisphere.

He later expanded on this theme in a speech to the University of Calgary on February 1, 1990:

Cuba has isolated itself from this hemisphere. Many states in this hemisphere have isolated themselves from Cuba. No one would deny that Cuba has had a role in the current troubles in Central America. And few can look at the economic facts and not conclude that Cuba suffered by exclusion from the hemisphere. . . . I will not ascribe blame here. I simply state that some of the current problems in Latin America could become more manageable if Cuba were brought back into the family of hemispheric nations. Clearly the problems here are not easy to overcome. There is a lot of history, remembered personally and bitterly by influential people throughout the Americas. Perceptions and prejudices have taken firm roots. But I refuse to believe these are insurmountable.

Clearly, Canada hopes that Cuba will follow the positive trend of other countries and take appropriate steps to overcome the isolated position in which it now finds itself. I believe that if there were any practical action that Canada could take that would assist or encourage Cuba in this regard, the government of Canada would probably be prepared to give it serious consideration. One possible area regards Cuba's status in the Organization of American States (OAS). The recent membership of Canada, Belize, and Guyana having brought about the long-desired near universality of membership in the organization, there has been a renewed focus on the present government of Cuba not having been allowed to take its seat. Member countries of the Rio Group have spoken publicly in favor of Cuba's reinstatement, but so far there has been no positive action. Cuba has indicated its interest in active membership if invited by the member states to return. Speaking to a parliamentary committee on November 8, 1989, the Canadian secretary of state for external affairs indicated that Canada was prepared to examine the issue "on the basis of the facts at the time" and "in the context of the relations we have enjoyed and maintained regularly with Cuba" and "in the spirit of the OAS to consult with all of our colleagues there."

On February 6, 1990, the Standing Committee on External Affairs and International Trade presented a report to the Canadian Parliament on Canada's role in the OAS. In regard to Cuba, the report recommended that "as one tangible contribution to getting the country into the hemispheric swim, Canada should work steadily towards the readmission of Cuba to active membership in the OAS." In its official response on July 4, 1990, the government indicated that as Canada was not part of the decision to exclude Cuba from active membership, a decision to reverse that stand should be taken by those nations originally involved. The statement went on to say that Canada was "currently actively engaged in seeking ways to limit Cuba's isolation in the hemisphere" and that Canada would "continue to maintain close contact with the Cuban government with a view to reducing tension in the region."

It is clear from the above that Canada would have no objection to Cuba's resumption of active membership in the organization and would in fact welcome it. But Canada believes it should be up to those nations that decided to terminate Cuba's active membership to take the formal initiative to propose the necessary practical steps. Any such action would be positively supported by Canada, as indicated by the Canadian secretary of state for external affairs, Barbara McDougal, in her formal address to the OAS General Assembly in Santiago, Chile, on June 3, 1991: "This year we are delighted to welcome our commonwealth partners, Belize and Guyana, to our midst. We are made stronger and more complete by their presence. We look forward to the time when the vision of the founders of the OAS for a universal hemispheric forum can be realized and Cuba will retake its place in the organization as a full member of the hemispheric family."

14

Cuba and the United States:
Opportunities Lost and Future Potential

MICHAEL D. KAPLOWITZ WITH
DONNA RICH KAPLOWITZ

Relations between the United States and Cuba have been strained since 1959. The U.S. embargo of Cuba has been in place for more than thirty years, yet Cuba remains a fiercely independent island nation 90 miles from the Florida coast. Much has been written about the foreign policies of the United States and Cuba, and while several previous studies address the impact of the U.S. embargo on the Cuban economy, surprisingly few address the costs of the extant U.S. policy to U.S. businesses. Moreover, almost all of the work in this area has been based on continued economic relations between Cuba and the Soviet bloc. The fall of Eastern Europe has left Cuba without its largest trading partners of the last three decades. This economic crisis can be seen as an opportunity of enormous potential for both Cuba and the United States.

Recent events signal a new period of entrepreneurial enterprise in Cuba, yet as Cuba reorients itself to the world's marketplace, the United States and its business interests are missing out on an opportunity. The chief trade competitors of the United States are losing little time developing new commercial relations with the island. It is estimated that U.S. businesses could sell $1.3–2 billion worth of goods to Cuba in the first year after the embargo would be lifted.[1] Other potential gains include savings for U.S. importers; the availability of an inexpensive, healthy, and well-educated work force; and a new market of nearly eleven million people with pent-up demand for U.S. goods and services. Allowing U.S. businesses into the Cuban market would also provide the United States with an important opportunity to participate in a changing Cuba.

In 1988, a Johns Hopkins University study estimated that if trade were permitted between the United States and Cuba at that time, U.S. firms could engage in up to $750 million worth of annual trade.[2] That year was the last year of regular uninterrupted trade between Cuba and the Soviet Union. Nearly all of the calculations in that study were based on the assumption that the Soviet Union and the Council for Mutual Assistance

(CMEA) would continue as Cuba's principle trading partners. The dramatic changes of the last four years are apparent in Cuba's new exchange patterns—the island is conducting far more trade with the West than ever envisioned, and the potential gains for U.S. businesses have increased. It is conservatively estimated that the trade embargo were lifted today, total trade turnover between the United States and Cuba would be $1.95–3 billion in the first year of free trade.[3]

This conclusion rests in part on the steady increase in trade between foreign subsidiaries of U.S. companies and Cuba over the last four years. The dissolution of the Soviet trading bloc has resulted in Cuba's increased participation in the world's markets. In 1992, U.S. subsidiary trade with Cuba reached $718 million, a threefold increase from such trade in 1988.[4] In general, the trade between foreign subsidiaries of U.S. parent companies and Cuba could be almost entirely replaced by direct U.S.-Cuban trade.

Furthermore, unlike four years ago, Cuba now actively transacts most of its international trade on world markets in exchange for hard currency. Cuban officials recently estimated that the United States and its businesses could, if the U.S. government allowed, capture 33–50 percent if not more, of all Cuban trade. Cuban trade officials report that the island imported about $4 billion worth of goods in 1991.[5] A conservative estimate of U.S. imports from Cuba during the first year of trade between the two nations would be $.65–1 billion worth of Cuban goods. Preliminary data for 1992 indicate a decrease in Cuban hard currency purchases to roughly $2.2 billion. This 1992 data would support lower estimates of potential trade turnover between the United States and Cuba of $1.1–1.7 billion.

It is important to note that these figures are based upon a static analysis and look only at Cuba's present capacity to buy and sell. In all likelihood, U.S. firms would be able to increase their share of business with Cuba in subsequent years. As Cuba rationalizes and diversifies its economy, in addition to earning more hard currency revenues it will increase its total trade levels. Some analysts estimate that U.S.-Cuban trade could soar to as much as $6.5 billion annually after the first few years of trade.[6] This is not surprising given that prior to 1959 a vast majority of Cuba's trade was with the United States with annual trade totaling more than $1 billion. Moreover, the above estimates do not account for the dynamic potential of U.S. involvement in various Cuban sectors such as mining, tourism, citrus production, and manufacturing.

The benefits flowing to Cuba from free trade with the United States would be varied. Cuba would, of course, have access to attractive and influential markets of goods and services. No longer forced to incur high transportation costs, Cuba would have additional hard currency with which to trade. Lifting the embargo would remove the current chilling effects it has on foreign investment, economic participation, and cooperation with Cuba. Furthermore, some would argue that the free flow of people, ideas, and information that would accompany removal of the blockade would facilitate positive changes for the Cuban people. For example, the large numbers of U.S. tourists visiting Cuba would bring to the island their ideas and values along with their hard currency.

Cuba is slowly opening to exchange forces, and the United States could use a new market of eleven million people only 90 miles away. The potential social, economic, political, and cultural benefits for both nations that would accompany lifting the embargo are positive and substantial.

CHANGES SINCE 1988

Comparisons with data from 1988, the last year of "normal" trade between Cuba and the Soviet bloc, provide a useful and illuminating point of reference. In 1988, 85 percent of Cuban trade was with the former Soviet Union. That year, Cuba's global trade was valued at $13 billion with hard currency trade amounting to $2.7 billion. The collapse of the Soviet Union resulted in Cuba increasing its hard currency trade. In 1991, Cuba imported roughly $4 billion worth of goods in exchange for hard currency. Its total trade turnover that year was approximately $8 billion. Preliminary figures for 1992 indicate that Cuba imported about $2.2 billion worth of hard currency goods.[7] Thus, although Cuba's total trade levels are less than half those in 1988, Cuba has increased its hard currency trade with the West. The economic incentives for businesses to trade with Cuba are greater now than they were four years ago. Some of Cuba's Western trade partners, recognizing this, are increasing their share of Cuba's expanding commercial activity. (See Table 14.1.)

The composition of Cuba's major western trading partners remains relatively unchanged since 1988. Spain is still Cuba's largest trading partner, and Mexico, which has increased trade with Cuba since 1988, has become its second largest. Today Japan, Canada, England, Italy, France, Austria, Germany, and Finland are also major trading partners with Cuba. In Latin America and the Caribbean, Cuba is increasing its trade with Venezuela, Brazil, Chile, Uruguay, Colombia, and Jamaica. These nations and their entrepreneurs are realizing the gains to be made from free trade with Cuba.

Perhaps the most important change apparent from discussions with Cuban officials and businesspeople involves Cuba's pragmatism and flexibility. The island's practical application of its joint venture law is creating new business opportunities. Cuba seems eager to accommodate increased hard currency trade, and recent constitutional changes signal Cuba's commitment to welcome investment. In this climate, the United States has a new opportunity—U.S. commercial interests and wherewithal can participate positively in a changing Cuba.

Table 14.1   Cuban Trade Worldwide

1991 figures are projections based on results for the first nine months

Canada (in thousands of Canadian $)

Exports to Cuba

	1986	1989	1990	1991
Animal, fish products	6,202	8,467	2,743	15,467
Cereals, flour	264,207	103,484	99,905	65,333
Vegetables	15,469	5,906	7,449	n.a.
Other edible products	1,830	n.a.	2,150	n.a.
Industrial, agrochemicals	18,741	5,105	3,052	3,733
Wood, paper, board	10,344	4,853	3,735	2,266
Intermediate goods	3,024	10,810	10,328	2,933
Communications eq., parts	3,677	2,262	3,006	4,266
Electrical fixtures	3,562	2,351	6,386	n.a.
Rail, road vehicles, parts	n.a.	779	3,250	n.a.
Pharm., health, vet. products	1,277	1,614	803	n.a.
Other inedible products	23,118	8,393	9,481	n.a.
Other products	n.a.	n.a.	n.a.	30,533
Total exports	371,025	154,024	188,704	124,266

Imports from Cuba

	1986	1989	1990	1991
Lobster, shrimps, prawns	14,144	11,537	11,011	10,133
Nickel products	n.a.	n.a.	n.a.	57,733
Cigars and tobacco	453	842	1,262	n.a.
Precious metal ores and scrap	8,973	9,245	n.a.	2,133
Chromes in ores	492	n.a.	n.a.	n.a.
Baler twine	416	553	221	n.a.
Finished textiles	1,595	1,202	1,117	n.a.
Raw sugar	41,851	35,211	111,712	87,733
Cane molasses	n.a.	n.a.	2,933	3,066
Towels	n.a.	1,137	465	n.a.
Rum and tafia	n.a.	1,103	621	2,800
Other products	n.a.	1,317	812	3,066
Total imports	71,123	62,147	130,154	166,666

Germany (in thousands of U.S. $)

Exports to Cuba

	1986	1989	1990	1991
Food products of animal origin	4,170	100	25	1,191
Food products, vegetable origin	10,124	39,957	32,216	11,403
Beverages and tobacco	974	667	942	784
Raw materials	7,631	587	305	217
Semifinished products	19,223	20,523	12,467	14,141
Finished products	63,737	62,555	54,015	95,041
Total exports	105,859	124,389	99,970	122,777

Imports from Cuba

	1986	1989	1990	1991
Food products of animal origin	3,283	2,898	3,210	5,166
Food products, vegetable origin	4,404	3,573	5,635	3,734
Beverages and tobacco	4,121	4,265	4,169	5,407
Raw materials	919	2,025	1,631	526
Semifinished products	8,601	12,203	6,585	4,947
Finished products	3,286	5,316	4,770	1,930
Total imports	24,614	30,280	26,000	21,710

Table 14.1 continued

Switzerland (in thousands of Swiss francs)

[Swiss francs 1.9 = US$1 (approx.)]

	1986	1989	1990	1991
Pharm. and chemical products	25,350	40,917	24,244	21,760
Synthetic materials	538	492	305	314
Machinery and equipment	9,003	8,446	15,476	12,388
Instruments and watches	3,908	2,359	2,413	3,128
Other goods	1,859	1,098	1,186	1,439
Total exports	40,658	53,312	43,624	39,029

	1986	1989	1990	1991
Seafoods	1,560	759	782	121
Sugar	1,721	1,748	1,195	556
Tobacco	9,982	10,569	11,349	9,201
Jewelry and antiques	n.a.	n.a.	n.a.	688
Other goods	251	39	70	408
Total imports	15,204	13,377	16,740	10,974

Sweden (in millions of Swedish krona)

[Krona 6.00 = US$1 (approx.)]

	1986	1989	1990	1991
Food products	5.6	53.1	n.a.	98.1
Raw materials	6.3	2.7	n.a.	0.7
Chemicals	5.1	6.0	4.9	3.2
Manufactures	39.1	22.5	5.7	23.6
Machinery and transport equip.	111.3	75.6	61.4	73.3
Other ind. products	22.2	25.0	16.2	14.0
Total exports	191.6	184.9	88.2	212.9

	1986	1989	1990	1991
Food products	16.6	19.2	144.4	29.8
Raw materials	0.1	n.a.	0.2	6.5
Beverages and tobacco	2.1	1.6	2.0	1.2
Other goods	1.5	0.5	0.3	0.3
Total imports	20.4	21.3	146.9	37.8

Belgium (in millions of Belgian francs)

[Belgian francs 34.00 = US$1 (approx.)]

	1986	1989	1990	1991
Malt	n.a.	364.3	441.7	184.2
Animal fats	170.3	329.8	369.6	276.1
Chemicals	n.a.	282.3	234.7	137.5
Paper and board	79.5	35.2	20.4	9.5
Metals	126.0	108.4	83.4	114.3
Machinery and electrical equip.	262.9	151.4	217.1	159.6
Animal products	n.a.	n.a.	n.a.	370.0
Other goods	110.7	73.6	136.0	98.0
Total exports	1,050	1,344.8	1,502.8	1,349.3

	1986	1989	1990	1991
Shrimp	15.5	0.2	n.a.	n.a.
Sugar, tobacco	113.1	67.3	70.0	104.8
Pearls, precious metals	n.a.	15.6	n.a.	25.5
Other goods	0.2	9.7	4.4	6.2
Total imports	144.0	92.7	75.4	136.6

Table 14.1 continued

Spain (in millions of US $)

	1986	1989	1990	1991
Mechanical machinery	60.6	83.7	110.4	108.4
Vehicles, tractors	12.7	16.6	10.4	5.0
Electrical machinery	17.5	24.9	29.5	23.2
Iron, steel castings	20.6	10.2	15.9	14.4
Optical, photographic equip.	10.1	7.9	8.0	7.5
Tools, cutlery	n.a.	5.9	7.6	6.3
Paper and board	2.0	6.5	6.5	4.5
Rubber	5.7	3.8	4.8	3.8
Plastic materials	3.5	5.1	6.6	5.0
Maritime navigation	n.a.	0.2	47.6	59.2
Furnishings, lights, etc.	n.a.	1.8	4.6	5.0
Other goods	158.2	41.1	35.3	27.1
Total exports	292.3	207.7	287.2	269.4

	1986	1989	1990	1991
Tobacco	37.2	42.3	42.3	54.0
Fish, seafoods	17.4	21.3	20.9	13.3
Coffee, tea	17.3	9.6	2.3	0.8
Fuel and minerals	11.4	8.0	2.4	7.8
Drinks	0.5	0.7	1.2	2.7
Nickel	n.a.	0.4	0.3	0.1
Paper and board	0.6	0.1	0.5	0.2
Meat and fish products	n.a.	0.5	3.8	7.0
Cotton and synthetic fibers	n.a.	1.9	1.5	0.7
Other products	3.4	7.2	4.9	6.6
Total imports	87.3	91.6	80.1	92.2

Italy (in millions of lire)   [Lire 1,200 = US$1 (approx.)]

	1986	1989	1990	1991
Food, drinks	1,064	12,216.4	5,031.7	n.a.
Tobacco leaf	n.a.	657.0	1,902.4	n.a.
Textiles and clothing	5,361	1,131	3,185	n.a.
Paper and card	n.a.	1,229	2,444	n.a.
Metal products	977	5,240	9,274	n.a.
Machinery	41,812	45,985	72,107	n.a.
Precision instruments	n.a.	2,930	2,420	n.a.
Transport equipment	13,955	7,712	3,594	n.a.
Construction materials	n.a.	144	3,199	n.a.
Chemicals	25,608	23,809	17,865	n.a.
Other goods	11,931	10,221	9,894	n.a.
Total exports	100,708	111,275	130,916	219,000[a]

	1986	1989	1990	1991
Food products	55,819	37,717.5	20,729.2	n.a.
Tobacco products	n.a.	n.a.	526.4	n.a.
Textiles and clothing	354	668	1,043	n.a.
Minerals	n.a.	470	5,736	n.a.
Nickel	n.a.	1,509	1,260	n.a.
Metal waste	n.a.	17,044	29,916	n.a.
Scrap metal	n.a.	2,420	1,159	n.a.
Leather hides	n.a.	930	1,031	n.a.
Other goods	25,322	1,764	1,555	n.a.
Total imports	81,495	61,339	62,956	57,000[a]

Table 14.1 continued

France (in millions of francs) [Francs 5.00 = US$1 (approx.)]

	1986	1989	1990	1991		1986	1989	1990	1991
Cereals	n.a.	n.a.	118.5	102.9	Coffee, cocoa	n.a.	n.a.	28.2	26.0
Poultry	n.a.	n.a.	n.a.	58.8	Animal products	n.a.	n.a.	7.4	3.8
Petroleum products	n.a.	n.a.	8.3	8.1	Fruits	n.a.	n.a.	7.1	8.6
Mechanical equipment	n.a.	n.a.	29.6	24.0	Tobacco leaf	n.a.	n.a.	16.1	3.6
Electronic equipment	n.a.	n.a.	66.3	20.0	Cigars	n.a.	n.a.	60.1	42.0
Precision instruments	n.a.	n.a.	13.6	9.4	Fish, seafood	n.a.	n.a.	53.3	45.1
Automotive equip.	n.a.	n.a.	1.7	3.8	Preserved fish	n.a.	n.a.	85.9	89.8
Metal packaging	n.a.	n.a.	11.3	2.4	Sugar	n.a.	n.a.	9.4	82.6
Glass ind. products	n.a.	n.a.	12.9	3.4	Cotton textiles	n.a.	n.a.	3.1	2.6
Basic chemicals	n.a.	n.a.	14.7	17.6	Other goods	n.a.	n.a.	7.5	38.8
Total exports	n.a.	n.a.	373.0	351.5	Total imports	n.a.	n.a.	282.2	343.4

USSR/CIS (in millions of rubles)

	1986	1989	1990	1991		1986	1989	1990	1991
Machinery, transport equip.	841.6	1,150.0	1,263.4	474.9	Sugar	3,574.2	3,709.1	3,335.9	903.4
Petroleum and products	2,172.7	2,127.6	1,637.0	560.7	Nickel	186.1	213.0	211.2	23.1
Minerals, metals	422.2	277.6	250	183.8	Citrus	67.4	60.3	88.1	42.1
Chemicals, fertilizers, rubber	77.5	178.5	79.9	18.3	Alcoholic drinks	2.5	5.6	3.8	0.7
Construction materials	18.2	16.8	18.7	6.7	Tobacco	6.9	6.8	4.3	2.9
Forest products, cotton	261.8	245.5	148.0	20.7	Electronic products	n.a.	16.7	n.a.	n.a.
Raw foods	81.5	137.3	256.0	56.0	Other goods	48.9	13.3	14.2	30.8
Food products	238.0	237.3	153.1	129.0					
Consumer products	227.5	163.5	136.7	6.0					
Other goods	18.0	83.9	64.0	94.0					
Total exports	4,359.0	4,617.9	4,006.8	1,550.1	Total imports	3,886.0	4,024.8	3,657.5	1,003.0

Sources: National trade statistics. See also *Cuba Business,* 7, no. 1 (January 1993).
Notes: Imports CIF; exports FOB. a. Projection based on results of first nine months. n.a. = not available.

POTENTIAL U.S. OPPORTUNITIES

Grains. In 1988, Cuban grain importers said that if the embargo were lifted, the United States could capture approximately one-quarter, about $80–100 million worth, of Cuban grain imports. In 1991, the deputy director of Alimport, Cuba's grain-importing enterprise, estimated that the United States could capture that entire market, roughly $500 million annually.[8]

Fertilizers. In 1988, Cuba imported 80–90 percent of its fertilizers from the Soviet Union. In 1991, the deputy director of Quimimport, Cuba's chemical import enterprise, reported that if the embargo were lifted, the United States could supply up to 100 percent of Cuba's annual fertilizer needs of about one hundred different fertilizer products totaling about 500,000 tons and valued at $150 million.[9]

Medicines. Cuba's medical enterprise has undergone dramatic changes. While developing its growing biotech industry, Cuba purchased supplies, raw materials, and basic medicines from the former Soviet bloc. In 1989, Cuba imported $18–20 million in medical supplies from the East. By 1991, because of the collapse of the CMEA, Cuba's medical imports from the East had dropped to $5–6 million. Recently, MediCuba director Orlando Romero predicted that if the U.S. embargo were lifted, Cuba would buy about $90 million in medical supplies from the United States.[10] This is a 50 percent increase from a similar estimate made four years ago. Other reports estimate that the United States could sell up to $200 million in medical supplies to Cuba annually.[11]

Textiles. Cuba's textile importer, Cubatex, reported in February 1992 that the United States could supply all of Cuba's current needs in cotton (20,000 tons), polyester and rayon fibers (5,000 tons), and cotton and polyester threads ($1 million).[12]

Tourism. Tourism has quickly become Cuba's second most important sector for hard currency earnings. Together with foreign investors, Cuba is building world-class luxury resorts across the island. The number of tourists visiting Cuba has been steadily increasing since 1988. Hard currency revenue associated with tourism grew from $152 million in 1988 to $324 million in 1991.[13] European and Latin American hotel chains and investors are actively developing the Cuban tourist industry while U.S. businesses sit on the sideline. Opening Cuba to U.S. tourists would result in a significant increase in the number of visitors to the island and the revenues associated with increased tourism. (See Table 14.2.)

Table 14.2   Cuba's International Tourism, 1988–1992

	1988	1989	1990	1991	1992
Total income					
(in millions of pesos)[a]	152	168	250[b]	324[e]	445[e]
Western	146	161			
Socialist	6	7	0		
Total tourists					
(in thousands)	309	325	340[c,d]	400[c]	500[c]
Western	247	289			
Socialist	62	37	0		
Currency earned					
per tourist	591	557	735[d]	809[d]	890[d]

Source: Comité Estatal de Estadísticas, reprinted in Banco Nacional de Cuba, *Informe Económico,* June 1990.
Notes: a. 1 peso ≈ $1.
b. Economist Intelligence Unit, *Cuba Country Profile 1991–1992.*
c. Carlos Garcia, vice director, Cubanacán, February 25, 1992.
d. Increased earnings per tourist reflect new upscale market. Estimates assume 10 percent increase annually in currency earned per tourist. However, with more luxury tourism, this figure will increase.
e. Estimates based on b, c, and d.

U.S. SUBSIDIARY TRADE WITH CUBA

Direct trade between Cuba and the United States has been impossible for more than thirty years because of the U.S. embargo. However, in 1975 the Ford administration amended the embargo regulations to allow U.S. companies to trade with Cuba through their subsidiaries located in third countries. This change was primarily a result of pressure from U.S. allies that complained about the extraterritorial restrictions of U.S. trade regulations toward Cuba.

The amended subsidiary regulations are still quite restrictive. They require that

1. goods sold to Cuba by foreign subsidiaries of U.S. companies be produced in the third country and may contain only extremely limited amounts of materials of U.S. origin;
2. U.S. directors and employees of U.S. subsidiaries in third countries be precluded from negotiating with Cuba; and
3. the U.S. parent companies of foreign subsidiaries apply for and receive a license from the U.S. Treasury Department before any trade is conducted.

These regulations in no way limit or remove the U.S. ban on the importation of Cuban goods or materials to the United States. That is, as a general rule, goods made in whole or in part with either Cuban labor or materials are not permitted into the United States.

U.S. subsidiary trade with Cuba has changed a great deal since the fall of Eastern Europe. (See Tables 14.3 and 14.4.) In 1988, 215 license applications were made to the U.S. Treasury Department and subsidiary trade totaled $246 million. Of this amount, $97 million were in exports to Cuba from U.S. subsidiaries, while $149 million were in imports. That is, U.S. subsidiaries bought more from than they sold to Cuba. The ratio of Cuban exports to imports vis-à-vis U.S. subsidiary trade in 1988 was approximately 60:40.[14]

Table 14.3   Licensed U.S. Foreign Subsidiary Trade with Cuba

	1980	1985	1988	1989	1990
License applications	164	256	215	233	321
Total exports to Cuba[a]	206	162	97	169	533
Total imports from Cuba[a]	86	126	149	162	172
Total exports and imports[a]	292	288	246	331	705
Export:import ratio	71:29	56:44	40:60	51:49	76:24

Source: Office of Foreign Assets Control, An Analysis of Licensed Trade with Cuba by Foreign Subsidiaries of U.S. Companies (Washington D.C.: U.S. Treasury Department, July 1991).
Note: a. In millions of U.S. $.

By 1990, the number of license applications had increased 50 percent, to 321. (The U.S. Treasury Department explains that there is a self-selecting mechanism regarding license applications. Companies rarely apply for a license to trade with Cuba unless they have made certain that their request falls within the legislative parameters.) More dramatic than the increase in license requests, however, was the increase in the dollar amount of trade between U.S. subsidiaries and Cuba in 1991. Trade between foreign subsidiaries of U.S. companies and Cuba almost tripled from $246 million in 1988 to $718 million in 1992.[15]

Not only did the volume and value of subsidiary trade increase, there was also an important change in the direction of the flow of goods traded. By 1990, the ratio of Cuban exports to Cuban imports had more than reversed the 1988 ratio. The 1990 figures show that Cuban exports make up

Table 14.4   Goods Exported from U.S. Subsidiaries to Cuba
(in millions of US $)

	1980	1985	1988	1989	1990	1991
Grain, wheat, and						
other consumables	192	109	56	114	500	348
Industrials and						
nonconsumables	14	53	41	55	33	36
% of consumables of						
subsidiary exports	93.20	67.28	57.73	67.46	93.81	90.63
% of consumables of						
subsidiary trade	65.75	37.85	22.76	34.33	70.92	48.47

Source: Office of Foreign Assets Control, *An Analysis of Licensed Trade.*

only 24 percent of U.S. subsidiary trade, while Cuban imports account for 76 percent of this trade. Furthermore, the composition of U.S. subsidiary trade with Cuba has changed appreciably. In 1990, 94 percent of U.S. subsidiary exports to Cuba were in grains, wheats, and other consumables. What is more, the ratio of consumable exports to total U.S. subsidiary trade with Cuba rose from 23 percent in 1988 to 71 percent in 1990. Recently released U.S. Treasury Department data show that Cuban imports from U.S. subsidiaries are still greater than exports. In 1991, 95 percent of U.S. subsidiary trade with Cuba was in consumables. Cuba purchased approximately $347 million worth of sunflower oil, wheat, and other consumables from U.S. subsidiaries.[16] The loss of Cuba's former primary trade partners, the Soviet Union and the CMEA, is apparent in Cuba's sharp increase in U.S. subsidiary trade.

According to the latest U.S. Treasury Department data, the vast majority of foreign subsidiaries of U.S. corporations conducting trade with Cuba were located in Switzerland. U.S. corporations appear to be taking advantage of Switzerland's banking and commercial facilities to enter the Cuban market. These Swiss entities accounted for 75 percent of all U.S. subsidiary trade with Cuba in 1990. The following countries, in descending order of importance, accounted for most of the remainder of U.S. subsidiary trade with Cuba in 1991: the West Indies, Argentina, Canada, and the United Kingdom. The most significant change was the 1,000 percent increase in subsidiary trade based in the West Indies. The ten-year (1981–1991) total for commerce between U.S. subsidiaries in third countries and Cuba was approximately $3.8 billion. The last three years of subsidiary trade account for roughly half of the ten-year total. U.S. parent companies of the subsidiaries taking advantage of the Cuban market include such notables as Johnson and Johnson, Beatrice Companies, Ford Motor Company, Union Carbide, and Continental Grain. (See Table 14.5.)

MACK AMENDMENT AND TORRICELLI BILL

In 1989, Sen. Connie Mack introduced an amendment that essentially would preclude U.S. subsidiary trade with Cuba. The Mack Amendment drew opposition from U.S. parent corporations, foreign governments, and the Bush administration.

Foreign governments have criticized the extraterritoriality implied in the proposed legislation. Canada went so far as to order local subsidiaries of U.S. companies to ignore the Mack Amendment if it became law. In October 1990, Canadian attorney general Kim Campbell issued an order barring Canadian corporations from complying with U.S. measures precluding subsidiary trade; the order required companies to report any directives relating to such measures to the Canadian attorney general. In a 1990 letter of protest to U.S. secretary of state James Baker,[17] Canadian foreign affairs minister Joe Clark called the proposed amendment "an intrusion into Canadian sovereignty."

In September 1991, British trade secretary Peter Lilley warned the U.S. Congress that he would use the Protection of Trading Interests Act (PTIA) to block the effects of the Mack Amendment. He said, "It is for the British government, not the U.S. congress, to determine the UK's policy on trade with Cuba. We will not accept any attempt to superimpose U.S. law on UK companies."[18]

U.S. corporations have also strongly criticized the proposed amendment. Continental Grain, for example, sent letters to members of Congress urging them to oppose the amendment "simply because it will not deter Cuba's imports of food commodities and is not in the best interest of United States trade."[19] A representative for Cargill told this author: "It doesn't make sense. We are talking about fungible goods. The Cubans can easily buy somebody else's grains and medicines. The Cubans aren't being hurt, it's the U.S. businesses that are losing the market."[20]

In 1989, 1990, and 1991, the U.S. State Department went on record opposing the Mack Amendment. In a cable to foreign embassies obtained by this author, the State Department explained the rationale behind its opposition:

> We permit these activities [subsidiary trade] . . . because we recognize that attempting to apply our embargo to third countries will lead to unproductive and bitter trade disputes with our allies. A number of our major trading partners have enacted so-called blocking statutes that could prohibit any company organized under local laws from complying with U.S. embargoes. . . . The Department of State has opposed the amendment sponsored by Senator Mack because of its extraterritorial implications.[21]

Table 14.5   U.S. Parent Companies of Foreign Subsidiaries Licensed to Trade with Cuba, 1985–1991

ALCOA	E.I. Dupont	Monsanto
AM International	Envirotech	Morton International
Aeroquip International	Emhart Industries	McGraw Edison
Analytical Technology	Eli Lilly	N.L. Industries
Armco	Exxon	Nynex
BF Goodrich	Fischer & Porter	Otis Elevator
Baker Hughes	Ford Motor Company	Owens Corning Fiber
Borg-Warner	GTE International	Pfizer
Bridgestone/Firestone	GK Technologies	Philipp Brothers
Beatrice Companies	General Electric	Picker International
Barry-Wehmiller	Genlyte Group	Potters Industries
Bonne Bell	Gilbarco	RCA Global
Buckman Laboratories	Gillette	R.J. Reynolds
Burndy	Goodyear Tire and Rubber	Raychem
Butler Manufacturing	H.B. Fuller	Reichhold Chemicals
Campbell Investment	H.H. Robertson	Reliance Electric
Carter Day Industries	Hercules	Richardson Electronics
Caterpillar	Hoechst Celanese	Rohm & Haas
Carrier	Honeywell	S.C. Johnson & Son
Central Soya	Hussman	Joseph E. Seagram & Sons
Continental Grain	IBM World Trade	Sigma-Aldrich
Corning	ITT	Sybron Acquisition
Crane	Ingersoll-Rand	Stanley Works
Cooper Industries	International Multifoods	TFX Holdings
Cummins Engine	International Securities	TRW Teleflex
Combustion Engineering	Investment	Toledo Scale
Coleman	Johnson and Johnson	Tenneco
Champion Spark Plug	Johnson Controls	USM
Del Monte	John Fluke Manufacturing	Uarco
Dow Chemical	Joyce International	Union Camp
Dorr-Oliver	Lubrizol	Union Carbide
Drew Chemical	Litton Industries	Vulcan Hart
Drexel Burnham Lambert	Manville	Westinghouse Electric
Dresser Industries	Minnesota Mining &	Worthington International
E.D. & F. Man International	Manufacturing	Worthington Pump
Futures	Mennen	

Source: Documents obtained by the authors through Freedom of Information Act requests to the Office of Foreign Assets Control of the U.S. Treasury Department, March 31, 1992.

President Bush vetoed the Export Administration Act, which contained the Mack Amendment as well as provisions dealing with chemical weapons and high-technology transfers to the Soviet Union in 1991.

In 1992, the Mack Amendment was included once again as part of the proposed Export Administration Act. Also, a similar measure to prevent U.S. subsidiary trade with Cuba was proposed as part of the Cuban Democracy Act introduced by Congressman Robert G. Torricelli. In congressional hearings on the Torricelli legislation held in April 1992, the Bush administration opposed the subsidiary trade restrictions. Principal Deputy Assistant Secretary for Inter-American Affairs Robert S. Gelbard testified that "had the embargo applied to U.S. companies in third countries, Cuba would have likely won the UN debate [condemning the U.S. trade embargo in November 1991]." Gelbard also said that when the subsidiary legislation existed (prior to 1975), it did not work because "some of our strongest allies fundamentally oppose the measures and have local blocking orders against the proposed legislation. . . . The proposed legislation would be the worst of all possible worlds."[22] By May 1992, however, the Bush administration flip-flopped and testified in support of the bill. This switch is probably due to election-year politics.[23]

On September 18, 1992, the Senate passed the Cuban Democracy Act, and on September 27, the full House of Representatives voted in favor of the bill. Reaction by U.S. trade partners to the passage of the Torricelli Bill has been strong. Canadian external affairs minister Barbara McDougall and Canadian justice minister Kim Campbell announced a federal blocking order that carries a fine of up to $8,500 or five years in prison for executives of U.S. subsidiaries based in Canada if they obey the U.S. law. The British press secretary in Washington, Michael Price, stated, "We made clear that there will be provisions within the legal system which will prevent subsidiaries operating out of Britain from complying [with the Cuban Democracy Act]."[24] The Mexican Congress condemned the Torricelli Bill because "it is contrary to international law" and "affects third countries."[25] The European Community called on President Bush to veto the Cuban sanctions bill. The European commission said, "The extension of the U.S. trade embargo against Cuba has the potential to cause grave damage to the transatlantic relationship." The Commission went on to say that the EC "cannot accept that the U.S. unilaterally determines and restricts EC economic and commercial relations."[26]

In the short term, the new legislation will have a deleterious impact on the Cuban people. Because 91 percent of goods sold to Cuba by U.S. subsidiaries are foodstuffs and other consumables, food supply on the island will most certainly suffer further shortages as an immediate consequence of this measure. However, because the goods are fungible, in the long term the Cuban government will be able to replace U.S. subsidiaries with new trade partners.

CUBAN JOINT VENTURES

Although the Cuban Joint Venture Law (Law 50) has been in effect since 1982, by 1988 few joint ventures had been undertaken on the island. Beginning in 1989, with the disruption in Cuba's trade patterns with the former Soviet Union, Cuban trade officials began to search for new partners and trade options. In effect, they creatively, pragmatically, and realistically interpreted and applied the 1982 law.[27]

As of early 1992, Cuban officials confirmed that more than two hundred joint ventures had been entered into by Cuban enterprises and foreign partners. The officials reported that roughly half of such ventures are in tourism and biotechnology. According to a report by Business International, thirty-nine of the signed joint ventures involve Spanish investors. (Spanish investments alone accounted for $28 million in 1990.) At the annual Cuban trade fair in November 1991, sources reported that more than sixty joint ventures were being discussed. Hundreds more are in the process of negotiation.[28] Cuban officials predict that the number of joint ventures will be in the thousands within several years.[29] This is no doubt optimistic, yet it is clear that the Cubans are open to the possibility of all types of trade arrangements. During recent interviews in Havana, officials in charge of Cuban joint enterprises repeatedly emphasized their willingness to flexibly apply the Joint Venture Law. "Everything is open to consideration," said Abeledo Larrinaga, vice president of the Cuban Chamber of Commerce. Demonstrating the degree of this new flexibility, Larrinaga continued: "We're even open to the possibility of mixed enterprises between foreign partners and private Cuban farmers."[30]

A Snapshot of Cuba's Joint Venture Law

• Although the 1982 joint venture legislation limits foreign partner ownership to 49 percent, the Cubans, in fact, now allow foreign participation of 50 percent or more. The Cuban Chamber of Commerce reports that Latin American and Caribbean companies receive priority consideration for enterprises with more than 50 percent foreign ownership.

• Foreign partners may fill senior management positions of a joint enterprise with whomever they wish, including foreigners. The managers of the joint undertaking determine their employment needs and may hire and fire Cuban workers at their discretion.

• Joint enterprises contract a Cuban entity to provide a preselected group of workers from which it selects its personnel. The Cuban entity in turn contracts each individual worker, expressly stating that he or she will be directed by the managerial staff of the joint enterprise. The Cuban entity, not the joint enterprise, is responsible for the rights as well as the wage payment of the workers.

• Cuban personnel are paid at officially established rates. Often these rates are less than those in other countries because free public health services, education, cultural activities, and subsidized housing offered by the Cuban government. Cuban wages range from $0.55 to $2.50 per hour based on a forty-hour workweek.

• There is a 25 percent workers' payroll tax that comes out of the enterprise's gross income. This includes the enterprise's contribution for its employees' social security.

• Theoretically, all joint ventures are subject to a 30 percent tax on net profits. However, in practice, the Cuban government often grants tax exemptions. These exemptions run for periods up to and beyond the time needed to recover the original capital investment.

• There are no restrictions on the repatriation of profits by foreign partners. Likewise, managers, technicians, and others brought in from overseas may remit up to two-thirds of their salary in convertible currency.

• Once a joint enterprise has been approved by the Cuban Council of Ministers, it acquires its own legal status and is completely independent of the state.

• Land ownership is not allowed. Under Cuban law, permission is granted for land surfaces to be used for periods of twenty-five years and upward.[31] These are, in effect, leases.

• Tariffs and customs duties on direct imports and exports have been routinely waived for joint enterprises. These exemptions had been considered on a case-by-case basis. In October 1991, the Fourth Party Congress of Cuba met and decided to allow joint ventures to export and import directly and free from tariffs and duties.

Major Countries Engaged in Joint Ventures with Cuba

The major countries engaged in joint venture operations and negotiations with Cuba include Spain, Mexico, Canada, Austria, Finland, Italy, France, Ireland, and Germany. Latin American countries involved in joint ventures with Cuba include Venezuela, Brazil, Chile, Uruguay, and Colombia. Cuba is currently negotiating with several Caribbean partners and has already entered into agreements with Jamaica.

Examples of Joint Venture Agreements

• Grupo Sol of Spain built and manages the $40 million Sol Palmeras Hotel along Cuba's famous Varadero Beach. In addition to the many tourism joint ventures in Varadero, other areas of the island are being developed as tourist destinations. These include Pinar del Rio, Santa Lucia, Santiago, Granma, Guardalavaca, Cayo Coco, and Ciego de Àvila. The Isle of Youth is being developed for tourism in conjunction with Grupo Basco of Spain.

- Cuba and Lithuania signed an agreement for the production of electric meters. Production began in January 1992 and is targeted for both the Cuban market and the export market.
- Cuba has signed a joint venture with Ireland. The Irish airline Aer Rianta will assist in airport management and aircraft handling. Additionally, Cubana Airlines will fly scheduled service between Ireland and Cuba.
- A Canadian mining company, Sherritt Gordon, entered into a five-year, $1.2 billion investment in the Cuban nickel industry.
- Technical and Manufacturing Services (TAMS), a British company, has signed a deal to jointly produce a chemical cleaner with Cuba.
- Cuba signed a six-year contract with a French consortium composed of Total Petroleum and Compagnie Europeéne des Pétroles. The consortium finances offshore oil exploration. If oil is found, Cuba keeps 50 percent of the profit.
- The French firm Geophysics General Company signed a joint venture agreement with the Cuban state-owned CUPET (Cuba Petroleum) in May 1992 to provide oil exploration services.
- A Cuban-Brazilian pharmaceutical company will produce the meningitis-B vaccine developed by Cuba's fast-growing biotechnology industry.

Other Business Arrangements

Cuban trade officials report that the possibilities for trade, in addition to joint ventures, are infinite. In 1990, Cuba introduced several new arrangements to increase foreign economic activity in Cuba. They include cooperative production ventures, free-trade zones, marketing agreements, management agreements, and third-country associations.

Cooperative production arrangements between foreign companies and Cuban enterprises most often entail foreign partners supplying missing inputs (raw materials, technology, packaging, etc.) in a Cuban production process. In exchange, the foreign partner receives a portion of the revenue and/or the finished product. There are more than two dozen of these projects in operation.[32]

In late December 1991, Cuba announced that free-trade zones in which foreign investors could establish import-export businesses would be allowed. "Nongovernmental entities such as hotels or other joint venture companies will be able to open trading firms, import whatever they want, and sell it to other joint venture companies or to the state," according to National Assembly president Juan Escalona.[33] Such entities will allow the introduction of other types of capitalist enterprises, such as suppliers of food and furniture for the hotel industry. Consignment shop arrangements enable foreign companies to provide goods for sale in Cuban hard currency stores and receive a profit from the sale of the goods.

Marketing arrangements take various forms. One example is the citrus agreement between Cuba and Chile. In this agreement, the Chilean partner provides marketing expertise and some supplies, and the Cubans provide the fruit, packing facilities, and labor. Plans include the export of more than one million cartons of grapefruit (primarily to the United Kingdom) in 1992. The tourism sector is replete with management agreements. For instance, the Spanish group Oasis has signed agreements to manage Cuban resort facilities in Varadero and Cayo Largo.[34] The management agreements are usually for set periods of time as well as for set fees.

Another new Cuban business arrangement involves associations in third countries. Such agreements call for joint efforts outside Cuba. An example is a deal signed by Cuba and Venezuela that calls for Cuban technology and labor in the extraction of Venezuelan phosphate. Both countries will sell the phosphate on the international market as well as retain a portion for themselves.[35]

CONCLUSION

A great deal has happened in the Cuban economy over the last four years. Today, Cuba's willingness and ability to buy and sell on the world's markets signals an increase in the opportunities for U.S.-Cuban trade. The Cuban market is more attractive than ever before. European, Latin American, Canadian, and Asian businesspeople are taking advantage of the openings in the Cuban economy. It is fair to say that, although the internal Cuban market is relatively closed, the Cuban economy is successfully operating on the world's markets on the basis of hard currency. In fact, the savvy of Cuban businesspeople is widely acknowledged.

Unlike European, Canadian, Latin American, and Asian companies, which must traverse relatively long distances, U.S. businesses have a geographic advantage for trade with Cuba. All else being equal, transportation costs alone make U.S. goods and services more attractive to the Cuban market. Yet all else is not equal. The United States is one of the world's leading growers of agricultural goods and one of its largest manufacturers. It can make its goods and services available at highly competitive prices. For example, unlike Japan, the United States produces wheat surpluses. Moreover, in Cuba there is pent-up demand for and a fascination with U.S. products.

The Cubans are adapting to a post–Soviet bloc world. While acknowledging the intent to repay its debt to the West, Cuba has maintained and expanded its market activities. Despite its current difficulties, in 1991 Cuba purchased $4 billion worth of goods, mostly food and medicine, from nearly everywhere else in the world but the United States. Figures for 1992 indicate that Cuba purchased $2.2 billion worth of goods in exchange for hard currency. The United States has an opportunity to open a new market to its businesses, remove a tool for President Castro's anti-American rhetoric, and take an active position regarding a new Cuban economy. The opportunity cost of maintaining the U.S. embargo may be more than the annual $1.3 billion that meets the eye.

NOTES

1. Donna Rich Kaplowitz and Michael Kaplowitz, *New Opportunities for U.S.-Cuban Trade* (Washington, D.C.: Johns Hopkins University, 1992).
2. Kirby Jones and Donna Rich, *Opportunities for U.S.-Cuban Trade* (Washington, D.C.: Johns Hopkins University, 1988).
3. Rich Kaplowitz and Kaplowitz, *New Opportunities.*
4. Office of Foreign Assets Control, *An Analysis of Licensed Trade with Cuba by Foreign Subsidiaries of U.S. Companies* (Washington, D.C.: U.S. Treasury Department, 1991). Personal interview with Clara David, U.S. Treasury Department, Office of Foreign Assets Control, July 16, 1992.
5. Personal interview with Raúl Taladrid, vice president of Comité Estatal de Colaboración Económico (CECE), February 26, 1992. Note that predictions for Cuba's imports in 1992 fell to $2.2 billion because of a lack of Soviet subsidies and a poor sugar harvest. See Mimi Whitefield, "Castro: Cuba Still Politically Strong," *Miami Herald*, September 6, 1992, p. 12A.
6. Rosalind Resnick, "Is There a Cuban Factor in Your Future?" *International Business* (January 1992), p. 32.
7. Taladrid interview; Whitefield, "Castro."
8. Personal interview with Emerio Izquierdo, deputy director of Alimport, June 24, 1991.
9. Personal interview with Raúl Abreu, deputy director of Quimimport, June 24, 1991.
10. Personal interview with Orlando Romero, director of Medicuba, June 24, 1991.
11. Cuban American National Foundation (CANF), *Blue Ribbon Commission on the Economic Reconstruction of Cuba* (Washington, D.C., and Miami, 1991).
12. Personal interview with Ada Prado Brito, vice president of Cubatex, February 25, 1992.
13. Rich Kaplowitz and Kaplowitz, *New Opportunities*, p. 22; Personal interview with Carlos Garcia, vice director of Cubanacán, February 25, 1992; and Economist Intelligence Unit, *Cuba Country Profile 1991–1992* (London, 1991).
14. Data on subsidiary trade is drawn primarily from Office of Foreign Assets Control, *An Analysis of Licensed Trade with Cuba by Foreign Subsidiaries of U.S. Companies* (Washington, D.C.: U.S. Treasury Department, 1990, 1991, and 1992).
15. The U.S. Treasury Department figures concerning the dollar amount of U.S. subsidiary trade may be misleading. The dollar figures included in U.S. parent companies' license applications to trade with Cuba are rough estimates that are not verified. Clara David of the U.S. Treasury Department also reported that the amount reflects license applications and not actual sales. Some companies may

request licenses, but the deals may not go through. Personal interview with Clara David, U.S. Treasury Department Office of Foreign Assets Control, July 14, 1992. Personal interview with W. Brendan Harrington, Public Affairs for Cargill, June 4, 1992. Mr. Harrington cited an example in which the value of an entire boatload/shipment is used for the permit application when, in fact, only a small percentage of that amount is intended for Cuba.

16. Office of Foreign Assets Control, *An Analysis of Licensed Trade with Cuba by Foreign Subsidiaries of U.S. Companies* (Washington D.C.: U.S. Treasury Department, 1992).

17. *Washington Post*, November 1, 1991, p. C1; *Miami Herald*, November 2, 1990, p. 1A; *Wall Street Journal*, November 1, 1991, p. A19; *Globe and Mail*, October 31, 1990, p. A1; *Globe and Mail*, November 1, 1990, p. A1.

18. *Department for Enterprise* press notice, September 1991.

19. Letter by Rebecca Fraily of Continental Grain to U.S. congressmen, dated October 12, 1989.

20. Harrington interview.

21. "Cuba Sanctions Amendment in the State Authorization Bill," from U.S. State Department to U.S. embassies in Brussels, Paris, and Ottawa, September 1989.

22. Statement by Robert S. Gelbard, principal deputy assistant secretary for Inter-American Affairs, before the Committee on Foreign Affairs, House of Representatives, April 8, 1992.

23. While in Miami in May 1992, Gov. Bill Clinton publicly praised the Torricelli Bill, which probably pushed the Bush campaign to endorse the proposed legislation several days later. See Christopher Marquis, "Bush Vira a Favor de Plan Contra Cuba" *Nuevo Herald*, May 6, 1992, p. 1A. See also Saul Landau, "Tightening the Chokehold on Cuba," *The Nation* 254, no. 23 (June 15, 1992), p. 819.

24. "Torricelli Bill Passes Congress," *CubaINFO* 4, no. 11 (October 2, 1992), p. 1.

25. "Mexican Congress Condemns U.S. Bill on Cuba Embargo," British Broadcasting Corporation, Summary of World Broadcast, *Monitoring Report,* October 3, 1992.

26. "EC Warns Bush Not to Ban U.S. Subsidiaries' Cuba Sales," Reuters AM cycle, October 8, 1992; "The EC Calls for Veto of the Cuban Democracy Act," PR Newswire, Washington dateline, October 8, 1992; "EC Asks Bush to Veto Cuban Sanction Bill," Agence France Press, October 8, 1992.

27. For information on the particulars of the 1982 Cuban Joint Venture Law, please refer to Legislative Decree no. 50, 2–15–1982, On Economic Association Between Cuban and Foreign Entities; *Cuba: Legislation on Foreign Investments* (Havana, 1989); and Executive Committee of the Council of Ministers, *Possibility of Joint Ventures in Cuba* (Havana, 1991). See also Rich Kaplowitz and Kaplowitz, *New Opportunities.*

28. "Cuba Lures Foreign Capital," *Miami Herald*, March 25, 1992, p. 1C; Business International, *Developing Business Strategies for Cuba* (New York, 1992), p. 24. See also David Jessop, *Cuba: New Opportunities for British Business,* prepared for the Caribbean Trade Advisory Group, the Anglo-Cuban Trade Council, and the West India Committee (London, 1992), pp. 23–24.

29. Personal interview with Abeledo Larrinaga, vice president of the Cuban Chamber of Commerce, February 24, 1992.

30. Larrinaga interview.

31. Jessop, *Cuba*, p. 39.

32. Taladrid interview; personal interview with Andrew Zimbalist, professor of economics, Smith College, April 15, 1992.

33. *Miami Herald*, December 8, 1991, p. 28A; *CubaINFO* 3, no. 18 (December 13, 1991), pp. 4–5.

34. Lila Haines, "Cayo Largo Under New Management," *Cuba Business* 6, no. 1 (February 1992), p. 3.

35. Taladrid interview.

The Contributors

DONNA RICH KAPLOWITZ is former deputy director of the Cuban Studies Program at the Johns Hopkins University School of Advanced International Studies, where she is a doctoral candidate. She has been an adjunct professor at the American University in Washington, D.C. For four years she served as editor of *CubaINFO*, a fortnightly publication on Cuba published by Johns Hopkins. She has written extensively on Cuban foreign policy and is a coeditor of *The Cuba Reader: The Making of the Cuban Revolution*. She also worked as an analyst on the Cuban Missile Crisis Project at the National Security Archive. Ms. Rich Kaplowitz is codirector of Cuba Research Associates, a research organization that specializes in U.S.-Cuba trade issues.

JOHN ATTFIELD was director of Intercom Marketing Research Services Ltd (IMRES), a London-based consulting firm with expertise in Cuban economic and trade questions, from 1984 until 1992. He has traveled frequently, to both Cuba and the Middle East. He is a frequent contributor to *Cuba Business*, and he coauthored a research study on the health care market in Cuba. Attfield moved to Germany in 1992 and is now working with the market research and marketing consulting firm RMM in Hamburg.

JOHN WALTON COTMAN is an assistant professor of political science at Howard University. As a Fulbright doctoral fellow he conducted field research in Grenada. He has published on U.S. policy toward South Africa in the *Review of Black Political Economy*. His books include *Birmingham, JFK and the Civil Rights Act of 1963: Implications for Elite Theory* (1989), and the forthcoming *The Gorríon Tree: Cuba and the Grenada Revolution*. His current work concerns Cuban policy in the Caribbean Basin and Cuban foreign aid programs.

H. MICHAEL ERISMAN is a professor of political science and the department head at Indiana State University in Terre Haute, Indiana. His main fields of interest are U.S. policies toward Latin America, transnationalism/political economy in the Caribbean Basin, and Cuban foreign affairs. He is the author of *Cuba's International Relations: The Anatomy of a Nationalistic Foreign Policy* (Westview Press, 1985) and *Pursuing Post-Dependency Politics: South/South Relations in the Caribbean* (Lynne Rienner, 1992), he has edited *The Caribbean Challenge: US Policy in a Volatile Region* (Westview Press, 1984), and he has coedited *Colossus Challenged: The Struggle for Caribbean Influence* (Westview Press, 1982, with John Martz) and *Cuban Foreign Policy Confronts a New International Order* (Lynne Rienner, 1991, with John Kirk). His current research agenda involves projects dealing with U.S.-Cuban relations and Havana's evolving relations with countries of the Far East.

DAMIAN J. FERNANDEZ is associate professor of international relations and director of the graduate program in international relations at Florida International University. He is the editor of *Cuban Studies Since the Revolution* (University of Florida Press, 1992).

RICHARD V. GORHAM joined the Canadian diplomatic service in 1954 and served in Tokyo, New Delhi, Phnom Penh, and China. He was appointed as roving ambassador for Latin America and permanent observer to the Organization of American States in 1987 and served in that position until 1990, when he was appointed as special adviser to the secretary of state for external affairs for the implementation of Canada's long-term political strategy for Latin America. Ambassador Gorham is now an adjunct professor at the University of New Brunswick.

WOLF GRABENDORFF is the founding director of the Institute of European–Latin American Relations (IRELA), Madrid. Born in Germany, he studied in Frankfurt, Berlin, and the United States. He spent time as a researcher in various Latin American countries; three years as a Latin American correspondent for the German TV network, ARD, based in Buenos Aires; and was also a visiting professor at the Johns Hopkins School of Advanced International Studies, Washington, D.C. Mr. Grabendorff is the author and editor of various books and numerous articles covering diverse aspects of Latin American politics and international relations.

GARETH JENKINS is an economic consultant based in London. He has worked on problems in East-West trade since the late 1970s and has published *Cuba Business*, a newsletter on trade with Cuba, since 1987. He is vice president of CaribExport, Inc., the Washington firm of U.S.-Cuba trade specialists that consults for U.S. clients interested in developing business with Cuba.

MICHAEL D. KAPLOWITZ completed an M.A. in international economics and Latin American studies at the Johns Hopkins University School of Advanced International Studies. He is currently a doctoral candidate in resource development at Michigan State University. Kaplowitz is the coauthor of "New Opportunities for U.S.-Cuban Trade," published by Johns Hopkins University in 1992, and jointly directs Cuba Research Associates.

FRANCINE MARSHALL was editor in 1992 of the newsletter *CubaINFO,* published by the Cuban Studies Program at the Johns Hopkins University School of Advanced International Studies. Ms. Marshall worked on the Subcommittee on Western Hemisphere Affairs of the House Foreign Affairs Committee from 1989 to 1991, when she specialized in U.S.-Cuban relations. Ms. Marshall has traveled extensively through Latin America and the Caribbean, including an extended research trip to Cuba.

CARL MIGDAIL worked for United Press in Mexico from 1951 to 1955, and then spent five years in Washington as chief of press for the Organization of American States. He returned to Mexico in 1960 to open a Mexico City bureau for *U.S. News and World Report,* and remained there until 1969. Mr. Migdail worked with *U.S. News and World Report* until 1985; his specialization was Mexico.

WAYNE S. SMITH is a former foreign service officer who served in Moscow; he was chief of the U.S. Interests Section in Havana (1979–1982). Now director of the Cuban Studies Program at the School of Advanced International Studies at Johns Hopkins University, he teaches courses on the Cuban Revolution and Soviet policy in Latin America. He is the author of *The Closest of Enemies: A Personal and Diplomatic Account of US-Cuban Relations Since 1957* (WW Norton, 1987), and he edited *The Russians Aren't Coming: New Soviet Policy in Latin America* (Lynne Rienner, 1992). Mr. Smith has also authored numerous articles on hemispheric affairs and Soviet policy in Latin America.

LUIZ L. VASCONCELOS is professor of economics at the Federal University of Rio de Janeiro. He worked for many years with the UNDP/FAO as project manager in Latin America and Africa. Vasconcelos has published in several scientific journals. His main field of interest is economic systems, with particular reference to socialist economies and the problems of transition.

KANAKO YAMAOKA is a research fellow at the Latin America Project of the Institute of Developing Economies in Tokyo. Her major interests are international relations, especially relations among Cuba, other Latin American countries, and the United States. Ms. Yamaoka holds a B.A. in law from Waseda University in Tokyo and an M.A. in international relations from the University of Chicago.

Index

About the Book

Focusing on Cuba's bilateral foreign relations—and especially its economic relations—since the end of the Cold War, this book explores the impact on Cuba of the major changes that have occurred in Eastern Europe and the former Soviet Union.

The authors examine Cuba's ties with important, yet overlooked, countries and regions such as China, Japan, and the Middle East, as well as with Britain, the European Community, the former Soviet Union, Canada, Mexico, Brazil, Central America, the Caribbean states, and the United States. Their comprehensive examination reflects the realities of the changing international order.